THE
FOOD
& WINE
OF
FRANCE

PENGUIN PRESS

New York

2016

THE
FOOD
& WINE
OF
FRANCE

———

Eating and Drinking
from Champagne to Provence

EDWARD BEHR

PENGUIN PRESS
An imprint of Penguin Random House LLC
375 Hudson Street
New York, New York 10014
penguin.com

Portions of this book first appeared in different form in the magazine *The Art of Eating*.

Excerpt from "An Omelette and a Glass of Wine" from *An Omelette and a Glass of Wine*
by Elizabeth David (Viking, 1985). Reprinted by permission of Jill Norman,
literary trustee of the Elizabeth David Estate.

Excerpt from *Simple French Food* by Richard Olney. Reprinted by
permission of the publisher, Grub Street, London.

ISBN 9781594204524

Printed in the United States of America
1   3   5   7   9   10   8   6   4   2

Designed by Nicole LaRoche

For Kim

CONTENTS

THE
FOOD
& WINE
OF
FRANCE

Introduction

We live in a time of innovation and forgetting. For food and drink, it's a time of excitement. Compared with twenty or thirty years ago, we know an astounding amount, and the information continues to accumulate: about ingredients, cuisines, cultures, nature, diverse science, technology, the economics and the politics of food. It seems as if the popularity of food as entertainment will never stop growing. In ambitious restaurants in France and other countries, the quality of raw materials and the aspirations and achievements of many cooks have leaped upward, drawing customers' expectations with them. The world's cuisines—their structures, ingredients, techniques, recipes—are taken up, celebrated, exploited, ignored, tossed out the window, put on the shelf with the rest, according to the cook and what feels right at the moment. High-end cooking, and the more affordable cooking influenced by it, is wide open and seems destined to become only more and more international. Not so long ago I thought that North Americans in particular were becoming increasingly knowledgeable and discriminating about food and drink. But no individual can master more than a sliver of the information now available. Consumers, and often chefs and writers, in the face of so much information, seem to have become overwhelmed and to have pulled back. They're more likely to skate over the wide, enchanting surface. We've retreated to what we *can* easily know—what's new, what's fun, what's happening, what tastes really good right now. (The popularity of innovative, often captivating new cocktails, with no roots and no background to think about, makes perfect sense for our time.)

When we live so much in the moment, we miss a lot. Good French food is very, very delicious. Other food may be as good, but none is better. French food is generous, sensual, obvious, subtle, both simple and complex. A lot of modern inventive food by comparison is wildly abstract and austere. The deliciousness of French food is overt; it's about appetite.

Into perhaps the early 1970s in France, which was about fifteen years before I began to visit there regularly, by most accounts you could eat well practically anywhere, going on the looks of a place and the menu posted outside. For a very long time, however, without good advice, it has been the easiest thing in the world to eat badly in France. The reasons aren't so surprising—the pressures of industrialization in an industrialized country, the passing of a generation rooted in life before the Second World War, and the aftershocks of Nouvelle Cuisine, which called so much into question. Slowly, here and there, as a charcutier or a pâtissier or a chef retired, the losses accumulated. Now when you eat out, you must know where to go. And if you do, it's a great time to eat in France, particularly in the high-energy small restaurants of Paris.

But where French cuisine once towered, its influence has famously shrunk. The sauces at the center of classical cuisine have been seen as outmoded for decades and are all but ignored, in France as everywhere. The old dishes too are mostly gone, except the stereotypical selection in a retro-ish bistro, and even those dishes may not be intact. To be clear, I mean coq au vin, gratinéed onion soup, *sole meunière, salade niçoise, frisée aux lardons, moules frites,* steak frites, steak au poivre, *moules marinière,* skate with brown butter and capers, sautéed kidneys in mustard sauce, *tripes à la mode de Caen, blanquette de veau,* pot-au-feu, *tarte Tatin,* a simple lettuce salad with vinaigrette (which was always available in any restaurant, whether it was on the menu or not). In Anglophone countries, to the extent a "French" restaurant still exists, it's just another ethnic alternative. We've forgotten a lot about France.

And yet French food still holds a fascination and power. There's a widespread sense of its present or former greatness and of the greatness of French wine and cheese. Western chefs continue to rely on French technique more than any other. Nothing from the West is nearly systematic enough to replace it.

But what is French food? My aim is to reintroduce it, to present some of the people responsible for it, and to say that it's much more than whatever you probably think it is. More than the cuisine of sauces and former stodginess, more than the cheese course, more than delicate pastry, more than three-star tables, much more than the anthropological set of bistro and brasserie dishes. Though it's all those things. And deeply anchored in time and place. The wines are equally linked to place and often go further back.

I don't hesitate to look at the obvious: at Champagne and the baguette, to understand their essence; at the classic cheese Comté, whose link to its terroir may have been the first to be confirmed by scientific study; real Provençal cooking, which is a cuisine of the poor; the succulent Burgundian "parsleyed ham"; the Alsatian kugelhopf, one of the best of all cakes. But also the less obvious: the goat's-milk cheese Banon, made by a nearly disappeared technique and ripened in chestnut leaves; the deliciously rank andouillette, made of intestines and stomach; the "burnt" regional pastry called *tourteau fromagé;* the curious French "gingerbread," seemingly unleavened, at least as it was originally made. Among wines, there's Loire Cabernet Franc, an outstanding partner to food; the contradictory Sauvignon of Sancerre, with its two opposing forms; the unsuspected wines raised "under a veil" in the Jura; and, from the seaside border with Spain, Banyuls, made by killing the fermentation with a dose of alcohol and then oxidizing the wine in such a way that the taste miraculously forms a bond with chocolate.

I've tried to present French food, not in any methodical way but suggestively, evocatively. Its crazy variety, the love of richness and offal, of perfect young vegetables, of the highest level of artisanship—all are completely contemporary. I have no particular plan, except to go roughly from north to south and to stress the wealth and sometimes the surprises. And the utter deliciousness of it all.

——•——

ONE

There's No French Food Without French Bread

Nantes, Brittany, and 6th Arrondissement, Paris, Île de France

It was 1 a.m. and I was sound asleep when Gérard Meunier woke me. I got up from the cot in a back room and joined him and Alexandre, the eighteen-year-old apprentice. The bakery was on the outer edge of the suburbs of the city of Nantes, in Brittany. The building was recent, anonymous, and I felt I might have been almost anywhere in France. I had arrived the evening before, and with Meunier and his family eaten a simple supper, cooked by his wife, Ginette, in charge of the shop. And like Meunier I'd gone to bed early.

In the workroom, Meunier had already turned on a mixer filled with his important ingredient, *pâte fermentée,* dough that had fermented overnight. As the spiral hook deflated the dough, it released the slightly alcoholic smell of fermentation. Four more doughs waited in different containers, and three dry mixtures were ready. Meunier and Alexandre were wide awake. Meunier said he normally went to sleep at 9:30, rose at 1, then slept for perhaps two hours in the afternoon. Five and a half hours were enough for him.

Meunier, in early middle age with thinning dark hair, had apprenticed in his family's bakery in the Vendée, the department just to the south. Then he had worked as a baker in Paris. He had moved to Nantes because there was a bakery for sale. The spot was on the edge of the country, and he grew a garden—tomatoes, beans, lettuce, squash. He ran the bakery with his brother-in-law, trading days off, because they baked every day of the week.

To preserve the flavor in the dough, Meunier mixed—kneaded—only briefly and with that spiral hook. Kneading develops the gluten in the dough, so the loaves expand more in baking and become lighter, with a thinner, flakier crust. But kneading exposes dough to air, causing oxidation and taking away flavor. The more you knead, the less flavor there is.

Meunier loved white flour, which flowed automatically from a pipe above the mixer. He had been a student of the important French bread expert Raymond Calvel, who loved white flour at least as much. (Calvel would be appalled that some bakers have moved from white flour, called type 55 in France, to the slightly darker type 65 for their baguettes.) I'd come especially to see Meunier make his baguettes, which some people would say are flour and yeast in their ideal form.

At that early hour I must somehow have brought up the name of Poilâne, the Paris bakery known for its big sourdough loaves made from somewhat dark flour. Meunier laughed and laughed at the name. Eating that bread with its bran was like eating an orange together with its skin, he said. He added that he himself baked some whole-grain loaves for certain customers, but pleasing customers was part of the trade. He used sourdough for a country loaf, and altogether he made more than a dozen kinds of bread. For the day to come, the total would include eight hundred baguettes. If it hadn't been summer with some of his customers on vacation, he might have made two or three hundred more.

"Bonne pâte, mon cher," he said, complimenting Alexandre on the dough he had made. Adding some *pâte fermentée* to it gives it strength, just as kneading does, he said. Everything Meunier made contained a proportion of *pâte fermentée,* including the croissants and brioches. Eighteen percent went into the baguette dough. During fermentation, enzymes turn some of the flour's starch into sugar that the yeast breaks into alcohol and carbon dioxide, which inflates the dough. Organic acids, even with commercial yeast, slowly develop over the hours of fermentation and contribute significantly to the taste. Adding some already fermented dough provides an extra boost of acidity and other flavor, and saves time.

"A lot of experience touching the dough makes a difference," Meunier said. "That's not necessarily something that's explained very well in writing." According to the way the dough felt, he could make a correction if he needed to, in the amount of moisture, the temperature, the timing.

Raymond Calvel, who taught for many years at the national milling school in Paris, was the world's greatest authority on white bread. I once took him to lunch. He had begun his professional life in the 1930s in the South of France, baking sourdough and kneading with two fists in a trough. His strongly held views on ingredients and technique were supported wherever possible by scientific study, and where science hadn't explored he relied on his years of observation. Many French bakers have resisted his well-thought-out methods or have never heard of him. Calvel died in 2005, but even before then his former students had come together in an association and begun to publish a small periodical in his honor. Meunier said, "I don't have a lot of problems with him, but some of my colleagues . . . He gives them a hard time. He's sharp. *Oh, oh, oh.*"

Even a small amount of bran overwhelms the subtle flavors of the blond inner kernel of wheat. Any good bread requires skill and good ingredients, but the subtle flavors of white bread derive mainly from technique. Calvel knew that white flour with a marked creamy color from carotenoid pigments produced better flavor, and, because he stressed that so much, every baker now knows that the loss of color during kneading means loss of aroma. (In France, bleaching flour is illegal.) In addition to white flour, Calvel liked the subtle effects of commercial yeast. Meunier had thoroughly absorbed his mentor's teaching. But Calvel himself was undecided whether he preferred commercial yeast or the bread raised with a *levain,* a sour starter, which was the kind he had first known in the South of France. His favorite bread memory was of his aunt's home-baked *pain au levain.*

A lot of mental arithmetic is involved in making a dough, with everything calculated by weight. Calvel put his recipes in the form of complex diagrams that were off-putting to some bakers. And, Meunier said, there are adjustments in winter because of the different temperature and humidity. Calvel advocated using a little more water than many bakers then did. When you make wetter dough, the microorganisms are more active and the fermentation develops a little faster. You also thin the gluten so it's stretchier—the eyes in the bread are bigger and more irregular, and the inside texture is more tender and appealing. The moisture also helps the bread keep a little better. Meunier outlined eight steps for making baguettes, giving the number of minutes required for each. "To make a product that keeps, you need about four and a half hours." That was the total time of the eight steps. The water for the dough was kept at a cool 10 degrees C (50 degrees F). For flour, he turned a dial and a set amount fell down the plastic pipe. The first loaves would go into the oven at 5:15 and come out at 5:45, he said.

Meunier loved the *autolyse,* an important innovation of Calvel's. The French word, now adopted by English-speaking bakers, literally means "self-relaxation." It refers to the approximately fifteen minutes of rest that Calvel prescribed for the briefly mixed flour and water before salt and leavening are added. During that time gluten develops, even without kneading, so afterward kneading can be reduced, to the advantage of flavor. "If you don't do the *autolyse,*" Meunier said, "then you have to let the mixed dough sit in the mixer for about another half hour." The *autolyse* was "a miracle."

At one point Meunier and his apprentice took a tiny break to drink some hot sugary milk and eat half a slice of the regional *brioche vendéenne,* which is sweeter but less rich than the Parisian one. Mostly, they worked in silent concentration. The first baguettes were formed by machine and laid by hand in wire-mesh molds attached to shelves that stacked in racks and rolled into the oven. The racks save handwork, mostly with a peel. But a baguette placed directly on a hot oven shelf opens more completely, and Meunier baked some baguettes that way along with his other breads. When you're a customer in a French bakery, even with the loaves on the far side of the counter in shelves against the wall, you can see a difference. Baguettes baked on a hearth are a little arched and distorted.

When the baguettes had completed their final rise, the dough was so swollen and loose it almost jiggled. The enzymes were producing maximum sugar to feed the rapidly reproducing yeast. Meunier slashed the tops with five short overlapping cuts, almost parallel to the length. The raw dough looked ragged, but when the loaves bulged in the oven, the cuts would become diagonal and neat.

At 3 a.m., Meunier began forming some baguettes by hand and laying them on the *couches,* the French baker's standard linen cloths, each loaf separated by a fold of cloth. Even bakers who trouble to shape some baguettes by hand can't afford time and space to do many. "It's truly *agréable* to shape by hand," Meunier said. "You sense the state of the dough much better." Yet his customers preferred the machine-rolled baguettes from the molds, he said, although he charged the same. The hand-formed baguettes are superior because much of the flavor is trapped in the bubbles in the raw dough and afterward in the baked loaf. The machine squeezed out too much gas and aroma. (But recently developed machines are more gentle, and at least a few bakers think their work is better than shaping by hand.)

The first baking of the day is complicated by all the different kinds of bread. Alexandre was shaping whole-grain dough into balls. Already rising were several brioches (including *brioches au chocolat*), croissants that had been formed the day before (and chilled overnight), as well as various sorts of bread. Meunier said, "Later, it's all baguettes, baguettes, baguettes." He shaped all the bâtards by hand. He also made some of Calvel's *pains rustiques,* which are cut only, not shaped at all, so as to keep even more aroma. They look like little pillows. Although Meunier was a believer in white flour, he admitted to liking the taste of his *baguettes de campagne* containing 5 percent rye flour.

The speed and coordination of tasks were striking—how practiced the two men were, tracking time down to the minute. As baguettes rolled quickly out of the shaper to be transferred to the racks, Meunier could hardly turn his back to look elsewhere for a moment. The same machine made *ficelles* ("strings"), like very narrow baguettes. I saw the importance of little things: the way the linen cloth behaved differently in the heat or coolness, the way the dough stuck at times or didn't, its useful friction as it was rolled on the counter, and, especially, the timing. One oven held the rolling racks of machine-shaped bread; a larger one was for the loaves rising in the *couches.* The goal was to always have a succession of breads ready to bake. Just as Meunier had said, at 5 a.m. the first baguettes were going into the oven.

Then around 5:40, with the earliest daylight, there began to be a sense of urgency. To supply the shop, the oven had to be kept continually full. Bread went in and out at a rapid pace, and it all had to be properly baked—"done and not overdone." The baked baguettes, with their dull shine, had a deep golden color and gave off aromas of caramel and all the rich flavors of the crust. The air was full of the smell of bread. Finally, at 8 a.m., the race to fill the shop was over, and Meunier and Alexandre stopped for a meal.

They ate fresh tomatoes, baguette, canned sardines, cheese, leftover roast meat, mustard, red wine. In the background, the electric bell, attached to the door, rang automatically and continuously as customers came and went. The breakfast baguette was just cooled and of course perfectly fresh. The shape gives the satisfaction of fresh, crisp, brown crust and white in every bite. The flavors were buttery and eggy, subtly wheaty, and included some of the sweet cakey aroma that's typical of the best French flour.

As much as we identify French bread with the baguette, those skinny loaves only began to be made in the 1920s, in Paris. Before that "French bread" meant, as much as anything, big sourdough loaves, sometimes white, sometimes dark, like those of Poilâne today. And depending on where you are in France, "bread" can still mean something other than a baguette.

Every difference in ingredients, especially flour, and every difference in method and shape make a difference in the taste of bread. Depending on where you draw the lines, even today there may be a hundred or more kinds: *pain de mie* (white sandwich bread), *pain de méteil* (mixed rye-wheat), *pain de seigle* (mostly or all rye), *pain complet* (whole wheat), *pain viennois* (long, pale yellow inside, slightly enriched), *pain brié* (its dough beaten fanatically smooth, from Normandy), *couronne du Bugey* (a "crown" baked very dark, from a mountainous area in the east), *pain paillasse de Lodève* (known for an especially long fermentation, from a town in Languedoc), *pain d'Aix* (folded and notched, from Aix-en-Provence), *pain de Beaucaire* (two-layered bread baked on its side, from another town in Provence), *pain aux noix* (with walnuts), *pain jocko* (long), *pain polka* (low, round, and crosshatched all over the top), *tordu* ("twisted"), *tressé* ("braided"), *plié* ("folded"), *fendu* ("split"), *cordon* (with a "cord" of dough on top), *portemanteau* ("coat hanger"), *main de Nice* (a "hand" with fingers), *fer à cheval* ("horseshoe"), and *marchand de vin* ("wine merchant," the longest loaf of all). To name just those is to ignore most of the regional breads, most of the typical Paris shapes, and all the many regional brioches and other breads whose richness and slight sweetness might classify them as cake.

Still, if you had to choose one primordial bread, it wouldn't be any of those or the baguette but rather the large, somewhat dark, round *pain au levain* ("sourdough"), which has only a limited appearance on the list. It belongs to the very loose category of *pain de campagne* ("country bread"). If you go back far enough, it's the bread most people once ate.

That's the kind baked by Poilâne on the Rue du Cherche-Midi in Paris. It makes only sourdough, apart from some token loaves of white *pain de mie* and a few items of pastry. The location is among what are now some of the city's most fashionable and expensive shops, especially for clothing and shoes, and still the lines for bread regularly run out the bakery door. It was Poilâne, back in the 1970s and 80s, that brought darker bread into fashion, when most of the capital's bread was white, tasted like nothing at all, and turned instantly stale. Good bread seemed in permanent retreat, and some people began to think that white bread could never taste good. *Pain Poilâne* was at the head of the counterwave of "old-fashioned" and "country" breads, but it wasn't a re-creation of something from the past, as nearly all the others were. Poilâne has now baked it continuously—from a sour leaven, with the loaves formed by hand, raised in linen-lined baskets, and baked in a wood-fired oven—for seventy-five years. The bread is raised solely with a portion of lively sourdough taken from one batch to start the next. The round loaves weigh two kilos each. A decorative *P* is cut into the top, replacing the old four slashes that formed a rough square and barely opened in baking. The bread is sold in the old way by weight; you can buy a whole, a half, or a quarter loaf. The stone-ground flour contains enough bran to color the bread a deep beige, while the crust is a moderate brown, covered with traces of pale flour. The marked taste is of wheat and sourness plus fermentation. Although the sourness is less than that of most San Francisco bread, some technically attuned bakers consider the Poilâne loaves too sharp and acetic, the texture too dry and the holes too small.

Typically for a city bakery, Poilâne's oven is in the cellar below the shop. The space is inexpensive and the surrounding thick stone and earth help to keep the temperature even, to the benefit of the dough. Many visitors have descended the worn stone steps to the cellar (you only have to ask) to see the deep wood-fired oven that extends under the street, so as you enter the shop you walk over it. The baker at work wears white shorts and a T-shirt, the sort of minimal covering bakers have worn near ovens for centuries.

Poilâne is run by Apollonia Poilâne, who took over the business in 2002 at the age of eighteen after her parents died in an accident. When her grandfather, Pierre Poilâne, bought the Cherche-Midi bakery in 1932, the neighborhood was poor and artists would trade paintings for bread. During the Second World War, *pain bis* or darker *pain noir* ("black bread") was all that could be had. *Pain bis* is the nearly forgotten name from the time when dark bread was considered second quality; it describes something between white and whole, the bread of those who couldn't afford white. Few people who lived through the war ever wanted to eat it again. White bread returned, but the recalcitrant Pierre Poilâne continued to bake old-fashioned *pain bis* in the face of everyone's advice. He wouldn't adapt to his customers, and eventually they adapted to him. His darker sourdough became more fashionable than anyone's baguette. Some Parisians call any similar bread *pain Poilâne,* as if it were a type, though the name is a trademark.

With an intuitive sense of marketing, Pierre's son Lionel turned the business into a huge success, building many more ovens, all wood-fired, at a facility in the suburbs, where production continues twenty-four hours a day. The bread is sold widely in Paris, served in restaurants, and sold around France and abroad. When Pierre died, the business seemed to go entirely to Lionel, with his brother, Max, operating a single bakery on a corner of the Rue Brancion, near the periphery of Paris in the 15th arrondissement. (Max was the elder brother, with a captivating smile that showed he too knew how to market himself, though in a more lighthearted way. His bakery continues, run today by his daughter Mylène and grandson Max. All the loaves come from the two cellar ovens. They're nearly identical to those of the Rue du Cherche-Midi—no baguettes.)

Lionel could be very charming and was sometimes intense. He said to me, as he must have said to many others, "This is a real, very old bread and very French." Eating it, I thought afterward, you feel that the taste you cannot quite put into words might almost be the taste of history. Lionel argued for the adaptability of *pain Poilâne* to all kinds of food. He refused to make baguettes, though he wasn't as doctrinaire as his image. He said to me, "A good baguette, well done, it's not bad."

Almost everywhere in the world that wheat or rye is grown, bread is the most important traditional food. In France, it's a constant at every meal. And France, the greatest country for wheat bread, has for centuries placed the highest value on white bread. More than any other people, the French have made an unrelenting analysis of the methods for making it. The best resource until not so very long ago was Antoine-Augustin Parmentier's *Le Parfait Boulanger* (*The Perfect Baker*) published by the Royal Printing Office in 1778—accurately observed, beautifully written, and still useful. Parmentier's name on menus indicates the presence of potatoes, which he popularized in France, but his greatest gastronomic contribution was to bread.

It's not just that bread is healthful and affordable, and that well-made bread tastes delicious, but that it's an extremely good complement to other food. Wheat bread, and especially white bread, goes with almost everything. It moderates and makes more pleasurable the concentrated flavors of sauces, cured meats, and aged cheeses, while its flavors and textures provide a delicious counterpoint.

A big, somewhat sour loaf is the oldest and most basic kind, and can be extremely good. But what you prefer is a matter of taste. A large *pain au levain* can be baked very dark, while the crust of a classic baguette is much lighter, merely deep golden, because too much darkness hides the subtle flavors of the flour and fermentation. A classic baguette is really fresh for only about three hours, so many French still line up to buy it before each meal. It's the most urban and refined—the most *parisienne* and the most uniquely French—of breads.

TWO

·—·—·

The Struggle
and Triumph of
Haute Cuisine

7th and 15th Arrondissements, Paris, Île de France

The twentieth-century critic Curnonsky once divided French cuisine into four parts: *"la Haute Cuisine, la cuisine Bourgeoise, la cuisine Régionale, et la cuisine Improvisée."* Haute cuisine is luxurious, and except now and then when it loses energy and needs renewal, it's modern and fashionable almost by definition. At its best, it has harmony, a sense of rightness, and expresses the French appreciation for *volupté* ("pleasure in the senses"). But Curnonsky was a skeptic. He found haute cuisine snobbish, international, and complicated to the point that it often hid the real flavors of things. He was drawn more to regional cooking. (With his mustache, full face, and increasing size, as he grew older Curnonsky looked more and more the part of the gastronome. His real name was Maurice Edmond Sailland, and he was also a humorist. In 1900, he visited China and discovered the diversity of its cuisine, which was a lasting inspiration.) Curnonsky had in mind classical haute cuisine, the food of Escoffier, which has been gone for so long that today hardly anyone knows it from experience. Apart from technique, only pieces of it survive—here and there a sauce, a particular dish. But haute cuisine is very much alive in luxurious restaurants around the world, not least the three-star restaurants of France. It continues to embrace the new and sometimes the exotic; top chefs want to surprise, to dazzle.

Haute cuisine heavily influenced the *cuisine bourgeoise,* which was once prepared in many households by professional cooks. It hasn't disappeared, though it too has long been in retreat. Where today in restaurants do you find its iconic dishes— *bœuf bourguignon, blanquette de veau, poule au pot,* pot-au-feu, *bœuf à la ficelle, perdrix au choux* (partridge with cabbage), a well-made omelette? Some you can find, usually carelessly made at very modest places. You don't taste and say to yourself, "Ah! This is what French cooking is all about."

As to *cuisine régionale,* three-star chefs always used to have on the menu a few regional dishes, impeccably executed. The best of those dishes represent ideal combinations. People explored their local foodstuffs for so long, locked into the seasons, until perhaps they knew better than anyone what, locally, went with what. Certain ingredients flattered or commented on each other or simply tasted uncannily good together. There's no single authentic recipe for a regional dish and no one right way, but some combinations of ingredients, some ways of doing things, work much better than others. And to meet current tastes, the old regional dishes usually need only small adjustments, such as a reduction in fat or shorter cooking times. Yet most chefs in France now make only an occasional classic or regional dish in any form. In restaurants, *cuisine régionale* is hardly in the picture at all.

By *cuisine improvisée*, Curnonsky meant the cooking you do with materials you get at the last minute—say, when you come from fishing, hunting, gathering wild plants, or picking mushrooms. And then maybe you even cook them over a campfire. That kind of utterly honest, simple cooking, with outstanding fresh ingredients, is curiously close to what many current haute cuisine chefs seek.

Meanwhile, American-style fast food, led by McDonald's, has succeeded famously in France, and a few years ago, fast food began to outsell regular restaurant food. And yet during the past few decades, many Parisians have become more demanding about quality—of cheese, coffee, produce. French food is not a simple thing. And at the moment, haute cuisine is thriving as never before, although it's no longer particularly French.

Where once in Paris a number of bistros served old-fashioned food at a modest price, now hardly a decent place is left. When in 2015 Daniel Rose opened his bistro La Bourse et La Vie, to address exactly this lack, a Parisian friend of mine went and commented that he hadn't seen food like that in fifty years. Many little bar-cafés offer lunch. Out front, in chalk or marker on a board, is a two- or three-course menu for very little money. You might choose a first course of *œufs à la Russe, assiette de crudités, salade de thon, céleri rémoulade, filets de hareng, terrine de canard, fromage de tête,* or *rillettes de porc*—that is, stuffed eggs, raw vegetables, tuna salad, celery root in cream vinaigrette, pickled herring, duck terrine, headcheese, or pork rillettes. The plats du jour might be, to cite a real example: *bœuf miroton au riz* (slices of beef in a sauce of onions and a little vinegar, with rice), *côte de porc* ("pork chop") with *sauce piquante* (onion, shallot, herbs, vinegar, pan juices or stock) and *coquillettes* ("small pasta shells"), or grilled *faux filet* ("sirloin") with french fries. A quarter liter of wine might be thrown in, and you might have a choice between cheese and dessert. But these inexpensive meals range from sloppy to a nightmare, with the food bought already prepared from a mass distributor. A restaurateur can't afford to serve very good or interesting food for so little money. A sandwich is a much safer choice, and a lunch of bread and cheese that you seek out at a *boulangerie* and *fromagerie* is a treat.

When I visited France for the first time as an adult, at the age of twenty-one, in 1972, there was hardly any English to be seen or heard, and each time I've visited since then France has become steadily less foreign. People don't spend so much time at the table now, even at cafés or bistros, and the cost of a decent meal has risen along with the cost of labor. The price of a three-star meal has for several decades risen faster than the cost of living in general, until for most people it's stratospheric.

The French haven't yet come to fear fat the way Americans do, as it has often been said, and when they eat fat they enjoy it fully. Croûtons, freshly sautéed in butter, deliciously garnish cream soups; the warm crunch amid the creaminess precludes a sensation of heaviness. The average level of pastry in shops is incomparably higher than in North America. Most of the world's best chocolates, meaning the dipped ones with classic or novel centers, are still made in France. The French are still willing to spend more than North Americans do on food, and compared with us they still regard eating well as a more natural, important part of life.

There's game in the fall—birds in plumage, hare in fur, in the butcher shops of the Rue Mouffetard in Paris, for example. Menus as well as markets reveal a widespread, if diminishing, taste for innards. Outdoor markets thrive in Paris, like the one on the Boulevard Richard Lenoir, the organic market in the Boulevard Raspail, and the crowded everyday market streets (Buci, Cler, Mouffetard, and more); the last aren't particularly special, though they're lush with produce. Great French cheeses continue to be made, though even in excellent shops they're embalmed in plastic, as they never used to be. Fresh bread remains essential. Bread bakeries are distributed more or less evenly throughout neighborhoods, and the quality of some of the bread in supermarkets is impressive. French butchers, compared with those in other countries, cut more precisely into more pieces, so each muscle can be cooked to best advantage.

But haute cuisine today places much less importance on meat than it did. A restaurant meal in France was, and in old-school places still is, a festival of protein, which might start with foie gras or eggs and then move from fish through meat to cheese. Sauce, too, may be a concentrated protein essence, even if it is made by just deglazing a pan with wine and adding and reducing a ladleful of stock. A vegetable as a rule used to be a garnish, though a plate of asparagus, green beans, or peas might appear as its own course. The title essay of *An Omelette and a Glass of Wine,* by the great British food writer Elizabeth David, begins:

Once upon a time there was a celebrated restaurant called the Hôtel de la Tête d'Or on the Mont-St-Michel just off the coast of Normandy. The reputation of this house was built upon one single menu which was served day in and day out for year after year. It consisted of an omelette, ham, a fried sole, *pré-salé* lamb cutlets with potatoes, a roast chicken and salad, and a dessert. Cider and butter were put upon the table and were thrown in with the price of the meal.

Eggs, ham, fish, lamb, roast chicken! That was more than a century ago, but even today in France, especially in run-of-the-mill restaurants, you can be left longing for fresh vegetables and fresh fruit. The social explanation for all the protein is that vegetables were seen as a lower class of nutriment and that meat and fish taste much better with wine than vegetables do. Unfortunately, vegetables cost more to prepare—they must be cleaned and trimmed and cut, and it can be hard to charge proportionately. In stylish restaurant meals, the proportion of vegetables has nonetheless risen. But who, at the end of a meal in France or anywhere else, is ever offered a perfect piece of ripe fruit, which takes no preparation and may be the one thing you possibly desire?

The story of French food is disproportionately the story of food in Paris. The capital always had the money, the cooks, and the ingredients, many of them from the surrounding countryside of the Île de France. On a more humble level, not so long ago the food of many Parisians was the food of the provinces. That's where they had come from, and they had brought their cooking with them. Some opened restaurants. The cuisines of Normandy, Alsace, Provence, and more are part of the food of the capital.

The most French food of all is soup, the traditional evening meal at home, with broth or mere water as the medium for it. One wonders how many Parisians, how many French, still make soup more or less daily. Good old onion soup—*soupe à l'oignon*—in its more rustic version may be constructed of layers of bread and cheese, plus liquid, but the onions are first cooked very slowly to a light brown. Leek and potato soup, also called *potage bonne femme* or *potage parisien,* is associated with the now-disappeared concierges of Paris and with the working class of the Île de France, the former province of which Paris is the capital. Sliced leeks and potatoes are cooked in salted water until tender; they and their liquid are seasoned well with butter, salt, and pepper, and the whole is ladled into bowls over a piece of drying bread—the bread in soup shouldn't be fresh or it turns to utter pap. The potatoes can be crushed to thicken the soup. The taste is honest but a little thin, nothing a chef could sell in a restaurant.

The stereotype of haute cuisine is that it has no roots, in contrast with regional French cooking. But haute cuisine does have roots. It was originally court cooking, born in Paris and at Versailles. French cooking of the kind we would recognize appeared in the seventeenth century. Spices gave medieval aristocratic cooking much of its character, but spices became more widely affordable, taken up by the new rich of the bourgeoisie. The aristocracy responded by inverting the social distinction. They switched to simpler flavoring with native European herbs and common vegetables: celery, carrots, onions, thyme, bay leaf, and parsley (and to a lesser extent, tarragon, basil, and chervil). These quieter flavorings exalted a dish's principal ingredients, whose luxurious quality became paramount. The preparations were elaborate too, in ways that the lower classes couldn't afford. The main cooking fat remained lard, but in the new cooking the amount of butter in recipes, not least for sauces, rose enormously. Sourness was less frequent, and sweet and savory slowly began to be segregated, with sweet dishes appearing at the end of the meal.

(Butter, which had been a peasant fat, finally triumphed in haute cuisine in the nineteenth and twentieth centuries. And there were always exceptions to the pattern of separating savory and sweet, but the sweetness was mild, such as from fruit: pork with prunes, duck with sour cherries, and blood sausage with sautéed apples. The sweet-and-sour orange sauce for duck is a rare survival of medieval cooking; it was originally a more tart *sauce bigarade,* prepared from *bigarades,* bitter oranges.)

The haute cuisine that dates from the seventeenth century was also formed by dialogue among cooks who moved from one aristocratic kitchen to another, exchanging their knowledge. Another dialogue was between chefs and their aristocratic employers or, later, their customers in restaurants. (For a very long time now, the great restaurants of France have relied heavily on foreign customers. And critics have lost influence. Instead, wherever we live, we learn what haute cuisine is from the media, including social media, above all through shared photographs.)

During the same period that haute cuisine became modern, higher-quality wine began to be made and sold under the names of particular estates, starting with Haut-Brion in Bordeaux. Instead of being drunk from the barrel in the year it was made, before it turned to vinegar, the best wine began to be aged in glass bottles with airtight stoppers that preserved flavors and allowed them to evolve and increase, an essential condition for great wine.

I've always believed that the greatest influence on French cooking is French wine. By no coincidence, the stacked-tire cartoon figure that is the emblem of Michelin is named Bibendum, from the Latin *Nunc est bibendum* ("Now let us drink"). Except for a couple of recent years when Italy briefly surpassed it, France has always been the world's largest producer of wine. It makes not just more wine but more of the best and in more variety, and it has a long history of doing both. Great wine calls for great cooking to match. The combination is so good that to complement the wine, professional French cooking is elegant, delicate, and restrained. (The cooking may similarly restrain the wine. People used to the exuberance of New World wine often find that excellent French wine tastes light, although it's fully flavorful and has a long aftertaste.) The logical order for serving wines determines the order for serving food, as the tastes build from lighter and simpler to stronger and more complex, and then sweet. As a rule, French wine is dry, and dry wine tastes much less good or boldly unpleasant with sweet food, so French food is rarely sweet or sweet-and-sour. Even current French cooking generally avoids strong spice that would compete with the superior fruit and other aromas of great wine. (And until not long ago, among herbs, there was no cilantro; no oregano until pizza; no dill, called "bastard fennel" in French, borrowed from Scandinavia for use with salmon; and little rosemary, which is rarely used in France, even near the Mediterranean.)

And lately French and world winemaking has been energized by the French phenomenon of "natural wine." Some people are bothered by the name—What does "natural" mean? they ask. There's no definition, but methods are generally organic and manipulation in the *cave* is minimal. I'm a supporter of natural wine. It has brought fresh attention to moderately priced bottles with an overt deliciousness that flatters food; certain of the wines can be a revelation at the price. (I admit that to write so much about French wine, as I've done in this book, is to simplify and ignore French beer, such as the resurgence of outstanding *bière de garde* in the north of France.)

Second only to wine, cheese offers the most interesting flavors of anything we eat or drink. It's no coincidence that the taste of the best cheeses is strongly linked to place. And France produces most of the world's greatest cheeses by far—Beaufort, Camembert, Comté, Époisses, Mont d'Or, Roquefort, Sainte-Maure. The country has so many cheeses that no one can give a firm count. French cheese, like French wine, sets a high standard of complex flavor, and other French food must measure up.

Truffles, foie gras, or garlic go with almost anything. But certain combinations, such as chanterelles with fines herbes and cream, are precise marriages of flavor. More examples are a simple browned sausage with a pan sauce of shallots and red wine, salmon with cucumber and dill, asparagus with *sauce maltaise*, *boudin noir* (blood sausage) with sautéed apples, puréed chestnuts with a touch of celery and chicken stock in soup, a Gruyère omelette, chicken with tarragon, and *bœuf bourguignon* with the classic Burgundian garnish of pearl onions, white mushrooms, and lardons (sautéed sticks of salt pork).

I once had a conversation with the chef Alain Passard in his three-Michelin-star restaurant, Arpège, housed in a stark white building in the affluent 7th arrondissement on the Left Bank. Passard comes from Brittany, something you may notice first in the salted Breton butter. Passard hasn't set up an empire with outposts; Arpège is his only restaurant. He's there five days a week (the restaurant is closed on weekends). Thirteen people, including three pâtissiers, work in the small kitchen. In haute cuisine, it takes skill and often a lot of labor to produce each dish. When the hard work succeeds, the signs of it disappear, as at Arpège, and the result looks effortless.

Michelin stars are levers of publicity that reward a chef with customers. In that way Michelin helps to maintain the top level of French cooking. Do you distrust the Michelin inspectors? I asked Passard a couple of years after he received his three stars. "Not at all," he answered. When he received that third star, "it was a propulsion. It was maximum. It was determinant." He looked for a stronger way to say it: "It gave me wings. I felt so much better. . . . It was a liberty but a responsibility to French cuisine and the world. *Quel bonheur!* I believe in myself more than I did five years ago."

I asked him about certain classic dishes that are seldom made anymore and hardly ever made well, and he named some, including *blanquette de veau*. He called them "martyred, crucified plates—by people who weren't really of the métier. They have a negative image." Most young cooks haven't had the experience of home cooking that French cooks did in the past. And when a young chef prepares a traditional dish, the result is more remembered, or reinvented. I asked Passard what formed the taste of his young cooks. "They're formed by the cuisine of Arpège," he answered.

He spoke of a cuisine based on flowers and plants, "a cuisine completely cleaned up." Actually, he used the word *dépolluée* ("rid of pollution"). This was before 2001, when Passard launched his vegetable cuisine, not pleasing everyone (though meat and fish continue to appear on the menu).

His focus on the luxury production of native plants is in a direct line from the distant past. Where many ingredients were previously brought to Passard's door by small producers from the departments surrounding Paris, now he has three bio-dynamic gardens in three locations in France, where the fruits and vegetables are raised from carefully selected varieties. He receives deliveries each day; the produce is never refrigerated, except on the hottest days of summer. The garden in the Sarthe, with sandy soil, is the *potager,* the source of vegetables. The garden in the Eure, with clay soil, produces small red fruits and root vegetables. The garden in the Manche, across the bay from Mont Saint-Michel, with alluvial soil, has bees for pollination and honey. On an early fall menu was a honey soufflé, with the note that the honey had been harvested from the restaurant's hives a few weeks earlier in August.

For sauce, Passard has long extracted and reduced vegetable juices, such as carrot, celery, or beet. He travels and tastes and is wide open to all sorts of cultures. But Passard's cooking is not complicated. It's intelligent and precise. Another dish on the fall menu was *Tartare pourpre végétal au piment de Cayenne,* a purple vegetable tartare (red beets, red onions, red cabbage with unrevealed spices) with a sauce of acidulated cream. A meat dish was *Corps à corps de volailles haute-couture,* composed of a *poularde du Pâtis* and a *canard de Challans* (a specially raised hen from a particular farm and a special duck from a town in the western department of Vendée).

When Nouvelle Cuisine appeared in the 1970s, it rejected classical sauces, because they could overwhelm, and avoided all flour thickening. For meats, it looked to pan sauces based on quick reductions of stock that would underline the taste; it then placed the main item on top of the sauce. Nouvelle Cuisine, with its dictate that chefs be "inventive," seemed very loosened up, but it was extremely conservative compared with fashionable cooking today.

You might argue that classical French cooking provided something useful to react against or at least comment on. Structure, in any creative endeavor, can open the way to greater complexity. French dishes can have echoes of history, of respect and admiration, and sometimes, rarely, a frisson when you recognize something that seems totally new. A menu gives a chef more to do, more to achieve. After the best meals, you feel the chef has taken you on a journey. There's a trajectory to the experience. It's true that French chefs have often felt the structures of the past to be stifling, and some have moved to the United States to feel freer (just as some foreigners have conversely always felt freer in France). But now after Nouvelle Cuisine and the inventiveness that has followed, there's hardly any structure left to limit anyone. When anything goes, you may believe you've achieved something, but in relation to what?

I used to think that unaccustomed combinations of ingredients, as opposed to classic complements from the past, would at their best tell you something new about one or more of them. But we're so used to the unexpected mixtures now that I hardly think carefully about them at all, beyond a simple reaction of whether or not I like what I'm eating. (That doesn't apply to Passard.)

Many chefs in France as elsewhere now make small tapas-style plates of food instead of large ones, and sometimes they devise such long tasting menus that each course is a tiny taste. With a tasting menu, how often is a sybaritic *steaming* dish set before you? There's hardly enough of any one thing to hold the heat during the time it takes to get the plate from the kitchen to your table. Bénédict Beaugé, a critic and close friend who lives in Paris, e-mailed me a few years ago, "For myself, I can't stand the tasting menu: I think it's, to a certain extent, a kind of death of cuisine, because in a single mouthful, or two, a diner can't succeed to understand complexity."

Jadis, whose name means "yesterday," occupies a narrow corner on the Rue de la Croix Nivert in the 15th arrondissement. Guillaume Delage opened Jadis in 2008 when he was just twenty-nine years old. He was already extremely accomplished, a chef who had worked with Michel Bras, Frédéric Anton, and then Pierre Gagnaire, all chefs with three Michelin stars. He spent seven years with Gagnaire, the last four running Gaya Rive Gauche, where he quickly earned a Michelin star.

Delage's restaurant is one of those whose food is unexpectedly affordable for the quality. You eat and you sense the people behind the food. The restaurants have an intimacy and accessibility. The small number of seats feels very European. Chefs such as Delage can afford to make the food so good because they opt for cheap rent, have no linens to launder, have less staff in the dining room, skip the most laborious preparations, and turn tables. (Except in brasseries or very inexpensive places, tables never used to be turned; a table was yours for the evening.) Now more customers, especially young ones, can eat out well more often. There's no mandatory allegiance to the old sequence of three courses (entrée, plat, fromage or dessert, or sometimes both)— no actual cheese platter, which is expensive and leads to waste. (One or a few cheeses may be preselected and cut in the kitchen.)

Vitality fills the best current Paris bistros, including the ones with more moderate prices and a stress on natural wines. "Bistro" is almost impossible to define, except that it involves a degree of casualness. And there's something of a blur between a wine bar, a "natural wine" bar, and a bistro, because all may serve food. A bistro tends to have more ambitious food. The good places serve food with clear, clean, precise flavors supported by precise technique, an approach that may be timeless but seems especially modern.

When I called Delage one day at the end of lunch service, it was he who answered the phone. (If you call a small restaurant in France at six o'clock for a reservation, it's often the chef who answers.) About his cooking at Jadis, he said, "It's a cuisine inspired by the past." He spoke of "so many roots" in French cuisine—"the preparations, the bases . . . the marinades and farces. You must know all of them in order to work well. The bases are very important."

Jadis is current in many ways—you can order anything in a tapas size, or order a first course in a main-course size—but Delage is consciously not exactly backward-looking but deeply aware of the extraordinary gastronomic wealth that classical French cooking represents. The first time I went to Jadis, I had Delage's sole in *sauce Dugléré,* which is named for a chef who died in 1884. Before Delage revived it, it may not have appeared on a menu since the 1950s. The classic version is composed of fish stock, white wine, and béchamel, and finished with butter and—the defining element—bits of tomato. Delage would have nothing to do with the béchamel: "The original is heavy." He cooks finely cut shallots and white mushrooms slowly in butter, adds white wine and reduces, adds fish *fumé* and reduces, adds cream, and once the fish is cooked, he squeezes in a little lemon and emulsifies the whole with a little butter.

I asked him about *blanquette de veau,* citing Alain Passard's remark that it's one of the martyred dishes of French cuisine. Delage agreed. But he put *blanquette* on the menu, and customers began to ask for it, and now it's always on the menu. He does make it his own. Rejecting the old *liaison* of flour and butter, for creaminess he instead adds a purée of two or three seasonal vegetables, such as parsnips and potatoes, and he flavors it with modern touches of ginger and cardamom.

Dishes on the menu have included shellfish bisque with horseradish-*harenga* ("herring caviar") whipped cream, a red-wine stew of pig's foot with squid and chickpeas, Padrón peppers in tempura, a filet of scorpion fish with sweet-and-sour eggplant and spinach, and roast wild pigeon, lacquered with beet juice, with *pommes dauphine* and a classic *sauce salmis* (red wine and wild pigeon stock, bound with liver and blood).

Delage is very aware of the most current luxury cooking in other parts of the world. Of the Nordic cuisines, he says, "They're based above all on products. For me, it's not cuisine. *Ce n'est pas très cuisiné*" ("There's not a lot of actual cooking"). He acknowledged, "The ingredients are the highest quality, the cooking is done well." Then to be clear, he gave an example: "One cooks a super fish that's very scarce, irreproachably fresh, with three herbs." You could hear a period in his voice. For him, that kind of simplicity is not enough.

Does he see a possibility of a revival of French cooking? "Of course."

Haute cuisine may no longer be especially French, but in the twenty-first century it has triumphed as never before. Yes, it always influenced other cooking, especially the *cuisine bourgeoise,* but that was haute cuisine in compromised form. Now, in certain bistros, the compromise is all but gone. You may not get quite Alain Passard's perfection from all the labor and just-picked freshness. But the chefs bring the intelligence, skill, and knowledge of haute cuisine chefs—often that's what they are. At Jadis you can eat three full courses for less than fifty euros, a fraction of the cost of a meal at an haute cuisine temple. So you can say that more people than ever are eating haute cuisine, and not just in France. And the food in the bistros may be more stylish, because the rules are looser.

THREE

The Vegetables
of the King

Versailles, Île de France

"Cooking! That's when things taste like what they are." The re-mark made by Curnonsky in the 1940s has been so often repeated that it may qualify as an axiom. If good food depends on an intimate understanding of raw materials, then it's impor-tant that many French retain a bond to the countryside. Only about 1.5 percent of French work directly in agriculture today, but people who live in cities and suburbs often have a tie to a rural village where they have relatives. And a fair proportion of all the vegetables eaten in France, especially such items as toma-toes and green beans, are grown in home gardens.

If you take the train from Paris to Versailles and if, instead of walking from the station up to the enormous palace and its grounds, you turn left to the cathedral and then, facing it, look to your right across the street, you see the high stone wall pro-tecting the almost nine and a half hectares (a hectare is two and a half acres) of Le Potager du Roi, part of the palace's eight-hundred-hectare park. The entrance to the King's Vegetable Garden is through the building on the corner, though to visit the garden you have to reserve in advance. The Potager, full of both fruits and vegetables from the start, was created between 1678 and 1683 to supply the palace. After the Revolution, it became a school for gardeners and under one name or another it has been one ever since. Until late in the nineteenth century, the focus was on luxury production, then it switched to industrial production; now it's somewhere in between.

Antoine Jacobsohn, the head of Le Potager du Roi, is dark-haired, an eager talker. He's a friend of mine, a native New Yorker who has spent most of his life in France. It was Antoine who first pointed out to me that Paris is the capital of French agriculture as well as of French cuisine. When he was younger, during the summer he used to drive a combine in the South of France, working for friends who had a business traveling from farm to farm at harvest time, and the experience seems to have marked him permanently with the perspective of a farmer. When I asked Antoine not long ago to describe his career, he hesitated and said that he's interested in the history of food, both production and consumption, and within the history of agriculture, the history of vegetable gardening. When I first met him, he was working at the small Écomusée de la Courneuve, located in a Paris suburb and devoted to the history of the capital's market gardening. During that period, he co-wrote a small book called *Le Petit Pois,* devoted to the green pea and containing both history and recipes (not least one from the celebrated pâtissier Pierre Hermé, for a complex sweet pea soup). For the publisher Flammarion, he gathered a collection of sixteenth- to nineteenth-century French vegetable-garden writing, and he interviewed twenty-three growers for a 162-page paper he titled "Producteurs de goût" ("Producers of Taste"). Since then, however, he has focused on the practicalities of running the garden and school at Versailles.

This garden was always called Le Potager du Roi, but *potager* more often describes a humble country vegetable garden. The word comes from *potage* ("soup"), and Antoine points out that *potager* is also an old word for a masonry cooking range, the earliest kind. (He can't resist adding, "And the invention of the cooking range had an enormous influence on the capacity to cook with more finesse, as concerns sauces and diverse reductions.")

Le Potager du Roi is laid out in a grid of rectangles and squares, divided by stone walls, with a fountain set at the center of the main space. As in other old gardens, the thick walls hold the sun's heat and protect the plants from wind, giving the garden something of its own climate. Fruit trees are espaliered against the south-facing walls. The garden has 450 kinds of old and new fruits, dominated by apples and pears. The number of vegetables, Antoine says, "is far more variable." There have been as many as 80 different species and 500 varieties, but "I have progressively lowered the number to 300 to 350 varieties a year—otherwise it gets too complicated."

Soon after I met Antoine, we got together for dinner at À la Tour de Montlhéry near the former Halles de Paris. That market supplied all the needs of Paris and beyond until the day it closed, February 28, 1969. The restaurant is one of the survivors from that time. A market had stood on the spot, which is still referred to as Les Halles, from about the year 1110 (an earlier market had stood near Notre Dame on the Île de la Cité). The first two permanent structures, called *halles* even then, were built in 1183. Of the succession of buildings that replaced them, still remembered affectionately are ten iron-and-glass pavilions built in the 1850s and 60s and two more added in 1936, the last of them torn down in 1973. The Halles were "the belly of Paris," in Émile Zola's phrase, a regional market that fed the city. The food originally came from nearby farms by wagon and on hoof (animals were driven into Paris and refattened). Goods arrived in darkness and selling began before dawn. The market was both wholesale and retail, with producer-sellers as well as middlemen. By the end of the time of the Halles, trucks crowded the city streets, and France's agricultural economy was changing, becoming much larger in scale and more international.

The day after the Halles closed, trading immediately started up at the huge modern facility built outside Paris at Rungis, a redistribution point from which produce is sent all over Europe. Large-scale production at a low price demands more durable produce and is judged on appearance much more than taste. Some small farmers from the Île de France, rather than sell through Rungis, began to sell directly at the open-air retail markets around Paris.

The restaurant's name, À la Tour de Montlhéry, Antoine explained, refers to the town of Montlhéry, known for its tomatoes and located in a rich market-gardening area about twenty-five kilometers south of Paris. A prominent tower there is all that remains of a medieval castle. Antoine pointed above the bar, where hanging among the hams was one of the bells that started and stopped trading at the Halles and also one of the "Roman" balances that were illegal but nonetheless used for small sales.

Antoine had prepared notes for what amounted to a small lecture about why the food of Paris is different, and what he said is worth recounting. I've often thought of it. His conversation was dense with facts. In the late 1940s, the Île de France had more than 3,000 market gardening and farming operations, which at the time he spoke had been reduced to 500. (Now the number is even less.) Competition comes from growers in Spain, Italy, Turkey, and Greece, but not Belgium or the Netherlands, where growers are more specialized in out-of-season produce.

Among the produce of the Île de France, Antoine said, are many lettuces and radishes, an important part of regional consumption since at least the eighteenth century. Watercress is also traditional, though the quantity produced now is small. The flat onion called Jaune Paille des Vertus, which is straw yellow as its name indicates, has been raised on the Plaine des Vertus since the sixteenth century. It was the most cultivated onion in France in the 1950s and 60s, and now just one Île de France producer is left. Charcutiers like this onion because it contains little water and doesn't dilute their *boudins;* the low moisture also makes the variety a good keeper. White mushrooms are known in France as *champignons de Paris,* and some are still raised underground in abandoned quarries that once provided building stone for Paris. Certain crops, such as the plum Reine Claude de Chambourcy, have almost ceased to be grown because so many Parisians leave for vacation in August at the height of the harvest and not enough people remain to buy them.

Antoine moved back in time. From the seventeenth century on, Paris and the court at Versailles formed a luxury market for all kinds of goods, including food. (Paris was the most populous city in Europe, followed by London and Naples.) Demand and competition led the growers of the Île de France to focus on a new, high level of quality. Haute cuisine developed from high-quality foodstuffs, Antoine logically asserted, though he conceded the lack of any direct evidence to support the argument. By the mid-seventeenth century, he said, the former medieval theories about the health effects of different foods on the body had been replaced by an emphasis on the aesthetic pleasures of eating. A wave of cookbooks appeared, starting with La Varenne's *Le Cuisinier François*. But Antoine added a gardener's perspective, saying that lists of pear varieties had been published decades earlier, that fruit and vegetable books flourished at the same time as the cookbooks, and that there were more gardening titles than cooking ones.

Antoine argued (and I agree) that France's national cuisine was largely created in the Halles de Paris, where growers, middlemen, housewives, chefs, and other professional cooks met every day. "You had a communication that was very immediate," Antoine said. "You would buy an ingredient from the same person and cook it in the same way, and if it didn't taste good one time, you would say, 'I'm not going to buy from him again.'" At the Halles there were no published prices; everything was done by negotiation and price was influenced by circumstance—rumor of a boatload of apples overturned, Antoine suggested, sending apple prices up for a week and a half: "Price and flavor were continually negotiated. They really are linked."

Huge servings, he pointed out, were typical of the restaurants around the Halles, like the one we were in. I had ordered an individual serving of lamb kidneys in mustard sauce, and the platterful that arrived might have served two or three people. I remembered the first time I'd been to the restaurant, a place where you sit elbow to elbow beside strangers, often at the same table. My diminutive girlfriend faced an enormous plate of lamb set on a bed of garlicky white beans. She proceeded to eat, while on either side we were watched, by way of glances, no eye contact. When the food was about half gone, the older couple at one side, who had scarcely spoken to each other much less to us, smiled and complimented her on her appetite. The few times I've been back I've always felt it was a point of honor to finish everything.

Antoine has brought me up to date on the Potager. "Since we've gone 'almost without treatments'"—meaning toxic chemical ones—"our production of fruit has dropped by half and our vegetable production has gone up (think about that . . .)." Some of the fruit goes into jams made at the garden; herbs are dried or sometimes turned into jellies or syrups. When yields are high enough, some fruit is sent out to be made into juice and bottled. When there aren't enough pears for that, some are made into eau-de-vie ("quite good") at Distillerie Artisanale Cazottes—Laurent Cazottes is doing highly interesting work with organic fruit in the department of the Tarn in the South of France. The Potager also has a limited production of greenhouse exotics (green papaya, Chinese guava), which are among the specialties that a few very good restaurants come to buy. As to overall annual numbers, "Today we are at around eighteen to twenty tonnes of fruit and the same for vegetables." Almost everything produced is sold at the gardens, and most of the customers are from nearby. There isn't enough to meet the demand. *Locavore* is a current word in French.

FOUR

The Croissant: Tender Richness and Crunch

14th Arrondissement, Paris, Île de France

"We're lost at the bottom of the fourteenth," the pâtissier Michel Gerstenmeyer said to me. This was a dozen years ago, before he retired, and it was true that his shop, Le Palais d'Or, was just a narrow front in the middle of a block of the Rue de la Tombe Issoire, an out-of-the-way, unfashionable street in the 14th arrondissement. Gerstenmeyer's name had come up when I began to ask friends about makers of good croissants, and I had gone to the shop as a regular customer to buy one to taste. The interior of the shop was small, just three or four meters square, and I was surprised to see no bread. Usually a neighborhood shop has both pastry and bread, although the specialty is one or the other. The croissant I bought had a brown surface, a rich butteriness, and an optimal balance of textures. The craftsmanship, together with the small size and humble location of the shop, made me think Gerstenmeyer was someone worth meeting.

I had been gathering names of pâtisseries that were supposed to make good croissants and had come up with nearly twenty, located all over Paris. Traveling to each required time all out of proportion to the minute or two it takes to buy and eat a croissant. I went to the food hall of the Bon Marché department store and to well-known individual shops and chains—Dalloyau, Fauchon, Pierre Hermé, Eric Kayser, Ladurée, Moulin de la Vierge, the antique Stohrer—and others that weren't famous at all. Even for early December, the weather in Paris was unusually bitter; midday temperatures remained below freezing. That made a difference because when baked goods are chilled, they immediately lose their fresh-baked taste. Each time, I had to eat my croissant quickly, when I was barely out of the shop, scattering flakes down the front of my coat—not the sort of thing that's done in Paris. Rain would have been equally bad, because dampness ruins the crunch. Some of the croissants I tried were too soft, too crunchy, too dry, too salty, too sweet, too pale, or, in a few cases, plain gummy. But most were very good. I quickly realized that a good croissant isn't hard to find in Paris.

When I telephoned Gerstenmeyer at Le Palais d'Or, he mistook me for the man coming to fix his scale. I explained that I was a writer interested in croissants. He was friendly, but he was very reluctant to let me come and watch him work during the busy pre-Christmas season. A Japanese magazine photographer had once taken four hours to produce, in the end, just one published shot. Gerstenmeyer said, "I have never had a Christmas, *moi*, always there's work"—no time for parties. I promised him I would stand in a corner and stay out of his way, and after a few minutes he relented.

A couple of days later in the chill, early morning darkness, I knocked at the door of the very dimly lit shop. In less than a minute Gerstenmeyer appeared and unlocked the door, and we descended to his L-shaped cellar work space. Normally, he explained, he began work around 4 a.m., but that morning he had started a little earlier because croissants always take longer to rise in the cold. "The first ones come out of the oven at eight for the store," he said. That's when his wife, Marie-France, would open to customers. The shop closed again from about 1 to 4 p.m. and then stayed open until 7:30. "It's not the thirty-five-hour week," Gerstenmeyer said, referring to the French law that limits the number of hours employees can work before they have to be paid overtime. The Gerstenmeyers had no employees at all. "We're nothing other than artisans," he explained. "You know what that means? It means we work alone."

Gerstenmeyer's father too had been a pâtissier. He came to Paris from Alsace, where it's sometimes said that all the best French pâtissiers originate, including Pierre Hermé, who for three decades now has been the most famous. "It's true," Gerstenmeyer commented, about pâtissiers coming from Alsace. "I don't know why." He appeared wholly Parisian himself, and yet there was something about him that reminded me of farmers, who also work much of the time alone; he had a sweetness with strangers. His own apprenticeship had been with his father, and his three brothers also became pâtissiers or cooks or both. But, he explained, "it's not clear that there's a future for the small artisan." His two children had chosen very different careers. One was at the Sorbonne, and the other was a business auditor. By comparison, the life of a pâtissier is "a lot of work."

He and his wife opened Le Palais d'Or in 1976. "*Ce n'est pas le bon coin,*" he said ("It's not a chic neighborhood"). But it was a place where he could practice his craft as he wanted and he liked that. When he and his wife closed and took a vacation, their customers understood. Referring to the possibility of media visits, "If you are Japanese or American, I'll allow you to come," he said. "But if you are French, I don't allow it. There would be all the publicity." Too many people would come to buy his croissants and he would sell out: "I couldn't supply my customers who have supported me all these years."

Already that morning he had produced a tray of beautifully dark brown *chaussons,* made from circles of *pâte feuilletée* ("puff pastry") folded over a filling. That dough, containing no yeast, had inflated in the heat of the oven purely from the steam trapped between the layers of butter. Often for a *chausson,* a pâtissier buys ready-made filling. I asked what the flavor of this one was. "Apple," Gerstenmeyer replied, explaining that he bought the fruit directly from a farmer in Château-Thierry, northwest of Paris. "He keeps the apples in a barn, and bit by bit, I go and get them. And that gives me a little *promenade.*" When, later in the course of each year, the apples ran out, Gerstenmeyer switched to a ready-made filling because, he said, regular commercial apples tasted of refrigeration.

Sitting in a bowl on a shelf was a large mound of cultured butter from the Montaigu dairy in Poitou-Charentes, a region known since the nineteenth century for the quality of its butter. Gerstenmeyer uses *beurre sec* ("dry butter"), which contains slightly less water than regular butter and is more elastic. When it's squeezed thin between the layers of dough, it doesn't become granular but makes a smooth, continuous layer.

The two qualities essential to a croissant, Gerstenmeyer said, are *"moelleux et feuilleté"*—tender richness, running to creaminess, plus crisp leaves. The outermost leaves of a well-made croissant are shattering arcs, as thin as the thinnest paper. You take a bite and then you see in the cross section that the distinct rolled outer layers disappear into the larger quantity of soft, bubbled, faintly elastic insides, although you can trace curves to the very center. The outer layers should be neither too many and distinct nor too few and melted together, from a too-dry dough or a too-wet one or from careless rolling in a *laminoir*. The surface shine, easy to achieve, comes from the egg brushed on just before baking.

Rich flavor comes from cultured butter, not cheaper fats, and a full fermentation by yeast. A croissant should be distinctly buttery and yet not greasy. Greasiness occurs when the dough becomes too warm as it rises, which can happen when the croissants share the same small underground space with a hot oven or when they go into a too-warm proof box, because the melting temperature of butter overlaps with a good rising temperature.

A croissant seems quintessentially French, but it may have come to Paris only relatively recently. The crescent shape is timeless, and there's a record of "cakes" called *croissans* being served in Paris at a banquet for the queen as long ago as 1549, although there's no reason to think those were like the ones we eat today. During the nineteenth century in Paris, soft rolls called *croissants* were made from milk and the whitest flour and served with coffee, and they seem to have originated in Vienna, but again there's no evidence that those were flaky like today's. According to Raymond Calvel, France's great twentieth-century bread expert (who arrived in Paris from the South in 1932, already a baker), a more buttery croissant was first introduced to Paris in 1889 by Viennese bakers at the Exposition Universelle, the one for which the Eiffel Tower was built, and yet there's no evidence that those were flaky either.

A few years later, a new edition of the standard Roret *Boulanger* manual (one in a series published in Paris for all sorts of trades) described a croissant that was beginning to evolve toward layers and flakiness. The Roret credited its information to a baker named Frank from Vienna, "where one knows the art of making bread is very much perfected," and also to a French baker named Majat. These croissants contained just a single stratum of butter, a sixth or less of the amount commonly used today. They were rolled up like ours, but they can't have been very flaky. The Roret also gave an alternative: "If you want croissants in which the butter is not apparent, you must mix in the butter while kneading"—no layers at all. Calvel wrote that as late as 1920 croissants were still neither layered nor flaky. But about that time Paris bakers added more butter in the sort of layers found in *pâte feuilletée,* and that transformed the croissant. Therefore, Calvel asserted, the origin of the croissant is certainly French. Today's dough contains four dozen or more layers, even before it's rolled up to make a crescent.

Gerstenmeyer had, as always, made the dough the evening before, and he described the method. He kneaded together flour, milk (warm in winter, cool in summer), sugar, salt, and cake yeast. He kneaded only briefly, so the dough wouldn't develop too much elasticity, and if a batch of flour nonetheless made the dough too strongly elastic, he would add a little water to dilute and weaken it. He would roll out the dough, spread 250 grams of soft butter over it, and then fold the dough over the butter and seal the edges to make a flat, rectangular package. He would give this *pâton* a first "turn," folding it over onto itself to multiply the number of layers and then rolling it between the cylinders of his electric *laminoir*. The number of folds in a turn and the number of turns varies with the pâtissier and the texture of the dough. The layers can't be too thick or the result will be tough, but they can't be too thin or the dough will disappear into the butter.

The dough had spent the night in the refrigerator at about 5 degrees C (41 degrees F), so it would rise just a little. In the morning, as I saw, Gerstenmeyer took the *pâton* and gave it a final turn, again using the *laminoir*. "In my father's time, it was with the rolling pin," he said. He laid the thin sheet on the smooth stone counter, which I took to be marble. But it was Comblanchien limestone, he said, quarried beside the Côte de Nuits vineyards in Burgundy. With a knife, he cut the sheet of croissant dough in two, and he sliced each half into fourteen triangles, by eye, almost as precisely as if he were a machine. The scrap from an uneven edge, so as not to waste it, he divided and tucked inside several croissants as he rolled them up. The two-handed rolling up is a trick of long practice. He encouraged me to try, but even my best efforts had to be unrolled and redone. "I make four hundred croissants on Sundays," Gerstenmeyer said. "I can tell you that's hard; you also have the work the evening before."

He set each rolled croissant on a tray in a pronounced arc. The trayful went into a small, warm stainless-steel proof box to rise for two hours. Gerstenmeyer took more of the same dough and cut it into rectangles, placing two sticks of chocolate on each and rolling them up for *pains au chocolat*. Children love them, he commented, but everyone eats them.

He offered me coffee and turned to make it, quickly turning

back to ask whether instant was all right. Of course. He stirred it with boiling water in a glass café au lait bowl and provided a reheated croissant. Even having been reheated, it was very good. "But it's from yesterday," he kept reminding me. There were none yet from today. He gave me a reheated brioche as well, and it too was good.

When the croissants were risen, he brushed their tops with a whole beaten egg. He put them into his electric convection oven at 180 degrees C (350 degrees F) for fifteen minutes. What's the ideal color? I asked. "The color is a difficult question," he answered. "If the color isn't good, it's not a question of cooking but of the method beforehand. If the dough has overrisen, then too much sugar has been eaten, and they are paler—it's a problem of sugar, not cooking. After fifteen minutes, they are done."

The trayful came from the oven in a perfect dark golden state. The croissants' *moelleux* and *feuilleté* were ideal, and they had a depth of buttery, fermented flavor. At intervals throughout the day, Gerstenmeyer would take croissant dough from the refrigerator, rolling and forming croissants, and sending them freshly baked to the shop upstairs. The goal was to have none left at the end of the day. And that, he said, is what usually happened. He was a model artisan, and he made perfect croissants.

FIVE

The New-Old Sense
of Champagne

Épernay and Avize, Champagne

The first high land northeast of Paris, about an hour and a half by car, is occupied by the vineyards of Champagne. They're the northernmost vineyards of significance outside Germany. But the Mosel and other German wine regions are deeper in the continent, and they become hotter in summer, so the grapes become riper; Champagne, closer to the Atlantic, stays cooler, which is an advantage for a sparkling wine. The location is at the limit of what, at least until the age of global warming, was climatically possible for a major wine region. Cool ripening produces delicate aromas as well as the high acidity needed to carry the flavor past the bubbles. In addition, the vineyard soil is poor, as you would expect in a great wine region, just a thin layer of topsoil covering deep, white chalk. As a rule, the best wine in any part of the world comes from a single estate and often a single vineyard, certainly from just one vintage. Yet not long ago, when you bought Champagne you almost always bought a brand—a bottle that was a blend of vineyards and vintages. (It may go without saying that in most of the world, wine labeled Champagne must legally come from that region of France.) *Champagne de vigneron* ("grower Champagne") is a recent, widely known but proportionately tiny phenomenon, appealing for the fun of drinking good wines at moderate prices from small-scale individual growers whose names appear on their bottles. Most Champagne is still a blend of vineyards and vintages, coming from houses that produce vast quantities. For them, any bottling with a vintage date is a small part of the total, made only in a better-than-average year. And even their prestigious vintage Champagnes, whose prices enter the hundreds of dollars or euros, and in some cases go higher, are normally a blend of vineyards. With the big houses, whether you pay a little or a lot, when you buy the brand, you buy the house style. Champagne, with its typical qualities of lightness and elegance, comes more or less dry, more or less powerful, more or less fruity (pear, apple, and so on), more or less yeasty (bready, toasty, briochelike, nutty), more or less austere (steely, mineral).

More than three hundred million bottles of Champagne are produced each year. There are about 320 houses, and of those the top ten produce almost one-third of all Champagne. They are Moët & Chandon followed by Veuve Clicquot, Nicolas Feuillatte, Mumm, Laurent-Perrier, Piper-Heidsieck, Taittinger, Pommery, Lanson, and Perrier-Jouët. The big houses are clustered in the city of Reims or lined up impressively on the Avenue de Champagne in Épernay. Most of the houses sold off their vineyards in order to survive the hard times after the First World War, and they still buy most of their grapes from small growers.

There are 15,700 growers altogether, and besides the houses, there are 140 co-ops. Quality from most producers is variable, and a famous name is no guarantee that a particular bottle will be interesting or a good value. In the face of international competition, the Champenois groom their image. And the regulations are considerable. The officially delineated area, recorded minutely, parcel by parcel, is 34,300 hectares. One key is that machine-harvesting, even for the least expensive Champagne, is forbidden; the grapes arrive whole at the press to protect their aroma.

If you have only ever bought an occasional nonvintage bottle, you might think there's one continuous, unchanging supply of each nonvintage brand. But with each new harvest, a house blends a new batch of Champagne. Where a classic winemaker of another region may intervene with the wine as little as possible so as to emphasize the taste of the vintage and the terroir, the blenders of Champagne apply their skills, perhaps their art, to re-creating each year the taste associated with the house, regardless of the vintage. Each house has a formula, often rigid. The blenders draw on different proportions of grape varieties, they use different amounts of wine from different parts of Champagne, and they add more or less reserve wine—good wine held back from previous years. Even small amounts are supposed to be noticeable to inexperienced tasters.

A blend—a brand—has the advantage that customers recognize it and know what to expect, and there's nothing at all wrong with that. With nonvintage Champagne, once you decide on your producer, you always know what you're getting. The skills of blending are at their peak in Champagne, and a great blended wine can easily be superior to a wholly unblended *vin de terroir* from the same region. The appeal of the unblended vintage wine, on the other hand, is its direct connection to nature—the way particular vines behaved in the soil of a particular spot during one year's weather.

Champagne is paradoxically a white wine made from mostly black grapes—pressed very gently, whole and still on their stalks—so no red pigment from the skin colors the clear juice, except in the case of rosé. A blend usually contains all three of the region's grape varieties (others are permitted but rare), except *blanc de blancs* Champagne comes from only Chardonnay, and *blanc de noirs* comes from the black grapes Pinot Noir and Meunier. Any summary of taste risks caricature, but Pinot Noir, at 38 percent of the vineyard, gives fruit flavors (small red fruits when the wine is young) and tannin; Chardonnay, the sole white grape at 30 percent, gives elegance and longevity; and Meunier, at 32 percent, an old mutation of Pinot Noir and the most frost resistant of the three, contributes fruitiness to young Champagne and provides acidity in a hot year when the other varieties lack it. Usually, Meunier is avoided in Champagne meant for aging longer than five or six years. Rosé Champagne is made by blending red wine with white or, less often, by leaving the juice of crushed black grapes with the skins just long enough to stain the wine pink. Rosé can be a light apéritif, but more serious rosé Champagne, containing a subtle astringency from Pinot Noir tannin, is a versatile wine with food.

Up to the point of bottling, Champagne is a still wine. Then, at bottling, a mix of sugar, selected yeasts, and wine is added, creating a final fermentation. The carbon dioxide formed is trapped and absorbed into the liquid, and then the wine is left to age on its lees, mostly dead yeast. At better houses, aging *sur lie* lasts several years or longer, even for basic nonvintage brut. The wine acquires the yeasty flavors that in a young wine are often called bready and that after some years become richer and nuttier. At the same time, the wine's initial unyielding acidity softens, allowing evolving fruit flavors that were previously all but hidden to come forward. Outstanding Champagne may take six years or more to become really enjoyable.

To clear the sediment from the last fermentation, the bottle is upended and periodically turned and lightly shaken, a process called riddling. When the sediment has all fallen to the neck, the bottle is opened again and the sediment is disgorged. For the last hundred years or more, the necks have been first dipped in freezing brine to turn the sediment into a less explosive slush. But once taken from its lees and disgorged, the wine ages much more rapidly. The fashion now for better Champagne, vintage and nonvintage, is to include the disgorgement date, as an indication of freshness. Labels say "late-disgorged," "*récemment dégorgé,*" or "RD." But with a nonvintage Champagne, the date has meaning only if you know how old the Champagne really is. It's so much easier to buy a nonvintage brand.

To cut Champagne's natural acidity, absolute bone-dryness, and sometimes astringency, nearly everyone likes a little sweetness. Since the early 1800s, more or less sugar has been added at disgorging, mixed into the wine used for topping up. It doesn't ferment because by then the yeasts are dead. How sweet the wine actually tastes depends on how much acidity and other elements are present to balance the sugar. (The preference for lighter, drier Champagne represents a reversal of taste. François Roland-Billecart, head of the house of Billecart-Salmon, once said to me that, as late as 1940, 90 percent of Billecart-Salmon was *dosé* to make it demi-sec, "half-dry," and was drunk with dessert. "And then the market slid toward the apéritif"—perhaps 1 percent of Billecart-Salmon is demi-sec today. "At that time, sugar hid absolutely everything. Now the wine speaks.")

"Extra brut" is austerely without or almost without any dose of sugar. These wines are a small minority, but the number of non-*dosé* wines has increased as the climate warms and the riper grapes don't necessarily need the sugar. Most Champagne by far is "brut" (literally, "crude, raw, untreated"), and it may contain up to twelve grams of sugar per liter, but it tastes dry. "Extra sec" ("extra dry") begins to be sweetish. "Sec" is lightly sweet. "Demi-sec," with a dosage of thirty-two to fifty grams of sugar, is definitely sweet.

To give a sense of the physical scale of the establishments, Veuve Clicquot (one of the half-dozen houses owned by the luxury corporation LVMH) has twenty-four kilometers of cellars dug into the chalk on the edge of Reims; two-thirds are former Roman quarries. I once spent time with a Clicquot winemaker, who was one of nine. He and his colleagues devoted five months of each year to tasting, blind, in order to form the blends. Stainless-steel tanks held five hundred different wines of the current vintage, he said, from sixty to seventy different village *crus*. In addition, another three hundred tanks held reserve wines. Clicquot's well-known nonvintage "yellow label" in the previous year had been composed of wine from seven vintages and about sixty villages. "I would say the nonvintage is hardest to make," the winemaker said. "That's where the work really is." He suggested that "99.9 percent of consumers cannot tell there is any difference" from year to year, although usually a difference was apparent to the nine winemakers: "After three or four years of age, it becomes quite difficult."

Champagne is commonly an apéritif, but you can drink Champagne with a meal, as the Champenois do. Not just any Champagne works. The more full-bodied are better, and that means especially vintage Champagne.

On my first visit to Champagne, Richard Geoffroy, *chef de cave* for Dom Pérignon (under the umbrella of Moët & Chandon in Épernay), was funny, smart, fast talking, and fast thinking. He gave a neat summary of Champagne, including its role with food. Dom Pérignon is among the wines at the pinnacle of Champagne. (The eponymous seventeenth-century monk was an accomplished winemaker who advanced the art of blending Champagne, of making the wine clear, and of preserving the bubbles. Moët & Chandon bought his abbey and vineyards in 1823.) Geoffroy remarked that of course nonvintage Champagne isn't really constant at each house from year to year. Every producer follows a formula, he said, but Moët and some others allow the taste to vary more, reflecting the vintage.

He described two families of styles. First were "the styles of processing, of vinification—fermentation in stainless steel or small barrels, with or without heavy-handed malo, with oxidative handling of the juice or not (bigger, fatter or more light, fragrant, on the fruity side)—the whole enological catalogue." (The "malo" is the secondary, malolactic fermentation, which converts malic acid to softer lactic acid.) He said, "The Champenois have a habit of imposing themselves on vintage character. . . . You mock a little the basic material." Champagne made this way, he said, is like the cooking of Escoffier. "You eat *brochet* [pike]—it's good—but you're not really sure what it is." If you arrange a tasting of one brand of this kind of Champagne without vintage character, as produced in different years, you taste only the age of the wine: "Something is twice as old as something else."

The second family comprises "styles that don't process but have the imprint of the maker, coming from the blend." You can taste the vintage. With this approach at some houses, including big ones, the style is "all over the place." He didn't mean that was bad. His Dom Pérignon is made in this "unedited" way. In such Champagnes, he suggested, you may not at first perceive the common elements from one year to the next. He added, metaphorically, "It takes a number of encounters to understand the character of a person."

Geoffroy takes a strong interest in combinations of Champagne with food. He's open to cuisines from around the world and attuned to the cooking of big-name chefs. The salt and sugar in the dish counterbalance the acidity in the wine, and Champagne's acidity requires more than the usual salt. "You always need to be at the upper limit." The astringency and trace of bitterness in some Champagne, from the tannin in Pinot Noir, work better with dishes containing fat, such as cream, duck fat, or marrow. Red wine's tannin, he said, also cleans the fat from the mouth, as it did with many rich old French dishes. He didn't accept the idea that red wine is necessarily the best for many important main dishes. He described rosé Champagne as "Pinot Noir pushed to an extreme"—and a perhaps more effective alternative to still red Pinot Noir: "low in tannin, not working by contrast but mingling food and Champagne together.

"The miracle of Champagne is the marriage of the character

of the fruit and the yeast." At the table, one seeks vegetable and fruit flavors that answer the fruit in the Champagne. For example, dishes containing tomato or black olives, he offered, go with Champagne made from Pinot Noir. Acidity in the wine is echoed by the "high notes" found in lemongrass or Meyer lemons. Yeast flavors in the wine are echoed by the "brown notes" in mushrooms, truffles, sweet woody spices, nuts, and roots, such as turnips and celeriac. The last, he said, was "magic" with Champagne and truffles.

Geoffroy was not much interested in Champagne with dessert, calling the combination "very difficult." If you do drink Champagne with dessert, he said, it should be warmer than usual, because cold brings out the wine's acidity and hides its sugar, making the wine too tart for the dessert. He said he has liked a rosé Champagne from Pinot Noir with a chocolate *glace,* prepared with the traditional South American chile and cinnamon. Just a little chile, he said, prolongs the wine taste in the mouth.

In the Côtes des Blancs *grand cru* village of Avize, Anselme Selosse runs the small house that bears his father's name, Jacques Selosse. His parents, from whom he took over in 1980, made hardly any Champagne. They grew and sold grapes. Today Anselme has 9.3 hectares of vines, 90 percent Chardonnay and 10 percent Pinot Noir. The wines are costly and hard to find. Selosse is a passionate man, the first small producer of Champagne to become well known—now he's the most famous grower in Champagne, and his wines are among the most celebrated. He was the first to take a wide-open look at technique. His wines gathered huge admirers and also some critics, who found the wines too oaky, too oxidized, and too aldehydic (meaning alcohols have oxidized, giving flavors found in sherry). Back in the early days, he said, "my role is to put a light on a monument. . . . I don't change it, I clarify what is beautiful, what is there." He spoke happily of Americans calling him a "crazy man," using the English words.

"I have very specific ideas. Champagne is not a method of vinification; it is wine that comes from Champagne." He believed in the soil's microorganisms as being very important, an uncredited part of terroir. Years of chemical agriculture had hugely reduced the proportion of organisms in his soil, and early on he was trying to bring them back. "A terroir is its organisms." He concluded, "I don't want to be best. I want to make the juice of my soil."

Selosse stressed the quality of fruit when few in Champagne did. Before he picks, he doesn't measure the sugar and acidity in his grapes, as almost every modern grower does, if only for reassurance. He tastes for flower and fruit aromas (as other growers do), and he looks for sweetness in the flesh next to the seeds. He checks as well that the seeds are brown, indicating ripeness. Often this means that he waits, and then the sugar rises much higher than Champagne growers used to look for. He was alone in that, but now there are others.

The wine ferments in 225-liter and 400-liter oak barrels (20 percent of them new each year) with only wild yeasts. "That's equally part of the terroir." The yeasts, scattered in the waxy bloom on the surface of the grapes, are still relied on by most of the best French winemakers. The wine ferments without the usual application of heat or cold to control the temperature, and sometimes it doesn't finish fermenting until May. For complexity and antioxidant effect, Selosse employs the Burgundian technique of *battonage,* regularly stirring the lees in the barrel with stainless-steel wands. He minimizes the use of sulfur. All that was considered madness when he began.

The key was that he had the land to produce high-quality fruit. His *grand cru* Initiale is his basic brut, a blend of three vintages. Version Originale is composed of three older vintages. The vintage bottling, Millésime, is from sites in Avize. Two characteristics of wine from Avize, Selosse says, are saltiness and a powdery taste. The wines are rich; they've often been called "Burgundy with bubbles." And there's rosé and extra brut and demi-sec. There are two very unusual wines, with a complex taste, that are very rich and very *un*-Champagne; they have the familiar *rancio* taste of sherry, and like sherry each comes from a solera system, another form of blending.

Although Selosse has always emphasized terroir, it wasn't until 2010 that he began to release the first six *lieu-dit,* or single-vineyard, Champagnes from particular villages. The typical Champagne of big houses "is technically good, but it lacks genius," he says. "One should be drawn into a wine as into a book. The first pages are sometimes hard, and you may have to come back to them, but then the pages turn themselves." Where twenty years ago he had no colleagues—no one taking a similar approach—now he cites more than twenty. Some of them spent time working with him.

The Aube lies to the southeast of the other four regions of Champagne, separate enough from them that it's closer to the Burgundy appellation of Chablis than to the rest of Champagne. Early in the twentieth century, growers and producers in northern Champagne fought to have the Aube excluded, and yet underlying most of it is the Kimmeridgian limestone found in certain of France's most famous vineyards. Now the Aube is the center of "grower Champagne." Bertrand and Hélène Gautherot, who are the proprietors of the small producer Vouette & Sorbée in the village of Buxières-sur-Arce, represent perhaps the summit of "grower Champagne."

Bertrand cultivates just five and a half hectares, most of which he inherited from his parents. "They were more peasants than wine growers," he says. They raised grapes and sold them to others to be made into Champagne, and when Gautherot took over the family property in 1993, he did the same. "I didn't like Champagne," he explained to me. "It wasn't a wine," in the sense that it didn't taste "of terroir but of vinification." Nevertheless the wine seemed to pose a puzzle that drew him in. Among his friends were Pierre Larmandier of Larmandier-Bernier and Jérome Prévost of La Closerie, both of whom are producers of now-sought-after Champagne: "The three of us together reflected on what is the taste of Champagne."

They made blind tastings comparing conventional wines with organic and biodynamic wines from Burgundy, Beaujolais, the Loire, Alsace, Sancerre, the Jura. Gautherot became convinced that organic and biodynamic wines were superior, and he decided to have his property certified as both. During that period, he met Anselme Selosse (the two are friends) as well as Raymond Laurent, a grower who works "with old-fashioned methods, unchanged since the 1950s"—"no enologist, no pesticides." The blind tastings brought the realization that Champagne could be "a real wine, like Burgundy," and that realization launched Gautherot as a winemaker. He made his first wine in 2001.

"I'm not an extraordinary grower," Gautherot said to me at one point. He aims to "let nature do everything. You choose a variety, put it in a good place, and have confidence in nature." And yet he is known for his vineyard work.

The Vouette & Sorbée vines are 60 percent Pinot Noir, the dominant variety of the Aube, with 34 percent Chardonnay and, exceptionally, 6 percent Pinot Blanc (made into a separate wine). Three-quarters of the vines are on Kimmeridgian lime and the rest on Portlandian (in the parcel called Sorbée) with the soil in both cases based on clay-and-lime marl. Yields, Gautherot said, are generally thirty-five hectoliters per hectare, "when things go well," which is far below the French average. Lower yields tend to give finer, more aromatic wine. (Yields are sensitive to the warming climate, he said, and the extra carbon dioxide is making the forests of the Aube, a source of oak for barrels, grow faster.) In the cellar he relies on wild yeasts as the wines ferment in wood for up to a month, and he leaves the wines on their lees for another nine to ten months (with no *battonage*). Gautherot uses barrels five to sixteen years old, so the wines aren't marked by the taste of new oak.

He chaptalized (added sugar to the fermenting juice, a not-uncommon practice in France, to raise the alcohol in the wine made from less-ripe grapes) in his first year (and again in 2004 to just 15 percent of the wine) and never again. "The goal is to learn. How can you learn if in the *cave* you make compensations?" He explained, "Above all it was a decision to make a library for my children"—a library of the taste of each vintage, a library of "memories." "If I chaptalize, I can't leave them the truth." And where Champagne bottles, after the producers disgorge the sediment, are normally topped up with *liqueur de dosage,* a blend of wine and sugar, meant to make the taste more consistent as well as sweeter, Gautherot has never added any such thing, only more of the identical wine. All three Vouette & Sorbée wines are "extra brut."

Fidèle, his primary Champagne, is pure Pinot Noir from Kimmeridgian soil in the parcels named Vouette and Biaunes. The wines are now in demand and not necessarily easy to find, but at first they were seen as unexpected, even eccentric—not for every lover of Champagne. Fidèle is rich, complex, and elegant, but it turns especially on the acidity and mineral sensations associated with Kimmeridgian lime, and its aromas are different from those of usual Champagne. Gautherot says he always recognizes Fidèle by its taste of "Burgundian grapes, fresh almond, and quince, but above all its saline, limestone finish." He says, "What never fools me is the dynamism this wine gives me; if I'm tired and I drink a glass, my vitality is back."

SIX

High-Scented Sausage

Troyes, Champagne

When you cut into a grilled andouillette and release the steam, there's no getting around the smell. I tasted my very first andouillette long ago in a Paris bistro. Andouillettes are chitterling sausages, and not all the French care for them. The waitress, when I ordered, tried several times to warn me off. But I persisted. The usual serving is one, and yet before long I was presented with a pair of grilled andouillettes. They were probably andouillettes de Troyes, the best-known kind. I don't remember that there was anything else on the plate. Cutting in, I unleashed a powerful earthy aroma, and my girlfriend moved to an adjoining empty table. I was deeply discouraged. Like other neophyte andouillette-eaters, I wondered if something was amiss. I could eat only half of what was on the plate.

In the words of Édouard Herriot, who was mayor of Lyon for most of the first half of the twentieth century and three times prime minister of France, "Politics is like an andouillette; it should smell a little of shit but not too much." A retired andouillette-maker first quoted that line to me. I had gotten the idea that andouillettes might be fading in popularity, and I asked him whether customers today were mainly older. "No, the young still eat them," he said. "They're a product for, let's say, the bon vivant."

The twin ingredients of an andouillette de Troyes are *chaudins* and *panse*—pork intestines, specifically the large intestine, and stomach. At four to six inches long, the sausage, despite its feminine suffix, looks distinctly penile, especially before it's cooked: fat, beige, and skinlike, with the skin pushed inside the center of each rounded end. The time-honored presentation is plain with potatoes—mashed, boiled, sautéed, french-fried (though the fat of frying layers richness upon richness). Sometimes there's also a sauce, such as red wine with shallots; sometimes there's a salad. A pot of mustard is normally on the table. Many people don't use it, and to me it neither adds nor subtracts.

I didn't try an andouillette again for years, and when I did it was in Champagne, which is the home region of the andouillette de Troyes. Like some other people, I had somehow, mysteriously, become acclimated. It may have helped that the wine in my glass was Champagne, a classic accompaniment to the andouillette de Troyes, a contrast of refined with rustic. Since then, occasionally—twice a year is about enough for me—I've eaten others. Barring extreme examples, the rich odors are no longer at all off-putting but instead distinctly satisfying. A good andouillette is rich, meaty, tender—highly sensual, like some distant, suspect relative of a truffle.

The andouillette is not to be confused with its much longer

and frequently wider relative, the *andouille,* which is a differ-ent kind of chitterling sausage. ("Andouillette" is easy enough for a foreigner to say—AHN-dwee-ette—but *andouille,* though shorter, is a little difficult. It occupies about two and a half syl-lables, the middle one being stretched out so as to nearly encom-pass the last, sounding roughly like ahn-DOO-yeh.) The current diverse sorts of *andouille* are all typically smoked and served cold in slices. On display at a charcuterie, you may see the unusual-looking cross section of the *andouille de Guémené,* from Brittany, with its neat concentric circles looking like a ma-chine product. Yet, like a good andouillette, it too is made by hand, one *chaudin* being merely slid over another, again and again, around a central "heart." If you are looking for a safe way to try chitterlings for the first time, without all the intense odor and flavor, the *andouille* is the answer. It can be tender and highly delicious, the smoke and chill masking the earthiness. If, however, you seek the full underlying chitterling taste, then head straight for the andouillette.

The ingredients can be chopped and stuffed into the casing (*chaudin* again) by machine, but the best andouillettes are made entirely by hand. The key phrase is *"tirée à la ficelle"* ("pulled by a string"). That's how the contents enter the casing. The an-douillettes of some outstanding charcutiers are made in this way and labeled AAAAA. No more than a dozen as I write. These andouillettes have been tasted and approved by the jury of the Association Amicale des Amateurs d'Andouillette Authentique. A diploma from the Five-A's is a highly valuable form of market-ing good for two years, when the next tasting is held.

The Paris section of the Michelin red guide places the an-douillette on its list of fifteen traditional foods, together with recommended restaurants in which to eat them. (Six of the fifteen dishes either are or include offal.) No other country places such importance on a sausage composed of intestine and stomach. Why France? The only answer I can come up with is that the unusually strong French appreciation for meat extends without prejudice to meat in all its forms. The funk of an andouillette doesn't exactly reflect the French appreciation for refinement, but there are plenty of other great, vigorous, rustic French foods.

I first tasted Christophe Thierry's Five-A andouillette de Troyes, made just outside the city of Troyes itself, at a natural-wine bar in Paris. Like all the others I've had, this one arrived burning hot from the grill and, when cut into, it steamed. But it was clearly different from lesser versions. A slice held together a little, something that an andouillette doesn't tend to do well. And the inside color was a faint, healthy pink.

The small French city of Troyes, capital of the onetime province of Champagne, is about two and a half hours' drive southeast of Paris. Marketers for the city describe its shape as that of a Champagne cork, but a street map shows that its shape is better described as phallic, with a narrow branch of the Seine running under the cap. The epicenter of andouillette production today lies not far past the city's train station, on the busy main street of the adjoining suburb of Sainte-Savine, at the prettily painted corner building of Charcuterie Thierry.

Christophe Thierry, with his wife, Olivia, runs the business, and he has a focused energy. His seriousness about métier is typical of the top culinary artisans in France—not that they lack humor, but they're sober and earnest on their topic. Thierry started out studying accounting and management, before deciding to become a charcutier after all, like his father. The shop once belonged to his parents. The range of charcuterie produced is wide, from *pieds de cochon* ("pig's feet") to *boudin noir*. About the latter, Thierry said, "We make it every day. You know why? The *boudin* is good only when it's fresh." Of the ten charcutiers in or near Troyes, he said, only two or three trouble to make andouillettes de Troyes. "It's sad."

In a separate building behind the shop, Thierry and his three employees worked in a chilled room as a team, assembling andouillettes, as they do four mornings a week. They worked in silent concentration, like Benedictines in respect for physical labor. I thought my presence might be inhibiting their talk. No, Thierry said, they always concentrate and they rarely speak.

Three times a week an abattoir in Brittany, "the cleanest possible," delivers fresh ingredients, usually two hundred kilos of *chaudins* at a time. (Amazingly to me, most of the weekly production of andouillettes is sold right there in the small Thierry shop to individual customers, about half of whom drive from a distance. Sales rise during the outdoor grilling season.) The first step, when the *chaudins* arrive, is to scrape off any fat, then all the innards are thoroughly washed. The best *chaudins*—free of holes—are set aside for use as casings. The rest, along with the *panses,* are blanched in boiling water. Afterward, Thierry said, for milder flavor, it's important to cool the intestines quickly in chilled water. "From *A* to *Z,* there's no mechanization." The intestines and stomach are cut with knives into long strips about a centimeter and a half wide.

The seasoning and flavoring had been already carefully weighed out: salt, a mixture of spices, Dijon mustard, raw onion, and white *vin ordinaire*. Thierry had said to me earlier, "I don't hide anything," and yet he held back the details of the spice mixture, saying only that it contained neither herbs nor pepper. He didn't claim the mix was that special, but he didn't want anyone to make an exact copy. I watched him add the seasoning and thoroughly incorporate it with his hands. The strips of *chaudin* and *panse* marinate in it for two to three hours.

I told Thierry that in Paris I had learned to recognize his andouillette partly by the rosy inside color. It must be present in the starting material, he said, a result of being fresh and "very, very clean. That's the primordial thing for making a good andouillette." The color is fixed by a little *sel nitrité,* which is regular salt mixed with a trace of sodium nitrite. "It's used in all andouillettes." He added, skeptically, "There are those who say they don't."

Thierry worked steadily, gathering a good handful of the seasoned strips by eye and setting them alternately in front of Frédéric Dieppois on his left and Philippe Urbain on his right. It didn't matter if the amount varied a little, because the andouillettes are sold by weight. The men's rhythms were automatic, and the trick of pulling the string took place so quickly it seemed like magic. I watched Urbain over and over before I caught what happened. He slipped the string, actually a band of fabric, around the handful of innards and bunched up the casing on his index and middle fingers, which, sticking out, hooked the string. Then he deftly pulled the bundle, looking like limp rags, into the gathered casing, while sliding the casing down. Thierry too pulled some andouillettes. As the men pushed in the ends to close them, they pressed to expel a little air, making a slurp. Rapidly, Dimitri Labille stabbed each one three times, so it wouldn't burst later in cooking, and he laid it in a big wheeled plastic case.

Why work *à la ficelle*? I asked. "The machine is much faster, but it hashes everything," Thierry explained. "One loses quality in terms of texture. Inside, everything is all packed together and not *moelleux*." That useful French word means "marrowy," referring to bone marrow, and thus "smooth, creamy, soft."

The pulled andouillettes would sit and further absorb their seasonings until seven in the evening, when cooking would begin. Thierry uses a court bouillon of water, onions, carrots, leeks, thyme, and bay leaves, and the andouillettes cook in it overnight at 80 to 85 degrees C (175 to 185 degrees F). If the cooking were hotter and faster, he said, they would burst. They cool in the same liquid, so they lose less weight and taste better. Freshness is important. They keep for two days under refrigeration, Thierry said, and three weeks if also vacuum sealed.

Like that glass of Champagne during my first positive encounter with the sausage, any wine you drink with an andouillette needs both lightness and acidity, so it's refreshing and counters the richness. Up to the point of my visit to Thierry, I hadn't found that andouillettes de Troyes were especially fussy about particular flavors or even about whether the wine was white or red. In Troyes at the wine bar Aux Crieurs de Vin, where Thierry and I went for a late lunch, I asked the sommelier Jean-Michel Wilmes what he thought. "There's no perfect alliance," he said. "There are lots of different wines that go." What about Champagne? "*Ah, oui, oui, oui.* The best is very little *dosé*"—almost completely dry. And he offered fine points. A Champagne made from Chardonnay grapes should be "a little old, a little less youthful and fresh." With andouillettes, he said, it's probably better that the Champagne be made from the red grape Pinot Meunier. "What *may* be better than Champagne is a vinous, rounder Pinot Noir. Maybe." It's a sommelier's job to think about the pleasure that comes from such careful choices, and I'm sure he was right. It was a moment when the complexity of the traditional French approach to food was on full display. It was normal that one of the most refined drinks in all the world should be juxtaposed with one of the most earthy and pungent of all foods.

SEVEN

A Sense of Welcome
and Wistub Brenner

Colmar, Alsace

Alsace is border territory, its long shape divided from Germany and Switzerland by the Rhine River and from Lorraine and the rest of France by the Vosges Mountains. Beside the Rhine runs the wide fertile Alsatian plain, which meets the hills that descend from the mountains. The climate and soil make Alsace rich in wine grapes and materials for the kitchen. Though its wines have always stubbornly resisted popularity in North America, Alsace is one of the world's great wine regions, excelling in aromatic whites and best known for Riesling, with Clos Sainte-Hune standing at the pinnacle. The finest vineyards, on the middle heights of the hills, make an erratic hundred-kilometer-long parallel to the plain and river. Most of the finest vineyards, however, like most of the farms that produce the great cheese Munster, lie in the southern half of the province, which is the department of the Haut-Rhin, or Upper Rhine, because it's farther up the river. The Bas-Rhin, which includes the major city of Strasbourg, is flatter. As you travel through the region, villages of half-timbered houses, the roofs of the highest buildings topped with storks' nests, seem borrowed from fairy tales. During much of the year, the streets of the more picturesque towns and villages are crowded with tourists, mostly German or Swiss. Alsatians descend from Gauls, Romans, Alemanni, Franks, and later others from surrounding areas who settled in the region after the Thirty Years' War. (The war ended in 1648, and many current wine properties have been occupied by the same families ever since.) The declining Alsatian dialect, stronger in the Bas-Rhin, is German, but Alsatians were long distrusted by both Germany and France, seen as too French to be German and too German to be French. Marc Haeberlin, the warm, readily accessible chef of the three-star Auberge de l'Ill, once said to me, "In school we were punished for speaking Alsatian, so we spoke Alsatian on purpose. And now it's being taught like a foreign language." Alsace is mountain and plain; country and city; French and German; Catholic, Protestant, and Jewish. It holds an unusually large concentration of Michelin-starred restaurants, and compared with most of France the traditional cooking remains strong.

Maybe by no coincidence, Alsace's two most famous dishes are made of disparate elements. *Choucroute garnie* is sauerkraut cooked in Riesling with juniper berries and served with up to eight or more cuts of cured pork and sausages (an homage to the Alsatian charcutier) plus sometimes, cooked at the last minute, *lawerknepfle* ("pork liver dumplings"). Instead of serving *choucroute* with forms of pork, it can be garnished in other ways, such as with pheasant or, long ago, sometimes fish, which was cheaper than meat; in the late twentieth century *choucroute* began to be used in new ways and the fish was revived. The sauerkraut itself is still made in some homes in September and October; fall is the best time to eat it. Closer to the hearts of Alsatians may be *baeckeoffe* ("baker's oven")—pork, beef, and mutton braised together in an earthenware pot with potatoes, white wine, carrots, and leeks. The dish used to be assembled the evening before a busy workday, and the meats left to marinate overnight. Next morning the earthenware pot was carried to the baker to cook slowly in the oven after the bread was out, so the *baeckeoffe* would be ready to be carried home again for the midday meal. The diverse ingredients of either *choucroute* or *baeckeoffe* don't really combine so much as cohabit.

Other typical dishes are *tarte à l'oignon* (tart filled with wilted onions set in custard) and *coq au Riesling* (a bought hen now replacing a home-raised cock). Red cabbage is cooked with onion, apple, and chestnuts, flavored with red wine and clove. *Tourte de la vallée de Munster* is ground, seasoned pork enclosed in pastry. Rye bread, often with caraway seeds, is popular, and at bakeries or at *points chauds* along city streets you can buy *bretzels,* which are fatter than typical American pretzels and eaten hot, while they're still soft inside. A popular meal for tourists or Alsatian families is *flammekueche,* or *tarte flambée,* a thin, pizzalike layer of bread dough covered with rich cream, sliced onions, and smoked bacon. At one time it was set to cook just inside the opening of a bread oven, while the fire was still burning to heat it; the *tarte* was licked by the flames, giving the name. Dessert tarts and preserves are made of native quetsch and mirabelle plums, *myrtilles* ("blueberries"), *griottes* ("sour cherries"), apples, rhubarb, figs, and raspberries. Many fruits are made into eaux-de-vie, a seemingly unending list.

Alsace is a welcoming place. Once, one of the best winemakers invited me to dinner at his home twice in a week, and those may have been the finest home-cooked meals I've had in France. A contender would be the *choucroute garnie* cooked by the mother of another top winemaker.

In Colmar, the Haut-Rhin's small, leading city, Wistub Brenner sits at the edge of the charming Petite Venise neighborhood along the Lauch River. A *wistub,* or *winstub,* is a simple restaurant that serves local food and local wine, generally at closely packed tables. *Winstubs* aren't automatically good, but a few are excellent. Of all the old-school places to eat traditional Alsatian food, Brenner seemed to be best. The ambience of the small dining room was more city bistro than village *winstub.* In winter, a curtain as heavy as a carpet hung at the door to shield the room from the draft. The walls were painted an uncertain color that could never look fresh, and the few decorations were a little kitsch (the restaurant is in different hands now, with brighter paint but still kitsch, and still with the old menu).

The customers hadn't tumbled in by chance. They arrived with confidence, and as they ate they looked content. Not that there was so very much to the experience. In addition to the printed menu of wholly conservative Alsace items, including the expected *choucroute garnie* and *tourte de la vallée,* two blackboards listed daily specials. To drink, I'd expected Edelzwicker, the old, light, everyday blend of white varieties, but the closest I could come was a plonkish, harmless Pinot Blanc, which came in a ceramic pitcher. Gilbert Brenner, the owner and host, was hurried but it was almost as if we'd just been introduced by a common friend. He guided me to that wine choice and took my order.

My portion of oxtail was enormous and good, and the meat fell from the bone. The sliced baguette was flavorful to an extent that's rare in France or anywhere else. At another lunch I chose *boudin noir* with sautéed apples, and it was outstanding. The simple bistro meal came with sautéed potatoes and a green salad, and always that exceptional baguette.

Brenner, rotund, gregarious, wrapped from the waist down in a red apron, appeared to know many of his customers personally. One day as I left, he was shepherding a departing group toward the door, which he turned hospitably to hold open for me. I went off on an errand and then half an hour later happened to walk by again. Brenner and the group were still there, on the sidewalk, still engaged in a loud, animated conversation. Brenner understood his calling perfectly.

—·—

EIGHT

The Odor Is Part
of the Reward

Lapoutroie, Alsace

E ven outside Jacques Haxaire's building, the smell was unmistakable. Indoors on the wall opposite the sliding wooden
door, a handwritten sign was posted:

TRAVEL WITHOUT ODOR.
You wish to carry our munsters-géromés
without being inconvenienced by their fragrance.
We propose to wrap them in a heat-sealed
paper that guarantees perfect air-tightness.

Haxaire's cheese-ripening business was located beside his home
in the village of Lapoutroie, in a small Vosges valley above the
highest Alsace vineyards, eight kilometers west of the half-
timbered, tourist-filled town of Kaysersberg. The craft of the
affineur, the cheese ripener, is separate from that of the cheese-

maker, and sometimes, as with Haxaire, it's a separate business. This was some years ago, just before Haxaire moved to a new facility in a more prominent location at a crossroads. The family's specialty is Munster. The flat orange rounds, soft to the touch, have a smooth, lightly moist surface. Their aroma is persistent but not really that strong, if the cheese has been well cared for and not kept warm and closed up for too long. An indelicate, satisfying stink is typical of all the *croûtes-lavées,* or "washed-rind," cheeses of northern France—Munster, Époisses, Langres, Livarot, Maroilles, about thirty in all.

Munster, or Munster-Géromé as it is also officially called, is commonly made in a round shape a little smaller than a Camembert, though there's also a larger size weighing roughly three times as much. The larger cheeses are made mainly in Lorraine on the west side of the Vosges Mountains, where for centuries the most important market for the cheese was held in the town of Gérardmer, called locally Géromé, which became a name for the cheese. Today nearly all of the Lorraine cheeses are made in just four big *laiteries* ("dairy plants"). Unfortunately, most of those cheeses are made from pasteurized milk, which subdues flavors and slows ripening, and gives a heavier texture.

Alsace has just two small *laiteries,* both good and both belonging to the Haxaires, one for raw-milk Munster and the other for pasteurized. Also in Alsace are most of the ninety farms that still make the cheese, although all of their production together amounts to only 5 percent of Munster. The farms as a rule are located in the mountains, which are old and eroded, with rounded heights called *ballons.* Each May, in a pattern that dates back more than a millennium, some of the farms move their cattle to the *chaumes,* the highest Vosges pastures, which give the best milk for cheese.

On the Alsatian side, the cheese is named for the small town of Munster, the site of a former abbey. *Munster* means "monastery," and the name was applied to the cheese as long ago as the 1570s, when in letters the town's secretary referred to *Münsterkase,* once describing it as "fat and blue." The color may have referred to a mold-covered surface rather than a blue-veined cheese like Roquefort. Still, the orangey, washed-rind type of Munster is old, though just how old no one can say.

Jacques Haxaire was a thin man who was so quiet that at first I thought he lacked self-assurance. Then I noticed his confidence in his craft and saw the purposefulness of the workplace. His wife, daughter, son, and a half a dozen or more employees worked in the *fromagerie*—today his daughter, Virginie, runs the business with both her brothers. Jacques Haxaire's father started the business in 1929, when all Munster was made on farms. Before the Second World War, around Lapoutroie, he told me, more than 160 farms had made cheese; now he estimated there were just 15. In the 1950s, when the dairies began to make Munster, many of the farms stopped. They couldn't compete with the dairies' efficiency and lower prices for cheese. It was easier and more profitable just to sell them milk. Now the family was ripening thirty thousand cheeses a week, with only a small minority of the cheeses coming from farms. In order to preserve traditional methods and ensure a supply of cheese from raw milk, Haxaire explained, his new facility at the crossroads would include a cheese plant.

I borrowed a hat, a white coat, and white boots so I could enter the work areas. The smell was strong but remarkably clean. I know that's a funny way to describe a stinky cheese, but "clean" is accurate—the smell was focused, with no undesirable aromas. The *caves* had bright lights and white walls. Floors and equipment were frequently washed; everything was spotless, austerely neat. Haxaire followed a stringent US hygiene model, though a simpler way had worked perfectly well in the past. "It's the modern world; one must adapt," he commented. "In the unfolding of my life, I've attempted to combine modernity with tradition. That's why the *caves* are not now underground. My father had levels beneath the house."

The Haxaires bought four- to six-day-old cheeses, fresh and white. The *caves,* only mounded over with earth, were essentially walk-in refrigerators set at 13 degrees C (55 degrees F). Stainless-steel racks held week-old cheeses that had turned a light golden color. Older cheeses, according to the farm or dairy that had made them, had become bright orange to pink to reddish with a hint of brown. The only ventilation occurred when the door to a *cave* was opened, and the atmosphere inside was very humid. "How humid is it exactly?" I asked. "I don't check," Haxaire answered. "I learned my trade empirically, and I still work with the same methods. One must always be very close to the product."

Every two days the cheeses were rubbed with well water (or with brine, if a batch needed more salt). The *laiterie* cheeses were brushed top and bottom by a machine with rotating soft, white plastic bristles. Even that required a lot of hand labor, to load and unload the cheeses and insert them into a separate device that rubbed the edges. The farm cheeses were dealt with individually by hand, firm fingers sliding rapidly over the cheese.

Hand rubbing is superior, Virginie said, "because you feel each cheese better, whether the rind is dry, for example."

The moisture and rubbing nourish the organisms essential to create the color and odor of Munster. The organisms are traditionally called *ferment rouge* in French and red mold in English; scientifically the chief one is *Brevibacterium linens*. Nothing is specially added to the cheese; the red mold is common in nature and inhabits the *caves*. New Munsters are chalky. The organisms work from the surface inward, turning the cheeses creamy. Being thin and moist, Munster ripens quickly. The Haxaires age most cheeses for only two to three weeks, although for customers who like a more evolved cheese they hold them as long as six weeks. "There are no secrets," said Haxaire. "There is the *cave;* there are the microclimates. My floor is clean. In another *cave,* the cheese would have another taste, from the temperature, the humidity, the gases that come from the cheeses. My father forty or fifty years ago did the same—he had shelves of fir; I use stainless steel."

The Haxaires were then buying from twelve farms, about the same number as today, keeping the cheeses of each separate; connoisseurs would ask for cheese from a particular farm. The makers set their milk into curd each morning; a few farms in the high Val d'Orbey were still making cheese twice a day. In France, *fromages fermiers* ("farm cheeses") are made from raw milk, which is a living substance, always changing. Haxaire said, "If you wait until tomorrow to use it, it will be different." The cheesemaker works by hand and each has her own technique. More important, each farm's location is at least subtly different. That affects the mix of plants in pastures, which contributes to making each farm's cheese unique.

One morning, Haxaire took me into the hills above Lapoutroie to see the farm of Odile and Gaston Jacquinez, set among steep pastures at nine hundred meters. Like Lapoutroie itself, the area is part of the *pays des Welches* ("land of the Welches"). That's the name of the people and of their disappearing Gallo-Romance dialect (very different from Alsatian, which is a form of German). It was the Romans who drove the Celts from the Rhine Valley up into the hills, where it's said they became the ancestors of the Welches.

Odile Jacquinez made about twenty-five cheeses a day, working in a tiled back room on the ground floor of the house. Once, she explained, cheese was made in a room that was lived in, because cheesemaking requires warmth. When we arrived, she was heating the mixed evening and morning milk in two brass cauldrons, each covered with a wooden lid and set on a trivet over gas jets. When the milk reached 32 degrees C (90 degrees F), she added a spoonful of rennet from a plastic bottle. The rennet would set the curd. She stirred it in with the *sabre,* a straight wooden blade.

Her cheeses from the day before, scattered with coarse crystals of salt, were still in their molds, which were made of fir. "Stainless steel doesn't work as well," Jacquinez commented. The wood keeps the cheeses warmer overnight. Her modern touch was to place a circle of plastic screening over the solid bottom of each mold to hasten the draining of whey. Gaston Jacquinez may have been the last person in Alsace to make wooden molds. It took him a day to make three; the most time-consuming part was turning thin pliable branches into outer bands to bind each mold tightly together.

The cheeses would remain in the molds for two days, Odile said, before she turned them out onto stainless-steel racks to dry. She sold most of her Munster to Haxaire, keeping only a few cheeses to ripen and sell at the farm. They sat on thick fir boards, their edges joined with wooden splines to form wide shelves.

At the *fromagerie,* Haxaire had offered me tastes of cheeses from half a dozen different farms to compare. Munster is sweet and fruity, sometimes called garlicky, but beyond that characteristic taste, the differences in flavor were hard for me to separate. Most apparent was a drier or a moister texture. I don't care so much for drier Munster, and yet a good farm-made Munster is never dense and heavy. Rather, even a somewhat firm cheese can have the kind of creaminess that in your mouth melts away like butter. Exceptionally, a cheese flows a little; that's the most luscious kind.

Munster's power is more in the nose than in the mouth, and the rind is the strongest part. Sometimes, when the cheese has been ripened too slowly or simply stored too long in the cold, the rind has an undesirable faint crunch. According to the cheese and personal preference, Alsatians either eat the rind or cut it away. Often Munster is served with caraway seeds on the side, and sometimes caraway is mixed into the curd. "I tell you in all honesty, I appreciate all the qualities," Jacques Haxaire said. "I can't personally say I like one or the other better."

With Munster, Alsatians often drink an aromatic Pinot Gris, one of the region's typical grapes, with a touch of sweetness, but the height of pleasure is a glass of full-bodied Alsace Gewurztraminer, especially a late-harvest one, though not too sweet or the wine will turn the cheese bitter. (It goes without saying that if you love cheese, you also have fresh bread to go with it.) The key aroma of Gewurztraminer is rose, which you might think is completely hostile to the cheese. But no! The combination is stunning. The cheese increases the floral perfume. Both the cheese and the wine are rich in their different ways, and each has a balancing acidity. The pure floral perfume and sweetness on one side and the pungent, slightly salty funk of Munster on the other make one of the great food and wine combinations, as crazy and fun as anything the loosest young chef could dream up.

NINE

The Kugelhopf of Christine Ferber

Niedermorschwihr, Alsace

I arrived in a wet snowfall at 6 a.m., the same time as the young employees and apprentices. It was December 3 at the Ferber shop in the village of Niedermorschwihr, in the hills just west of the city of Colmar in Alsace. Christine Ferber, *pâtissier-confiseur,* wasn't famous yet the way she is now, most of all for her fruit jellies and preserves in a range of sometimes inventive kinds. She chooses only fully ripe, sweet fruit; her execution is precise; and a generous amount of sugar captures rather than swallows up the fruit taste. The result is confitures with a refinement and elegance rarely found even in France—clear but not forceful flavors and a perfect delicate consistency. Christine Ferber excels at these and all sorts of sweet products, not least the kugelhopf, a cake that is a symbol of Alsace, popular at Christmas and throughout the year.

Niedermorschwihr is located at a point where vineyards start to give way to the forests that cover most of the Vosges Mountains. Just 550 people live in the commune, but customers arrive from Colmar and all around. The village is not as picturesque as some in Alsace, but the *grand cru* Sommerberg vineyard lies above it on one side and the Brand is not far away on the other. The building long occupied by the Ferbers was previously a bread bakery. Christine and her father, or rather one of their employees, still made bread, but demand in the village was small, and at the time of my visit they were baking just twenty *pains de campagne* each day and buying in thirty baguettes. The shop itself, as I'd seen on an earlier visit, was stocked with a few mundane groceries alongside Christine's hand-dipped chocolates, pastries such as fruit tarts, and, during the Christmas season, the Ferber preparation of foie gras, tree ornaments made of baked bread dough, the most buttery, crisp, delicious cookies I've ever tasted, and certainly kugelhopfs.

Christine, with her pretty eyes and warm voice, had the somberness of someone who lacks sleep. She always wakes up early, she said, and works long hours. Her father had started the business, and she joined him in 1980. He was still working with her. Maurice Ferber concentrated on the *traiteur* side of the business, meaning the specially ordered takeaway dishes, while Christine made the sweet things. She had trained in Paris and brought back with her a sense of luxury. Maurice, dressed in crisp white, set the tone of the workshop—happy but disciplined, with a strong seriousness of purpose.

The two main work spaces seemed hardly big enough for the twenty-four employees on hand at that busy time. The work was highly structured; everyone had tasks. Soon six people, pink-eyed and almost crying, were peeling and slicing shallots around a table, filling a big oven pan.

I had come to see Christine make her kugelhopf. It's a cake, but more precisely, it's a form of brioche that's baked in a mold shaped like a turban, with a whole almond set at the top of each spiral. A thorough dusting of powdered sugar picks out the twisting relief and gives a sensation of added moisture. Like the brioches of other regions, a kugelhopf is leavened with yeast and is rich with eggs and butter, but it also contains raisins, often macerated beforehand in eau-de-vie—a number of Alsace wine-makers distill fine fruit eaux-de-vie. Because the dough rises higher than its mold and often closes over the central cone, when the cake is baked and inverted, it sits on a wide foundation. The tender crust is brown except in the hollow center, which is as pale yellow as if it were underdone.

Recipes for kugelhopfs vary enormously in their amounts of butter and eggs, but compared with a classic, rich Parisian brioche, a typical Alsatian kugelhopf is slightly dry and austere. In compensation, where the brioche contains very little sugar, a kugel is more definitely sweet and cakelike—it's much more pastry than bread. The texture of a good one isn't closed and tight but somewhat bubbled and open, even a little stretched in the way of an Italian panettone. The almonds become lightly toasted. They're just the right presence to set off the rest of the taste—you wouldn't want them in every bite. The kugel is traditional for breakfast, but it's also eaten later in the day. I always think it's best late on a cool afternoon with a glass of good, sweet Alsace wine.

The kugelhopf may be Viennese in origin. It's made in a vast Germanic stretch of Europe, including Austria, Switzerland, southern Germany, and, in France, Alsace, where it's exceptionally good. The name and spelling—*kouglof, gugelhupf, gouglouf,* and more—are unsettled even within Alsace. The *kugel* part is supposed to refer to a medieval hat, while *hopf* refers to yeast. Certain Alsatian kugelhopfs include walnuts, and exceptional ones are entirely savory. Originally in Alsace, kugelhopfs were made at home, and some Alsaciennes still do that, but more often now they come from bakeries.

The Ferber recipe was in about the middle range of richness for Alsace; it was the one Maurice had been using for thirty years. Ingredients had been weighed out by Christine's star apprentice, and Christine began two identical kugelhopf doughs to compare the effects of hand- with machine-kneading and, I'm sure, to show off her skill. (At the time, the traditional kneading of yeast-raised doughs hadn't yet been called into question. Now serious bread-bakers everywhere knead very little, and some don't knead at all, because exposing the dough over and over to air costs flavor, and the final rise is only a little greater.)

On the counter, Christine made a neat circle of flour, pouring the sugar and salt on separate parts of the arc. In the middle went milk and a piece of bread dough saved from the day before, to bring full flavor to the fermentation. She began to stir with one hand, bringing the ingredients together until they formed a very loose dough. Then she turned to the bowl of the big Hobart mixer and to it added water, milk, flour, and another piece of bread dough. As the machine turned slowly, she added more flour by eye from a foot-long scoop.

Christine returned to the hand-kneaded dough, adding eggs and more milk, and continuing to stir the sticky combination with just one hand. Whenever I've tried to knead a rich wet dough by hand, I've produced a steadily expanding mess. Her dough remained uncannily neat. Three times she added a little milk because she found the dough too dry. To me it felt soft, but still she added more milk. Now she began to knead with both hands, forward and back, each time spreading and lifting the mass. "You can't work by the clock," she said. "Five minutes for this? And so much time in the oven?" Her tone was incredulous. "That depends on your oven." Impressively, her hand-kneading continued for almost an hour, by which time the dough was smooth and cohering, coming up easily from the marble. She raised the dough and slapped it down—to make it smoother, she said. Then at last she kneaded in the butter, already cut into small cubes. Earlier the room had been cold, but the oven and stoves had warmed it. The dough itself, she said, ideally should be 18 to 20 degrees C (64 to 68 degrees F). She kneaded in the raisins, soaked overnight in eau-de-vie.

Turning to the dough in the mixer, she added sugar, salt, and eggs, increasing the speed, saying that if necessary she adds a little water. From time to time she scraped down the sides of the bowl. "I find that in the mixer the dough is better. With the dough hook, the dough heats more," bringing out more of the elastic gluten. At home, dough was always kneaded by hand. "That's why the kugel of the housewife is always more tight and hard."

The large amount of fat in the kugel dough requires extra yeast to leaven it. For each kilo of flour, Christine's kugelhopf contains 300 to 320 grams of butter, where her brioche contains 350 and her stollen, the German Christmas cake, contains 500. The larger amount of butter in the stollen makes it even more challenging. Christine said to me, "It's my favorite cake." The danger with so much butter is that the heat of kneading may melt it. Christine offered me a slice of stollen, which had the contradictory qualities of being compact yet not dense. It was cakelike, butter-tasting, crumbly, not fatty and heavy but dry and light—altogether excellent. Christine was happy that the day before her mother had complimented the stollen. Sympathetically, with a sense of humor, she imitated her mother looking critically around the shop at Christmastime: "It's not quite like last year; that's a little overcooked. . . ."

Christine turned to the machine and added cubes of butter, saying cold butter "keeps its butter texture. It doesn't reach its melting point. If you add butter at the start, the dough takes much, much longer to stop being sticky." She added macerated raisins and only then, as the mixing continued, did the dough stop sticking to the sides and cling instead to itself. She stopped the motor and wrapped the bowl of the mixer in one of the linen cloths used in breadmaking, pushing the cloth down until it almost touched the dough, to keep it warm.

As the morning passed, a succession of gratifying smells came from the pastry and from Maurice Ferber's savory cooking. There was the bread, of course, and many varied nut and spice cookies. Dried fruits had been chopped for *berewecke,* the Christmas confection whose name literally means "pear cake." That huge pan of sliced shallots had been cooked in vinegar and gave off a strong, sweet smell; the shallots would be an accompaniment to foie gras. From the oven came *bonhommes,* baked from a lean brioche dough in the shape of oversize gingerbread men for the day of Saint Nicolas, December 6. That's when children in Alsace traditionally receive sweets and gifts. Christine replaced the stollen I had been eating with a slightly less rich, just-baked *bonhomme,* saying, "That will be better with your hot chocolate." And it was better, very good. The large cup of extraordinarily rich and good hot chocolate had been made with Valrhona Caraque chocolate melted in equal parts of milk and cream. Christine described the family products as "things done with extra effort and all one's heart."

On a previous visit I had asked Christine, What does it take to make a good kugelhopf? "*Old* earthenware molds," she had answered. The workshop held shelves of the brown molds. After years of baking, butter had entered through tiny cracks in the glaze, filling the pores of the clay and giving the kugels a faint, pleasing odor of rancidity, part of the essential kugel richness. Earthenware heats more evenly than metal, Christine said, and, besides, earthenware is traditional. You can buy new molds made in the pottery village of Soufflenheim, near Strasbourg, but their center opening is fatter, and the Ferbers had found they are not the same. When from time to time a mold would break, the Ferbers sought old ones as replacements.

After her two doughs had risen for an hour and a half, Christine deflated each without tearing it. Then she cut and weighed 350-gram pieces for the small earthenware molds and 800-gram pieces for the big ones. She rolled each lump into a ball. I rolled a few too; the dough felt remarkably soft. In its raw state, the taste was slightly salty, but the flavor had been transformed by fermentation. While the balls rested for fifteen minutes, Christine brushed the insides of the molds with thick, half-melted butter. A worker took the balls from under the linen one by one and with his two thumbs made a quick partial hole in the middle of each; then he pressed the ball onto the center post of the mold. The filled molds, covered with oiled paper to keep the dough from forming a crust, went onto a low rack, which was wheeled into the warm space beneath the oven. There the kugels would rise for a last time.

The atmosphere of the kitchen was strict, but the kugelhopf process had been so casual that I wasn't sure how either of the two doughs would turn out. Flour and liquids hadn't been precisely measured, and on that wintry day some of the ingredients had been very cold. I've seen bakers check the temperature of the dough with a thermometer, but nothing like that had happened here. Christine commented to me that she hadn't kneaded a kugelhopf by hand in years, and twice Maurice Ferber had gone out of his way to explain that it's hard to succeed with kugelhopfs. Now he came back to me, clarifying, "You understand that it's not to discourage." For instance, he said, success or failure is affected by atmospheric pressure. "It's as hard for anyone to capture the savoir faire in words as for me to follow a recipe of Troisgros. You may have to execute the kugelhopf ten times to get it right. It's because there is so much butter."

Of his kugelhopf recipe, Maurice said, "It's good. You have to know how to do it. You have to learn how to succeed—that's all." When he began his bread-baking apprenticeship in 1950, he said, *levain* ("sour starter") was used to raise everything, including baguettes. (They were a novelty; the bakery where he worked produced just ten a day.) The brewers in Alsace sold some beer yeast, which is the same as baker's yeast, but hardly any baker used it, because *levain* was free. Bakers didn't make kugelhopfs at all, although "the big bakers of the city made five or six brioches for the rich, you know." He explained, "We were just coming out of a bad economic period. We began to eat well and drink well only after the second half of the 1960s—when people began to eat more." I took him to mean that, literally, people could then afford to buy more food. *Levain* may be more traditional for kugelhopfs in Alsace, but because of the sourness, Maurice Ferber preferred commercial yeast.

"You know," Christine said to me when her father was out of hearing, "he doesn't like to give out recipes. He doesn't like it when I give out recipes—he doesn't even like to give *me* recipes. 'What is that recipe?' I asked on the day he told me how to make kugelhopfs. He said, 'Flour as much as necessary, yeast in sufficient amount.'" She wasn't really criticizing him. She continued, leaning toward me, "'Feel it first in your heart,' he said. 'You will feel the knowledge flow from your heart to your arm to your hand. The day when you know that, you will know how to make kugelhopfs.'" She put her hand on my arm for emphasis. Her father was demanding—I'd seen it with the apprentices— but beneath that was warmth. Her mother had seemed severe at first too, but when I was invited to join the family for a delicious lunch in their home upstairs, she was kind and welcoming. A substantial vegetable soup was followed by slices of beef in a dark, flavorful sauce (I was intimidated and didn't ask its name).

The two sorts of kugelhopf went into the oven, and because the automatic steam device was broken, Christine poured water directly onto the hot metal shelf before she closed the door. Steam trapped in an oven keeps the surface of any loaf flexible longer, so the loaf has time to expand fully before the crust sets. When the kugelhopfs were done and taken from the oven, they were immediately unmolded. I watched as a worker pulled each burning-hot, heavy cake from its ceramic mold with his fingertips, and in a single motion upended the cake, while still holding on to the wide bottom, and set it on a rack. That's not easy to do—I know, I unmolded two myself without grace. A hot kugel is easy to damage, because it doesn't yet have a firm shape.

When the kugels were cool and firm enough to cut, we tasted them. The hand-kneaded version turned out to be almost identical to the machine one, proof that before there were machines, professionals could always produce work of the highest level. Both kinds were superb.

Yes, Maurice Ferber confirmed, this was the taste of his kugelhopf. Each one was cakey, buttery, and rich, marked by the closely related flavors of butter and a full fermentation, which always make me think just a little of sweet cherries.

TEN

Comté: High Pastures, Joint Efforts, and a Big Mountain Cheese

Labergement-Sainte-Marie and Le Fort Saint-Antoine, Franche-Comté

Cyril and Florent Robbe milk forty-five Montbéliarde cows at their farm on the edge of the village of Labergement-Sainte-Marie in the Jura Mountains, not far from the Swiss border. The red-and-white breed is as much a part of the landscape of the Franche-Comté as its pastures, forests, and broad farmhouses. The Robbe farm lies at 950 meters (3,100 feet), but you don't sense the altitude, because you don't see peaks and bare rocks. The cows wear bells, although with fenced pastures the sound is no longer needed to locate a cow. "It's for the folklore," Florent said. From the window of my hotel room in the village of Jougne, at night when the traffic on the narrow road to the border had ceased, the sound of bells came from two different hillsides in a soft jangle, almost like breaking glass. On some farms, Florent explained, the cows wear a computer medallion, read automatically in the barn, so the cow receives an individualized ration of grain; a bell would only get in the way. Early on a July morning the two brothers worked the double line of cows, Florent Robbe in coveralls and a visored cap, his younger brother, Cyril, in jeans and bareheaded. They wore tall rubber boots, and one-legged stools hung behind them from their belts, ready to fall into place as they sat beside each cow to clean her teats and attach the milking machine. The cows were busy eating grain, but three-quarters of their food is pasture and hay.

The Robbes' milk goes to the village's small cooperative to be made into wide wheels of nutty, buttery Comté, one of the great cheeses. The name used to be Gruyère de Comté, but it has been simplified to Comté to distinguish it from the Gruyère made in Switzerland and the small amount of lesser plain "Gruyère" produced in France. Comté is France's most popular cheese with an *appellation d'origine protégée* ("protected designation of origin"), and production has been steadily increasing. There's only a third as much Roquefort, the number two. (Camembert dwarfs both of those combined, but only a little has the appellation Camembert de Normandie; most is generic camembert made anywhere in France. In fact, the country's largest production by far is of nonappellation Emmental, holey "Swiss" cheese.) Comté is outstanding for eating and it is the essential French cheese for cooking—nothing is better for an omelette or a soufflé. Especially around Christmastime in France, it's a popular indulgence to serve *vieux* Comté, from wheels as old as twenty-four and even thirty months. Its flavor has turned particularly nutty, toasted, and caramel, gaining a little of the character of Parmigiano.

But most Comté is eaten young, at less than ten months (the minimum period before it can be sold is four months). The

Franc-Comtois enjoy older Comté, but they have a special appreciation for the young cheese. In a restaurant I heard a woman being asked which of three ages of Comté she would like. "*Doux,*" she replied, meaning "sweet" or "gentle"—the youngest kind. A Franc-Comtois explained to me, "They know the product; they know a cheese isn't better just because it's older." Well-made young Comté can have a depth of flavor, and the young cheese melts better in cooking. When I asked Cyril whether he eats Comté every day, he answered, "Yes—at breakfast and at four o'clock."

Geographically, the Franche-Comté is divided roughly into levels. First, there's the broad plain shared with Burgundy. That rises to an undulating plateau, and along the uneven line where the plain and plateau meet is the small Jura wine region—the source of the unusual and sometimes superb *vin jaune* ("yellow wine"), which is the finest complement to Comté. From the plateau, itself in two levels, the Franche-Comté ascends further to the high range, where the Swiss border follows more or less the line of highest mountains.

The Jura Mountains aren't high and dramatic; rather than being jagged, they're rounded. Yet in a number of places the highlands as well as the plateau are broken by tall, white limestone cliffs. The stone comes from the Jurassic era, which is named for the mountains, created millions of years ago at the same time as the Alps. Huge underground pressure not only caused the mountains to pile up but in many areas of the Jura the layers were shuffled, contributing to the region's enormously varied terroir, for both wine and cheese.

For centuries, the only economic activity open to the mountain farmers was making cheese. But travel in winter was often difficult, sometimes impossible, and even in summer it wasn't easy to send a product regularly to market. So the farmers made big, dry, durable cheeses, suitable for long-distance trade when travel made sense. Dry cheeses are less biologically active, slower to evolve, slower to dry out—easier to keep—and of course the mature wheels can be very delicious. For the farm families themselves, the cheeses preserved the excess milk from summer for consumption in winter, when cows used to give little or no milk.

The long-ago herds were small, and the yield of milk from a cow was much less than today. Neighbors had to combine their milk in order to have enough to make a large cheese. By the fifteenth century, and maybe long before that, the villages of the Jura had begun to establish *fruitières,* groups of farmers who united their milk, each farmer taking his turn as cheesemaker. All the wide Franche-Comté is dairy country, and the approved zone for the cheese embraces most of the province, including a portion of the plain. But the Franche-Comté is more than 40 percent forest. Sawmills and stacks of firewood are common. As in other mountain places, the region's hams and sausages are smoked. Cheesemakers used to heat their milk and curd over a fire.

Even in the Upper Jura, summers are warm, sometimes uncomfortably hot, but winter temperatures at Labergement-Sainte-Marie fall to −30 degrees C (−22 degrees F). When clouds driven by the prevailing southwestern wind meet the Jura heights, they're blocked and drop their moisture as rain or snow. (A second prevailing wind, from the northeast, means good weather.) The Jura is one of the wettest regions of France, and wettest of all are the highlands. The soil is mostly shallow, unsuited to plowing; open land is left permanently in pasture and hayfield. The Robbes are in the zone of highest and best pasture, the lushest and the most diverse in plants.

Under the rules of the Comté appellation, at least 70 percent of a cow's diet must be pasture or hay. To produce it, for each cow there must be at least one hectare (two and a half acres) of grassland. The plants of the Jura are key to the aroma of Comté. The Robbes' cows graze outdoors from May through October, and overall the best cheese is made during that time. Carotene from the fresh plants gives those cheeses a yellower color, which French consumers have learned to prefer. But winter cheeses from cows on hay can also excel. Upstairs, the Robbe barn was filled with the strong, comforting smell of new hay.

So that each cheese will reflect the plants and conditions of its locality, the milk for each *fruitière* must come from within a circle no more than twenty-five kilometers in diameter, within which is the *fruitière*. The appellation's rules have evolved toward greater specificity and higher quality—they go on for twenty-five pages.

The best land for dairy, as at the Robbe farm and in most of the Upper Jura, has never been plowed or used as anything but pasture. The grain fed to the cattle is purchased, but the farm's methods aren't far from organic, with only a little synthetic fertilizer being applied. From place to place in the Jura, the plants in the pastures differ in number and kind. The selection reflects in part the region's tumultuous geology. A 1994 scientific study, one of a pair that is cited in the appellation rules and forms part of their foundation, examined the environments of twenty of the region's small dairy plants. It found that the fields around Labergement are composed of nearly two hundred species of plants. Some are much more abundant than others, and thirty-one contribute aroma to the cheese. First of all is the humble dandelion; then there are *petite pimprenelle* ("garden burnet"), *cumin des près* ("caraway"), yellow and green *alchémille* ("lady's mantle"), thyme, yarrow, mustard, *cardomine*. . . . (More recent studies have linked pasture to the flavor of other aged mountain cheeses, and to the flavors of even fresh cheeses from warm Mediterranean zones.)

Cyril and Florent finished milking that morning before 8:30, not much later than usual, despite my interrupting with questions. Cyril guided the cows down the road and into a large pasture. Already the milk was cooling in the stainless-steel bulk tank. At some village co-ops, the farmers still arrive every morning pulling a *boule*—a cartoonish stainless-steel sphere on wheels—behind a car or tractor. But at the Robbes', each day at 5 a.m. a tank truck stops, driven by the village cheesemaker himself.

It was hardly a stone's throw from the farm to the Labergement dairy cooperative, housed in an upright building that looks more like a school or town hall. (In 2014, the co-op moved to new, larger quarters.) The Fruitière des Lacs, named for two nearby lakes, has fifteen member farms. I was at the small plant the next day at 8 a.m. Typically, a *fruitière* sells some of its Comté at its own small shop, but Labergement was focused solely on making cheese.

The floor and walls of the cheesemaking room were covered with white tile, and the cheesemaker, another worker, and an intern were all in white—hats, shirts, pants, aprons, boots. Bernard Lavaine, the *fruitière*'s accomplished cheesemaker, had been at his job for almost twenty-five years. He worked with alert eyes and a fixed serious expression—an energetic man holding his energy in check. An enormous amount of vigilance and repetition underlie the dramatic transformation of milk into a wheel of new white cheese in only a few hours. The same actions are taken each day with each vat, with only small variations. Months later, the least differences affect the taste of the mature cheese. Lavaine monitors "acidity, temperature, the bubbles, the foam, the color of the whey." He said, "Each day the milk is different, and you don't know what you'll have to do." The temperature, the amount of whey, of rennet, of time allotted for different steps, everything can be adjusted.

The equipment today isn't romantic. Nearly all is stainless steel except the four big copper vats. The main advantage of copper, besides its ability to transmit heat, is that tiny amounts of it react with the milk and curd, and during the aging of the cheese they have such beneficial effects on flavor that the rules require copper vats. They're surrounded by stainless-steel jackets that fill with steam to heat the contents. The room itself in summer was very warm and humid, which, Lavaine said, was the hardest part of the job.

The vats had earlier been filled with chilled milk, which was now being stirred mechanically as it warmed. Lavaine already knew from the quantity that he would be making twenty-four cheeses that day. In April, the time of greatest milk, the number could rise as high as thirty-seven. That morning, Lavaine said, the amount of fat was between 2.8 and 3.0 percent, not especially high as milk goes, because other qualities are important for making Comté. The milk was raw. Pasteurizing it would be so damaging to the cheese—altering aromas and texture and killing microflora essential to the flavor—that it's forbidden to have pasteurization equipment on the premises.

When the milk in the first vat reached 27 degrees C (80 degrees F), in went the *levain*—whey from the previous day's cheese-making left overnight to develop and increase in acidity. At this exceptional *fruitière,* no other culture was added but only that complex wild one. At *fruitières* that do use laboratory cultures, the whey is nonetheless mandatory and its microorganisms must dominate. Lavaine started the four vats twenty minutes apart, so that throughout the morning the tasks wouldn't overlap. As much as the vats, he watched the clock on the wall. After about an hour and ten minutes, the milk had warmed to 32.0 to 32.2 degrees C (just under 90 degrees F). A dose of calf rennet, previously mixed with water in a bucket, was dumped in. The stirrers were flipped out of the vat, and in less than thirty minutes, a delicate curd had set. The stirrers were now replaced with the blades of the harp, which began to slice the curd to bits. During the next half hour, as the harp turned, the temperature was raised to 55 degrees C (131 degrees F) to "cook" the curd. In the heat, the curd contracted, releasing more of its distinctly yellow whey. Lavaine dipped in his hand to show me that the pure white bits of curd had been reduced to the desired size of a grain of wheat. I tasted the curd, which squeaked between my teeth; its flavor was almost neutral.

As the steps of the process grew further apart in time, Lavaine relaxed a little. The whey was drained off through the bottom of the first vat. Some was set aside for tomorrow's *levain.* Then the curd was sucked through pipes into six side-by-side vessels that released it into six molds, previously lined with cheesecloth. One by one Lavaine hauled the molds out along a track. He pulled back the cheesecloth and slipped in the official green oval Comté plaque, made of casein, which gives the number of the *fruitière* and the month and year the cheese was made; beside the plaque is the precise date. By noon, as always, the molds had been loaded into the presses, where they would remain overnight as more whey was squeezed out.

The cheeses from the previous three weeks were sitting on the wooden shelves of the animal-smelling "pre-aging" room, held at a humid 10 degrees C (50 degrees F). Every two days for about ten days, the new cheeses are hefted and turned, rubbed, and the top sprinkled with salt. The salt draws moisture from the surface, which helps to form a rind and favors certain microflora. The cheeses from the day before were still white; those a few days old had turned a surprising yellow; eleven-day-old cheeses were tan. The new cheeses weighed thirty-nine kilos, while after fourteen months, Lavaine said, they would be down to about thirty-three.

A century ago the cheesemaker was also in charge of aging, but *affinage* is a somewhat separate craft that requires a particular environment. Hardly any *fruitière* today ages any Comté after the initial few weeks. Instead, the cheeses are trucked to one of thirteen specialist *affineurs,* which sell the cheeses under their own brands. The Fruitière du Lac de Remoray sends its wheels to the Fort Saint-Antoine, which lies just half a dozen kilometers from Labergement-Sainte-Marie, up a winding forest road, at 1,100 meters.

Fort Saint-Antoine is a low, massive, somber stone building with a dry moat, built in the late nineteenth century and abandoned by the military in 1964. The following year an *affineur* named Marcel Petite, looking for a new *cave* and interested in the effect on flavor of a cooler environment, began to age some of his Comté in the fort. Today the Marcel Petite firm has a reputation for high quality and it buys from thirty-five *fruitières*. The fort is home to 100,000 wheels of Comté; another 100,000 are matured elsewhere. That's a lot of cheese, but 1.5 million wheels of Comté are made each year, and Petite is merely the second-largest *affineur*. Only the better wheels go to the fort to benefit from the steady climate inside its stone chambers, and they stay there for at least a year.

Claude Querry, the thin, dark-haired *chef de cave,* appeared from within the fort. He has co-workers at the fort, but in a sense the entire enterprise rests on his tasting skills. His quiet intensity seemed to reflect that, and as long as the subject was cheese, he was entirely serious. A problem quickly came up: the popularity and scarcity of *vieux* Comté, the oldest cheese. A dealer from the capital who was there to select cheeses said, "In my view, in Paris it's a *fromage de snob*." Old Comté tastes both more intense and different. Philippe Goux, head of sales for Petite, expressed the group opinion, which I heard elsewhere in the Franche-Comté. "Twenty-four-month-old cheese is very good, but it's not Comté."

Time magnifies not only strengths but defects. A good young cheese won't automatically become a good old cheese. Rather, you might say that each cheese has its ideal age, a point when it's the best it will ever be. (And for some cheeses, that best won't be very good.) The demand for Marcel Petite's *vieux* Comté far outstrips the supply. The proportion of Comté older than sixteen months at Petite, Goux said, is a mere 1 percent. Not only is that cheese all spoken for, it must be allotted, and a wholesale customer new to Petite must begin with basic young Comté.

Yet it was Marcel Petite himself who launched the fashion for aged Comté, as a result of his long, slow aging at the fort. The change didn't come about quickly. "At the time, everyone treated him as a crazy man," Goux said. The fashion took hold in the 1990s.

The single tool of the *chef de cave,* besides his senses, is the *sonde,* called a cheese iron or trier in English. For a hard cheese like Comté, it combines a borer at one end with a hammer at the other. The borer, which doubles as the hammer handle, is a narrow metal cylinder, open on one long side, that removes a *carotte* from the cheese for tasting. Querry makes 80 percent of his analysis before he tastes, he said, but at least one cheese from each batch must be tasted.

He led the three of us through the many aisles, as if proceeding from one familiar address in a city to another, rarely pausing with uncertainty. He was looking for wheels with particular qualities, aiming at a portrait of what the dealer present that day wanted. We tasted several dozen cheeses. Querry chose mainly, but not entirely, wheels from just one *fruitière,* which the dealer had always preferred. When he stopped at a wheel, Querry slid it half off its shelf so it rested at an angle. He ran his hand across the surface to check the rind, took out his trier, and hammered rapid-fire all over the top, listening for hardness and an even consistency within, including possible hollowness from eyes or the hidden cracks called *lainures.* Once or twice, he changed his mind and slid a wheel back. Apart from that he angled his trier at a spot about halfway between the rim and the center of the wheel and quickly, firmly inserted it, twisting and retrieving a long plug. He presented it to each of us in turn, so we could break off a small piece. We smelled, massaged it between thumb and fingers to examine the texture and at the same time warm it, and then tasted.

Querry, as he considered, fixed his eyes on a random spot. The dealer closed his eyes. I had scarcely ever before tasted more than two Comtés side by side, in a shop, and I worried in advance that my skills might be tested. Happily for me, the focus remained on the dealer and no one seemed concerned with my skills. Goux was the only person who was fully relaxed, as if he were on vacation, enjoying the chance to do more tasting than he normally has time for. At times Querry gave background. About the area from which one wheel came: "It's heavy land beside the river—not very large either." And he described the weather during that September when the wheel had been made. After we were done tasting each wheel, Querry pushed the remainder of the plug back into place and smoothed over the spot. We moved from row to row and from one part of the fort to another, sometimes passing through small bleak rooms, sometimes walking through puddles.

The adjective most frequently applied to any sort of Gruyère is *fruité* ("fruity"), which isn't specific and can mean merely "strong." Every cheese we tasted was to me fully distinct, but it was hard to put names to the flavors. The cheeses from the *fruitière* we especially concentrated on seemed smooth and balanced, containing not so much fruit as aromas in the realm of a gentle, rich, nutty butteriness. I was more attuned to the texture, which until that day I had hardly thought about. These mature cheeses were floury on the tongue, a sensation variously accompanied by creaminess or hinting at granular.

In a flavor study (the second in the pair cited in the appellation rules) made by the professional association that manages the appellation, experienced tasters identified eighty-three precise aromas, grouped in six families, as "most frequently found." The idea was to provide the language needed to show that the environment around a *fruitière*—conveyed through the pasture and hay—could be linked scientifically to characteristic aromas in the cheese. Depending on countless influences—but if all's well, primarily age and provenance—you might find in one wheel or another: grass, hay, celery, cauliflower, mushroom, yogurt, melted butter, apricot, honey, citrus, nuts, meat stock, leather, pepper, sautéed or burnt onion, coffee, dark chocolate, smoke. Since my visit to the *caves,* I've found all those, except perhaps celery. As with other aged food and drink, superior wheels of Comté have more complex, somewhat stronger aromas, coupled with a long aftertaste.

In the end, the Paris dealer had to accept what Querry and Goux offered, which seemed to be all that Marcel Petite could reasonably give. It was a business deal concluded with serious faces but based on friendly relationships and the dealer's pleasure, which he expressed more than once, in visiting the fort. The batch of wheels he had been selling had run out. Now he would sell both younger and older Comté, offering customers a taste of each to compare, teaching them to appreciate the differences. The work would be harder. In the bustle of the capital's open-air markets, he doesn't always have time to explain.

Comté distills the pastures and fields of the Jura, capturing and transforming the aromas. The big cheese is an artifact of information about a *fruitière* and its twenty-five-kilometer circle. Those of us from outside the region, unfamiliar with its varied locations, can't hope to make precise connections. But we can nonetheless have a deep enjoyment of a fine Comté, knowing it provides the full pleasure of nature and, especially in summer, represents the pasture and even the weather on one day in a particular place.

ELEVEN

Vin Jaune: The Virtue of Rancidity

Château-Chalon, Franche-Comté

The village of Château-Chalon is set on a limestone promontory whose cliffs fall to meet slopes, composed of deep marl, that hold some of the appellation's best vineyards. The cliffs are part of the erratic edge of the Jura plateau, which rises gradually to the high Jura Mountains and the Swiss border. Some of the village houses, along with traces of an abbey, are poised at the edge of the cliff. Within the village, the Rue de la Roche follows the curves of the promontory and for most of its length is lined solidly on either side with houses. At one end of the street stands the proudly maintained tenth-century village church of Saint Pierre. Close by, past an arched portal, a panorama stretches into the distant haze. Toward the other end of the street is the house of Jean Macle, bought by his great-great-grandfather, a cooper who came to the village in 1850 from the Upper Jura.

Several of the barrels he made are still in use in the cellar, filled with maturing wine.

If you explore the byways of French wine, which are at least as many as those of French cheese, you come eventually to the Jura in the east. Jura is the name of the wine zone and of the department, part of the pre-Napoleonic province of the Franche-Comté, known for its unspoiled nature and its great cheese Comté. The vineyards form an irregular, eighty-kilometer-long strip at the point where the Franc-Comtois plain, coming from Burgundy, encounters the plateau. Of France's classic wine regions, none is smaller and none produces more varied and unusual wines.

The finest of these wines and the most singular is *vin jaune* ("yellow wine"), produced from the Savagnin grape. By law, the wine must spend at least six years in casks or barrels, and some makers wait longer. Almost everywhere in the world, barrels of wine are kept continuously full, steadily topped up as the liquid evaporates, so good aromas aren't lost to combining with oxygen or dissipated into the air, and so the wine doesn't turn to vinegar. But from the start, barrels of *vin jaune* are never filled completely, and afterward there is no topping up. *Vin jaune* is one of the world's intentionally oxidized wines, like sherry or Madeira. In taste, the wine doesn't begin to come into its own until ten to fifteen years after the vintage, and most producers say all the virtues are apparent only after twenty to forty years. The best wines last a hundred years. The very bottle defies the norm. Rather than the standard 75-centiliter bottle, *vin jaune* goes into the traditional, squat, sharp-shouldered bottle called the *clavelin,* which holds the anomalous amount of 62 centiliters. Excellent examples of *vin jaune* also come from three other Jura appellations, but those also produce other kinds of wine. Château-Chalon makes only *vin jaune*.

According to Curnonsky, the most important French gastronomic critic of the early and mid-twentieth century: "Château-Chalon, with its astonishing bouquet and its taste of walnut, is one of the five greatest 'white' wines of France." (The other four were Château-Grillet in the Rhone Valley, Château d'Yquem in Bordeaux, Montrachet in Burgundy, and Coulée de Serrant in Anjou—not entirely the list a wine lover might expect.) Noting the wine's utter dryness, Curnonsky said that Château-Chalon has a "perfume like a strangely *empyreumatique* savor of walnut and plum." That odd French adjective is in most contexts purely negative. It signifies "acrid" and "burnt," and *vin jaune* does contain a small bitter edge. It's far from being one of those easy-to-drink wines that cause a list of fruit comparisons to trip off a critic's tongue. Rather, the estimable wine writer Jancis Robinson, while calling Savagnin "indisputably noble," says that its wine suggests "nuttiness or perhaps some rather delicious polish."

On first trying it, many people dislike it. Immediately, you think of sherry, which is made similarly and shares certain flavors, and inferior *vin jaune* can taste like cheap dry sherry—not all bottles justify the reputation. But good *vin jaune* has very much its own character. It's "serious" wine, for sipping in calm moments when you have plenty of time and can pay close attention. Usually *vin jaune* is drunk at the contented end of a meal on a special occasion. The taste is both concentrated and, in a good sense, acidic. As to food, the classic, ideal partner is Comté cheese with, during their fall season, walnuts. And the main flavor of *vin jaune* is sometimes described as "rancid walnut," although Jura producers obviously might prefer a more positive description. The wine also tastes notably of nonrancid nuts, caramel, and sometimes curry. Besides those, according to the particular bottle, you might find coffee, butter, honey, cocoa, toasted bread, toasted nuts, apple, citrus zest, dried fruits, even iodine or celery.

When I met Jean Macle, he was in his early seventies. He stood straight and tall, though he moved deliberately. His white beard and clean-shaven upper lip gave him a Quakerish look, and he had an air of authority combined with unusual gentleness. For twenty-four years, he had served as mayor of Château-Chalon, and he, or now his son Laurent, is the appellation's best-known, most respected producer.

The labels on the bottles describe Jean Macle as a *"vigneron."* That word implies genuineness and means a hands-on grape-grower who by extension is also a winemaker, usually the proprietor of a small family operation. More than once, Jean said to me that he is retired, and he expressed the ease and contentment of someone who has set down his burdens after achieving something in life. An interruption by his small granddaughter seemed to be a not-unexpected, very welcome part of his day. Macle's wife, Elyane, formerly a *couturière* and somewhat younger, did a share of the accounting and seemed to be head of sales. Until ten years before, she had also driven a tractor in the vineyard. Jean in his retirement continued to receive visitors and sometimes wait on customers; he waxed bottles of Château-Chalon by hand to seal the corks and assisted Laurent with the essential work of tasting and blending.

The earliest written evidence of vineyards at Château-Chalon dates from the tenth century, and almost certainly vines were first planted there long before that. The name Château-Chalon refers to a medieval castle, reduced to little more than the vestige of a single tower at one side of the village. The vineyards belonged to the village's former abbey, known to have existed in 869 and, according to tradition, founded in the seventh century. The members of the order were nuns who by all accounts made *vin jaune*. Surviving portions of the abbey's archives, at the Bibliothèque Nationale in Paris, record that in the fifteenth century the nuns themselves guarded their vines as the fruit ripened, evidence of the value of the grapes. They were women of means, knowledge, and power—only the daughters of noble families were accepted—and through their families the wine gained its reputation. It used to be known as a *vin de garde,* a "wine for keeping," which is still the phrase on the bottles of Jean Macle.

When and why the nuns started making *vin jaune* isn't clear. During the Middle Ages, the Franche-Comté was a "free county" (the meaning of the name) under its own count. For several hundred years, the countship passed from heir to heir, not without conflict, ending with the princes of adjacent Burgundy. In 1493, the Franche-Comté fell under the control of the Habsburgs, and then from 1591 to 1674 under the rule of Spain. (Finally under Louis XIV it joined France.) You can speculate that the Spanish brought sherry methods and taught them to the nuns. But it's hard even to guess where the Savagnin grape, the sole variety in *vin jaune,* may have originated or how it came to the Jura. It's a form of Traminer, named for the village of Tramin in the Italian Tyrol. However it was that the Savagnin and the *vin jaune* methods came to the Jura, it appears the nuns disseminated both through the region.

At the time of the French Revolution, the abbey was shut and its buildings were ruined. The vineyards were distributed among small proprietors, who struggled to emulate what had gone before. Still, the overall number of vines in the Jura gradually increased, until by the late nineteenth century they covered twenty thousand hectares. Then the phylloxera root louse destroyed them all, as it did vines throughout Europe, and afterward, in the Jura as elsewhere, the vines were only partly replanted. In the twentieth century, two world wars and emigration brought fresh difficulties and a shrinkage in the number of vines. Then in the 1960s, the area began to increase, although even now the size is less than a tenth of the peak amount.

Through most of the twentieth century, no one in Château-Chalon worked solely as a *vigneron*. Jean Macle's father had cows and scarcely a hectare of vines. Jean continued in the same way. The milk of his dozen cows went to the village *fruitière* to be made into Comté. Then in 1966 the family operation was divided: Jean's sister took the cows and Jean took the vines. Other growers at the time had begun to apply toxic chemicals in their vineyards, including herbicides to eliminate the labor of turning the soil. "It made me afraid," Jean explained. "I had had a little instruction in chemistry. I said, 'That can't go on very long.'" He and Elyane rejected herbicides and decided to rely on organic techniques, apart from a little nonorganic fertilizer. (Laurent is now in the process of having the property certified as organic.)

Today the family has three hectares in the Château-Chalon appellation and seven more in the Côtes du Jura appellation. The ground of the latter is planted mostly in Chardonnay, raised in the Jura since at least the sixteenth century. The Macle Chardonnay lies in a section that, until a strict reevaluation in the

1980s, lay within the Château-Chalon appellation. "Sometimes the Chardonnay is almost as good as our Savagnin," Macle said.

He was pleased when I praised his wine, but, not wanting to make unflattering comparisons with the work of others, he attributed the refinement of his Château-Chalon only to the vineyards themselves: to their deep clayey gray marl, their southern and southeastern exposure, and their surface debris of limestone fallen from the cliffs. The lime provides warmth for better ripening; the soil itself is just a thin covering.

Exposed marl looks like a soft, even a crumbling, version of shale. It's a mix of clay and lime, with some examples tilting toward one and some toward the other. The color can be a surprising range—red, green, gray, blue, or black. Blue marl is always said to be the best, but the blueness is partly in the eye of the beholder and might equally be called dark gray. The blue and much of the gray were formed during an earlier geologic period, and in the region it's an article of faith that blue or gray marl is essential for good Savagnin. They hold more water but are more impenetrable, providing the more difficult conditions needed to create the finest Savagnin. Still, at least a few *vignerons* produce fine *vin jaune* from vines on other kinds of marl.

To withstand the required six or more years in barrels, the raw material for *vin jaune* must be concentrated to begin with or the wine would be as unpleasant as any bottle of white wine that has sat open indefinitely. Rich raw material comes largely from lower yields, which allow greater concentration and ripeness. And for greater ripeness, throughout the Jura, Savagnin has always been the last variety to be picked. (Until relatively recently, higher alcohol was generally associated with higher quality, because ripeness and sugar, and the alcohol that follows, were harder to achieve. Now we understand much more about how to raise healthy, ripe grapes, and the climate has grown warmer, making ripeness easier to achieve every year.)

Today, Jean Macle said, only one other Château-Chalon producer picks Savagnin as late as his family does. "A few more days, that counts," he commented. The Macles normally begin about October 1, a date whose earliness compared with the past he attributed to the warmer climate. The level of alcohol in most Château-Chalon wine today is 13 to 14 percent. According to the local office of the Institut National de l'Origine et de la Qualité, the average yield in recent years has been thirty hectoliters per hectare. "We've always had twenty-five to thirty here," Jean Macle said, referring to his own property, where the pruning is close and no more than "a pinch" of fertilizer is applied. "When we do twenty hectoliters, we are very happy."

The clean-smelling Macle *caves* are located partly beneath the house and lead one into another. Typically for the Jura, they are only half underground. The oldest dates from the seventeenth century, while the newest was built of concrete in 1984. At Macle as everywhere, *vin jaune* starts out as regular white wine. The stems are removed to avoid their tannin and herbaceousness, and then the grapes are pressed. Like others in Château-Chalon, the Macles ferment in stainless steel. The fermentation, through chilling equipment, is allowed to get no warmer than 30 degrees C (86 degrees F), and it lasts about fifteen days.

The new wine, once the secondary malolactic fermentation is over, is transferred to 228-liter Burgundian barrels, leaving several inches of air at the top. Gradually, a *voile*—a veil of yeast—

spreads over the wine's surface. The *sous-voile* method limits oxidation, while it allows certain flavors to develop. It's a version of the *flor* of sherry, created by the same yeast, *Saccharomyces bayanus,* which is one of the many species that play a role in the alcoholic fermentation. But once that's over, *S. bayanus* continues on, no longer consuming sugar but instead alcohol. "In the Jura, the thinner the veil, the better the product that results," Jean Macle said. "If it's thick, it has too much taste from the yeast, and it lacks finesse. In Jerez, I've seen a veil of one centimeter. Here, it should be the thickness of a playing card."

A healthy veil depends on the amount of alcohol in the wine, the warmth and dryness of the cellar, and the mysteries of each individual barrel and cask. The yeast stops growing in winter and starts again in summer. In fair weather, the Macles open the murky street-level windows of their cellars to let in warmer, drier air and more oxygen.

During the years of aging the wine is left almost entirely alone, hardly touched—never racked from barrel to barrel, as would be done with normal wine. "Maturing is no more than a *surveillance* with us," Macle said. The wine's alcohol discourages but by no means blocks acetic bacteria, which like the yeast require oxygen, from sharing the same surface and beginning to turn the wine to vinegar. To monitor that possibility, twice a year enologists from the departmental laboratory in Poligny visit each producer. They insert a sterile plastic pipette through the veil to take a sample from each vessel and analyze it for acetic acid, the defining acid of vinegar, and for ethyl acetate, which has the unpleasant odor of nail-polish remover. (It forms from a combination of ethyl alcohol and acetic acid and is the important substance winemakers mean when they speak of the defect of "volatile acidity.") Over the years, as the wine evaporates and the air space grows, about a third of the liquid is lost.

Only if the smell of a barrel suggests there may be a problem do the Macles taste their aging *vin jaune*. Then, so as not to disturb the veil, they draw some wine from the traditional *guillette,* a small tap unique to the Jura. Little more than a dowel, but made of horn rather than wood, it plugs the small hole found in the head of nearly every Jura cask and barrel. Jean said that if tasting left him and Laurent in doubt, they would take the wine to their wives, who would decide. "There is nothing to be done against volatile acidity and maderization," Macle said. (By maderization, he meant an "old" taste reminiscent of Madeira wine but without its good aromas: oxidation in a wholly negative sense.) A barrel of Savagnin that has just started to veer off in the wrong direction can be blended into the Macles' Côtes du Jura, to the benefit of the latter wine. But certain barrels fail altogether. "The number of barrels that must be rejected is very variable," Macle said. "It depends on the year, the alcohol, the acidity. Some years go marvelously well, but others . . ." A few producers sell their moderately unsuccessful *vin jaune* to chefs, who use it to flavor the cream sauces found in nearly every Jura restaurant and nominally made with *vin jaune*. Badly defective *vin jaune* is sent for distillation into industrial alcohol. The Macles blend together all their *vin jaune* that succeeds, including barrels from lesser Château-Chalon plots. "We think that, as in society, everyone has something to contribute," Jean said.

Before his father bottled the wine, he used to clarify it with blood from the village abattoir. As with the other old fining materials of egg white, milk, isinglass (from fish), or gelatin (from terrestrial animals), it was mixed into the wine; the protein attracted suspended particles and then settled to the bottom. But adding blood is now forbidden. The Macles fine instead with the clay bentonite and then lightly filter the wine, so in the bottle no deposit will form that might trouble a customer. For taste, however, it would be ideal to leave the wine alone. Jean's father didn't filter. "He sold less to restaurants; if there was a deposit, the customer said nothing."

Their Château-Chalon makes the Macles' reputation, but their Côtes du Jura is also one of the best, a blend of Chardonnay with some Savagnin. That wine is also matured *sous-voile,* usually for three years. Such white Côtes du Jura has many of the qualities of *vin jaune* but in milder form, coupled with a degree of freshness and fruit. Being less intense, the wines are more adaptable and more refreshing. They easily suit entire meals from charcuterie through fish and white meats, and they're tolerable with beef, good to excellent with certain firm cheeses and some blue ones. And because they accommodate diverse foods, they're very useful with contemporary cooking in which multiple, varied flavors appear together on a plate.

Considering the low yields needed to make any *vin jaune* worth drinking, the six-year wait, the loss of wine to evaporation, and the barrels of it that must be rejected, *vin jaune* isn't that expensive. A good bottle is around forty euros at the *cave* (and roughly one hundred dollars in the United States).

On my first visit to Jean Macle, as he began to pour a glass of Château-Chalon he apologized because the bottle had been opened only that morning, not enough time for its aromas to develop fully in the presence of oxygen. It should have been opened at least twenty-four hours in advance. But Macle said,

"I'm not a partisan of decanting," because the wine seems to change too quickly. An open bottle, unless the wine is very old, will hold most of its good qualities for a week to fifteen days. When I returned in December, the wine had been opened far enough in advance, but this time Macle was concerned that it had sat overnight in the cool room and was 2 degrees below his ideal temperature of 18 degrees C (65 degrees F), "the same as a great red wine."

Château-Chalon is pale in the glass, yellowish, as the name *vin jaune* promises, but with a degree of amber. Although Château-Chalon has the dominant reputation, the taste of the wine isn't stronger than that of *vin jaune* from other Jura appellations. If anything, the color of Château-Chalon is lighter and the taste is more delicate and refined. *Vin jaune* has an ethereal side. Its elements add up to something subtle that is purely its own, perhaps not so much complicated as deep.

With Macle, I tasted three vintages. One of the first two was clearly stronger than the other, but Macle remarked that in ten years the reverse might be true. When I bought a bottle of the 1996, Elyane advised, "It was a very hot year; the acidity is still aggressive. It will be another fifteen years before it is ready to drink." When we tasted the 1990, Jean said it was only halfway to its peak and would last a hundred years. He and Elyane once tasted an 1881 with a "marvelous bouquet." The 1990 was very fine, much more settled than more recent vintages, with everything in its place and the wine expressing a quiet elegance.

The best Château-Chalon couples balance with restraint and an extremely long aftertaste, a typically French combination in good wine. Another producer, with vines in both the Château-Chalon and Côtes du Jura appellations, described the latter *vin jaune* as "more fruity and floral, more flattering, less aggressive, more reserved," saying it evolves less. "The Château-Chalon is more acid and aggressive; it has that bitterness, citrus aromas. When it evolves, it becomes more mineral, more ripe apple, walnut, hazelnut."

Vin jaune, being produced in too small amounts to have much economic importance, has generated little scientific study. The *vignerons* imitate the methods of their fathers; some speak proudly of their wine's inscrutability. Yet certain essentials are known, partly through research into related wines. Of *vin jaune*'s two main flavor-giving substances, ethanal (often called acetaldehyde in English) is also found in regular wine, formed during fermentation. But *vin jaune* has roughly ten times as much, produced when the alcohol ethanol (not to be confused with ethanal) combines with oxygen during the years in casks. It gives the ripe apple aroma.

The other main substance requires more explanation. The taste of rancid walnut accompanied by slight burnt sugar that typifies *vin jaune* is called *rancio* when it appears in certain oxidized wines made outside the Jura. Isabelle Cutzach-Billard, an enologist in the South of France who has studied aromas in the oxidized *vins doux naturels* made there, says, "*Rancio* is defined by notes of rancid walnut with nuances of coffee liqueur, burnt sugar." That slight burnt-sugar component comes from a group of aromatic chemical derivatives of oxidation, described in her work. But the primary source of rancid walnut is a single chemical substance called sotolon. Like ethanal, it's produced slowly during aging, in varying amounts in different wines and barrels, and through more than one chemical pathway. In *sous-voile* wines, sotolon comes from the veil of yeast, and it's produced faster at warmer temperatures; after a year it's strongly present. The aroma varies according to the concentration. A small quantity of sotolon conveys prune, more gives dried fig and nut, more gives rancid walnut, and still more gives curry. The last two concentrations are found in *vin jaune*. Some people have difficulty ever becoming acclimated to *vin jaune,* but to most people a degree of rancidity in certain wines tastes good.

Vin jaune is more a wine for cooler weather (don't respect that too closely). I once served *vin jaune* at the end of an ambitious December meal to American friends who like to eat but who had never heard of *vin jaune*. One of them tasted the wine and was quietly stunned—repulsed. Later he told me that the taste was so unpleasant that he began to question everything he'd ever heard from me about food and drink and even, he said, half-joking, "our friendship." Then he tasted the beautiful twenty-month-old Comté that was on the table, and the fall-harvest walnuts, and then the wine. And gradually he came to love it. *Vieux* Comté and walnuts are the way to convince someone who has never tasted the wine before. The flavors succeed because they are partly similar, variations on a theme.

On another visit to the *cave*, Jean Macle offered me a glass of his Château-Chalon accompanied by a Comté made the previous autumn, about nine months earlier. He said that his daughter a few days before had brought a two-year-old Comté to the family dinner, and it had "killed" the taste of the Château-Chalon. Another Franc-Comtois, however, while not saying it would happen every time, told me that an exceptional old Comté with decades-old Château-Chalon can form a perfect fusion of tastes.

Other sure combinations for *vin jaune*'s peculiar set of flavors are meat (including beef) with cream sauces, morel mushrooms, and chicken (*vin jaune* intensifies chickeniness). The best-known dish of the Franche-Comté, *poulet au vin jaune et aux morilles,* combines chicken, cream, morels, and *vin jaune* to make one of the great flavor alliances in all of food. Jean Macle further listed, without having to pause to think: "terrines, any fish, escargots, coq au vin, *poularde au vin jaune,* Comté and Beaufort but not other cheeses, roasted meats, *filet de bœuf* with sauce, pigeon, woodcock, venison, but not hare or wild boar." I can add lobster, salmon, and humble, well-browned fried potatoes. Some people find a bond with the faintly bitter side of asparagus. *Vin jaune* has a reputation for complementing dishes flavored with curry (though that risks masking some of the flavors of the wine) and for accommodating exotic combinations and certain dishes from Asian cuisines. The wine's dryness makes any combination with a sweet dessert difficult. *Vin jaune* is one of the rare wines said to go with dark chocolate, but to my mind the chocolate underlines the rancid-walnut side of the wine to the exclusion of the rest.

The Francs-Comtois assert that no other dry wine, white or red, can follow *vin jaune,* which means that you can place it only at the end of a meal before dessert—drinking *vin jaune* throughout would keep everything at a single high pitch. A purely Jura sequence would be: with fish, a red Arbois (from low-tannin Pinot Noir or the native Poulsard); if there's an intermediate course, then a *sous-voile* white from any of the Jura appellations; next *vin jaune* with both the main meat course and the cheese (Comté); and finally with dessert a *vin de paille* (sweet wine from semi-dried grapes). But the underlying rule is breakable: you can drink *vin jaune* with fish, and then drink a strong (non-Jura) red with meat.

It's hard not to feel affection for any wine, such as *vin jaune*, that has persevered for centuries so far outside the mainstream, and especially a wine made not for drinking today but for future generations. *Vin jaune* is also interesting because it raises questions about the concept of terroir. It's an Old World, and perhaps especially French, phenomenon that tradition, economics, a belief in the importance of the land, the qualities of the land in a particular place, and the satisfaction of appetite should all come together to form a particular food or drink. That might be Roquefort cheese, Champagne, a Bresse chicken, Argenteuil asparagus, or *vin jaune*. One view is that *vin jaune* is a response to the Jura's terroir—that the *sous-voile* method brings out the taste of the minerals in the vineyard and reveals terroir as no other method can. By that way of thinking, even the veil itself is a part of the terroir, an expression of tradition and a result of the environment of the *cave*. I asked Jean Macle, "Does the taste of *vin jaune* come more from the terroir or the method?" He answered immediately, *"Tous les deux confondus"*—both, mixed together.

TWELVE

Vinegar in Barrels

Orléans, Orléanais

The Rue du Faubourg Bannier in the city of Orléans is a trafficky two-lane street bordered by parked cars and gray buildings. It begins near the railway station, up away from the oldest part of the city and the once-busy port beside the Loire, and it leads toward outer suburbs. It was the main road to Paris, 120 kilometers away, before a tangle of pedestrian zones, one-way streets, and broad new roadways changed things. At number 236, modest signs mark the vinegar-making establishment of Martin Pouret. There was no outward activity, but through a gateway and inside a small courtyard with room for one or two trucks, a clean, strong, sweet smell of vinegar came from one building. Up a wooden stairway and through a door, hundreds of barrels were set in racks, four high to the ceiling. The few dim lights made the room seem darker; daylight from the small number of windows was trapped in the narrow aisles between rows of barrels. The air was filled with acetic acid, piercing my nose and lungs. It was hard to breathe, and my eyes watered. I crouched near the floor to find clearer air, and from somewhere a drop of vinegar landed on my head. In time, Jean-François Martin told me, you get used to the atmosphere; it no longer seems intense.

In the middle of the twentieth century, the great French gastronome Curnonsky wrote, in his quintet of regional cookbooks called *Recettes et Paysages:* "Don't forget that the vinegar of Orléans is without rival!" But Martin Pouret is the last of the old vinegar-makers in the city and the last old-line producer in France to have adhered continuously to making vinegar in wood. You may hear praise for the "Orléans process," but if you look in old books, you find it's really just the once-standard way of letting wine ferment into vinegar on its own inside partly filled barrels, an almost inevitable transformation.

Jean-François Martin is the great-great-grandson of the man who founded the company in 1797. His office, in which only one other person seemed to work, was on one side of the courtyard. The two cheerful modern rooms stood in contrast with the rest of the operation, where only winery-style pumps and hoses and some stainless-steel holding tanks recalled the present. Martin was born in the house that fronts the street. He explained that at the turn of the last century, one hundred vinegar-producers stood on either side of the road, surrounded by fields. He was a quiet man, not given to self-promotion or even to much conversation about his product. He did say that until the 1950s, Martin Pouret vinegar was sold only in barrels to small grocery stores that filled bottles for customers as they asked for it. The customers were in towns, Martin said, because country people made their own wine and vinegar. He was convinced that his company had survived solely because of the superiority of its vinegar, which was "more perfumed and less aggressive" than his competitors' vinegar produced quickly in stainless steel.

The wine used by the Orléans vinegar-makers was on its way from the Loire Valley to slake the thirst of Paris. Someone from neighboring Touraine once told me that at Orléans the barrels were checked and any wine that was *piqué*—beginning to turn to vinegar—was sold to the vinegar-makers. The river boatmen would tap into the barrels at will, as part of their compensation, and the air in those barrels started the process.

Loire wines were affordable as well as light, a quality that Martin Pouret continues to look for. It uses wine at about 9 percent alcohol, which gives vinegar with about 7 percent acetic acid. Better wine makes better vinegar. (The best I ever made or tasted came from leftovers from a tasting of expensive red Burgundy. When I used it to dress salad, even though I said nothing, people commented.) Vinegar loses its initial harshness and gains nuance during months and sometimes years of aging. The wine for the basic vinegar is not in fact special, but Martin Pouret long ago added to its line other vinegars from more interesting wines, and it now offers tomato and yuzu vinegars, and vinegar in a spray bottle for raw oysters. The basic red-wine vinegar, however, has a familiar, reassuring taste; it's an old friend, my point of reference for vinegar. You see it in liter bottles in French supermarkets.

Today we don't think of vinegar as being especially important, but most of the world's cooking evolved before there was refrigeration, and vinegar was useful to preserve food or at least prolong freshness. People had more taste for acidity than they do now, and they used vinegar more freely, adding just a little to point up soup or sauces. Meat was wiped with vinegar to keep it until it could be cooked later in the day. Vinegar is an essential component of pickles such as cornichons and of almost all mustard. It's required in the butter sauces *hollandaise, béarnaise,* and *beurre blanc.* It marks *poulet au vinaigre,* rabbit or kidneys with mustard, *aigre-doux* ("sweet-and-sour") preparations (not that they're so common in France), marinated fish, sautés (such as calf's liver) in which the pan is deglazed with vinegar, and, usually, cooked red cabbage. But its most important use has always been to set off the sweetness of lettuce and other vegetables in vinaigrette. Salad, Martin said, is the best way to taste vinegar.

The *vaisseaux* ("vinegar barrels") lay on their sides and looked a lot like regular wine barrels. The average one at Martin Pouret was thirty years old and some were eighty. Many were banded by wooden rather than metal hoops. From the end of each, an L-shaped glass tube protruded to show the level of the liquid inside. Above the tube, a round hole, several inches across, let in air.

Seeing that the opening was uncovered, I asked Martin whether vinegar flies, which are the same as fruit flies, were a problem. He paused, as if I'd posed a riddle. "Yes, we have them," he said, "and no, they are not a problem." A few flies circled near the *vaisseaux,* but not as many as you might see around a bowl of ripe fruit in summer. Maybe, I thought, the pungency repelled them.

The *vaisseaux* are kept about 60 percent full. No one measures, and Martin gave this estimate reluctantly, as if for the first time. The liquid inside is covered by a fine veil of bacteria, not the thick gelatinous mother that often appears on vinegar when you make it at home. Martin Pouret's steady supply of new wine makes the bacteria too lively for that. Every three weeks a quarter of the vinegar is drawn off, leaving the barrels about half full, and the same amount of wine is added back. The *vaisseaux* are never cleaned or even rinsed. After the acetic fermentation, the vinegar is aged in great casks for six months, "so that aromas can develop, as with wine," Martin said.

I asked him about the advantages of using wood, whether it breathed, for instance. Yes, he seemed to say, commenting, "If you put vinegar in something that is dead, that is inert . . ." But the essence of his response was to explain that the company does what it has always done: *"Donc ça marche bien"* ("Therefore it goes well"). These are very American questions, Martin said. "There is a certain tradition, and if one wants to continue it, one must repeat the old process. It's like the rest of gastronomy." It was so obvious to him that he almost shrugged.

THIRTEEN

"The Bread Was Better, It's True"

Tours, Touraine

"One can't regret the past," Charles Barrier said. He sometimes showed the hardness of a peasant who had begun life expecting little more than hard work. "I had a brother-in-law who was a baker. There were no machines; I worked by hand. It was a very, very hard trade. One kneaded one hundred kilos of dough by hand all at once for each batch. You cannot regret that." Without pause he added, "The bread was better, it's true."

Barrier had earned his third Michelin star in 1968. I went to see him several times, before and after he retired, at last, from his luxurious restaurant in the city of Tours on the Loire River. That was in 1996 at the age of seventy-nine—he died in 2009. (Restaurant Charles Barrier is still there on the Avenue de la Tranchée, still with the same name, in the hands of a young chef with one Michelin star.) I met him while he was still working. He already moved slowly, but he had the face and energies of a younger man. He wasn't tall; he was big around but not quite fat, partly bald. He was forceful, and his eyes, behind glasses that gave him the appearance of an office manager, were sometimes intense. He liked to talk.

He was one of France's great chefs, part of the group that created Nouvelle Cuisine in the early 1970s. The new style overthrew much that was classical in favor of simpler, fresher food that opened the way to all the freedom chefs around the world now feel. Not that Barrier necessarily approved of that. Nouvelle Cuisine stressed lightness, freshness, shorter and more precise cooking times, an awareness of diet and health. It also brought simplified menus (drastically so, compared with before the Second World War) and simplified presentations inspired by Japanese cuisine. The chefs rejected marinades and the hanging of game; they turned away from the old rich sauces and especially flour thickening. They were open to new flavors, combinations, and technology. A top chef had once been only a craftsman, and now he was a star and a businessman.

It's not that Barrier influenced a generation of younger chefs. The only famous one was his friend Joël Robuchon, who would call every morning just before noon. Rather than having a particular legacy, Barrier is important for what he represents.

James MacGuire, a chef and baker from Montreal who was very close to Barrier, says that Barrier's cooking was a little different from that of other Nouvelle Cuisine chefs. "He knew all of classical cuisine, so he had the most paring down to do. But he also began with an ordinary restaurant, listened to his customers, and never took simple things off the menu." James further explains, "He didn't follow trends. No green or red peppercorns. He dabbled in *foie de lotte*" ("monkfish liver"), which came briefly into fashion. "He tried sautéed foie gras but went right back to his *foie gras en gelée*. His philosophy was devoid of the least ambition to challenge or astound. His approach was more purist, every dish just so, each plate unfettered by any unnecessary element." When MacGuire was young, he served as an intern in Barrier's kitchen. There was rigor in everything. "The biggest lesson to any cook who worked for him was to constantly ask oneself: 'Why am I doing this?'"

Touraine was so influenced by the nobility who came from Paris to stay in its châteaux, Barrier would say, that it didn't have much in the way of a distinctive regional cuisine. And yet he loved his region and its food. On the restaurant's menu, you might find Tourangeau pork rillettes and *rillons*. And I remember an old-school first course of beef cheeks and lambs' tongues in jelly served with, in a Tourangeau inspiration, cherries in vinegar. Pike-perch was sauced with *beurre blanc,* a dish from Anjou that had made its way to Touraine and because of its simplicity was embraced by Nouvelle Cuisine. A first course at Barrier might be *friture de la Loire* (a mass of deep-fried tiny river fish). And he made ultra-Tourangeau pork with prunes; his innovation was to use not white wine but red, which is a much better counterpoint. He found a fifteenth-century recipe for raspberry vinegar and used it to make traditional *poulet au vinaigre*—found in Touraine and other parts of France—starting a fashion for the dish. The selection of cheeses tilted toward the region, including logs of goat's-milk Sainte-Maure at various stages of ripeness. He loved the white wine of Vouvray, produced so close by; among reds he favored Cabernet Franc from the nearby Loire appellations of Chinon and Bourgueil.

Barrier began life as a baker, and until the end the restaurant made its own bread, probably the first luxe restaurant to do that. (And also the first to smoke its own salmon, a Loire fish—his had a delicate refinement.) To young people who go to restaurants in North America now, it may seem normal to have bread treated as just one of the appetizers, something to be ordered. But in France, and not only France, until not long ago it was unthinkable to eat without bread. Bread signified food. Even now if the bread on your table runs out during a meal in France and you ask for more, it will arrive faster and more apologetically than anything else you request, as if to correct a violation.

Barrier was born in Cinq-Mars-la-Pile, a village below Tours on the river, and he spoke of his early life without sentiment. The family lived in a *maison troglodyte,* one of the innumerable cave houses dug side by side into the soft limestone cliff that runs for kilometers parallel to the river. He was the eighth and youngest child, and his father died when he was two. Other families nearby were also named Barrier; his was distinguished as *les Barrier misères.* They didn't always have enough to eat.

While he was still a young boy, he worked in the bakery of his sister and brother-in-law. "They were poor and they worked so hard," he said. He spoke objectively, without tenderness. He cut the wood for the oven. When it was hot enough, the embers were raked out, so the bread could be put in. And when the embers were cool, it was his job to shake them in a sieve to separate the unburned coals from the ash. "I was black from head to toe." His sister sold the coals to customers of the bakery—ten sous for a paper packet—"and with that they bought their house." He was exaggerating, but every bit of money was important.

At the age of twelve, he was first in his class at the communal school, but his mother couldn't afford any further education, so she apprenticed him to a nearby pâtissier. (Barrier never ceased to educate himself; valuable old books filled a long wall of his house.) The apprenticeship was so miserable that before it was over he ran away to Tours and found a job in a kitchen. The reason wasn't that he was especially drawn to food, and he would give different explanations for why he became a cook. Often he said that he knew he would never go hungry in a kitchen. He learned in restaurant kitchens, but he was one of the last chefs to train partly in great private houses, which was better, he said, because no limits were placed on labor or materials: "They never counted anything—there was no comparison."

The loaves baked by his brother-in-law were almost white— *gros pains,* long and *fendus.* That means that before baking they were split lengthwise, nearly in half, by pressing with a rolling pin, to make more crust. They weighed three, four, and, for big families, six and eight *livres* (pounds, more or less). For feast days, the same dough was baked in a ring shape. At the time, bakers in Touraine made baguettes only occasionally; the fashion for them didn't arrive in the region until the 1950s.

"The principal ingredient of good bread is time," Barrier said to me. "The bread made in three hours is *merde.*" Was the flour different when you were young? "It was not at all the same." The farmers harvested 35 hectoliters of wheat per hectare, he explained, and now the breeders had raised the yield to 120. The plants were less dense in the field long ago, but they were beautiful, he said, and the cows used to give less milk. "Wheat is the same. The yield is much higher, for sure." He seemed to be contradicting himself, as he often did when he talked. This time he meant that even though the high-yield wheat was less pleasing to look at, it made life easier. "Now the wheat is lower to the ground"—he held his hand to show me—"because today the straw has no value. But if you want to make bread as good as eighty years ago, you can."

The peasants always made their own bread, which kept a long time because it included rye. Ten percent? *"More."* It was *pain de méteil*—a mix of wheat with rye, barley, and sometimes oats, sown together in the same field. "If one grew less well than the others . . ." He let the obvious be understood. "And they made bread from that, and it was good. *I* did that." The flour was sifted to remove almost all the bran. "When I was a child, we made bread once a week. One never ate the bread of the week. One ate the bread of the week *before,* because it was harder and one ate less."

Pain bis, the old name for tan bread made from flour that is more whole than white, was made for centuries, and was always less expensive than white. What do you think of *pain bis*? I asked. "That depends on what you call *pain bis.* If you add rye, it's natural, it's good. It's better, if you will."

On the summer day when we talked about bread, we sat under an umbrella behind his house. He opened a perfect Vouvray *pétillant,* lightly sparkling and slightly sweet, and he offered a small improvised lunch of charcuterie and cheese. As we were about to eat, Barrier picked up a round loaf of bread and held it against his chest, and he sliced toward himself in the primordial peasant gesture, unchanged all his life.

FOURTEEN

A Point of Reference for Pure Cabernet Franc

Chacé, Anjou

"We don't have any wine to sell," Nadi Foucault said when I telephoned. Demand far outstrips supply. He didn't sound enthusiastic about my coming to visit, but he agreed to a time the following week. The brothers Jean-Louis and Bernard Foucault, called Charly and Nadi, owners of Clos Rougeard, were among the most respected producers in Anjou. (Sadly, Charly died at the end of 2015; Nadi continues.) Clos Rougeard is specifically near the edge of the Saumur-Champigny appellation, next to the province of Touraine. Some admirers of French wine consider the best bottling of Clos Rougeard to be the essence of Loire Valley Cabernet Franc.

The variety is much older than its offspring Cabernet Sauvignon (whose other parent is the white grape Sauvignon), although in most of the world Cabernet Franc lives in the shadow of Cabernet Sauvignon. The famous wine in which it plays a determining role is Château Cheval Blanc, from Saint-Émilion in Bordeaux, a blend of 49 percent Cabernet Franc, 47 percent Merlot, and just 4 percent Cabernet Sauvignon. But Cabernet Franc also excels in the middle Loire, where it has been grown for centuries. The area is cooler than Bordeaux, and Cabernet Franc has the advantage that it flowers a little later in spring than Cabernet Sauvignon, so there is less chance of damage by frost (though the warming climate makes that less likely). The wine it gives in the Loire is lighter than in Bordeaux—less tannic, less deeply colored, but no less fragrant. And it goes readily with a range of food.

On the Rue de l'Église in the village of Chacé, one of the few breaks in the front of houses is the Foucaults' wide unmarked gate. I entered and a moment later Nadi, with his luxuriant mustache, was striding toward me. Without asking my name, almost without greeting, he took me through double doors and down a ramp into the *cave*. It was a real cave dug into the *tuffeau*, the soft, yellowy limestone that runs for kilometers up either side of the river. "Here in the region," Foucault said, "there are more kilometers of *caves* than there are of roads."

Bare bulbs left the passages dim; the stone was black with fungus. Foucault went straight to tasting, seeming hurried at first, but soon more relaxed. He belongs to the eighth generation to occupy the family house, he said, but Foucaults were *vignerons* in the village before that. When Nadi's great-grandfather registered the trade name Clos Rougeard in 1904, he was already bottling and selling directly, a practice that was all but unheard of for a small-scale grower at the time. Most in the area began to do that only in the 1970s and 80s.

The property's red grapes are entirely Cabernet Franc, nine

hectares in all. Neither the brothers nor their father ever applied chemicals. "We are organic without saying so," Nadi said. I asked, Do you consider yourselves traditional? "Yes, absolutely—very, very traditional."

The wine ferments in open tanks, most of them concrete, some stainless steel. Mainly to extract more flavor and color, the cap of skins and seeds that rises during fermentation is pushed down by *pigeage,* meaning in this case still with the feet. A plank provides support, but "the cap of a tank in full fermentation easily supports a man from the force of the carbon dioxide gas." Is there any temperature control for the fermentation? "Yes," he said. The natural coolness of the *cave.* "That way the refrigeration never breaks down."

All the wine goes into *barriques,* the standard Bordeaux-size barrels, for anywhere from eighteen to thirty months, according to the needs of the particular wine. It was July, and the wine from the previous fall was just finishing its malolactic fermentation. No sulfur had yet been added. We were tasting from the barrels. Since the wines hadn't been decanted so far, they had some not-unpleasant stink, from lack of exposure to oxygen. The wines also had a lot of ripe berry flavors, and neither overripe fruit, a taste associated with New World versions, nor the too-grassy, herbal, bell pepper flavors that can dominate either Cabernet Franc or Cabernet Sauvignon. Even at this early stage, the wines were delicious.

Clos Rougeard takes its name from one section of vines, a hectare or so behind the house. The basic red is a very good blend, not from those vines but from several other plots. Two additional wines are more substantial and still more delicious. Les Poyeux comes from a somewhat sandy location and is kept in oak barrels previously used just once. Le Bourg, from seventy-year-old vines in a spot with more limestone, is kept in entirely new barrels. That last wine has the most substance, including tannin, for longer keeping, and it's the one that sets the standard for Loire Cabernet Franc.

I've been in other *caves* up- and downriver that were filled with old barrels, and I was struck by the sight of so many new ones. I have never had much taste for oak flavor in wine, because it can dominate the rest of the taste. New oak succeeds only with more concentrated wines; as the wines age, the oak diminishes, while the flavors from the grapes expand. I wondered whether the traditional barrels around Saumur were the new 225-liter *barriques* I saw or the big 600-liter *demi-muids* common in Touraine. The bigger barrels, especially when they have been in use for decades, contribute no flavor to wine. What's the tradition? I asked. "When are we speaking of?" Foucault responded. One of his grandfathers was a cooper in the next village who made lots of 225-liter *barriques*. In those days, wine was shipped in barrels, and a *demi-muid* was hard to handle even for two men. *Barriques* were far more common, and "since they sold plenty of wine in barrels, new *barriques* were traditional."

Foucault said, speaking to the fashion for adding less and less preservative sulfur to wine, or none at all, "They're not wines without sulfur." Yet the amount is unusually small, merely ten milligrams of free sulfur at bottling out of just twenty-five milligrams of sulfur in total. By the standards of the past, that's almost none. The red wines are neither filtered nor clarified in any way other than by the passage of time.

Besides Cabernet Franc, the property includes one hectare of

Chenin Blanc, which produces a dry white wine with the appellation Saumur. Foucault served this wine, called Brézé, last, after all the reds, in an upending of the near-universal practice. "Because there's much more acidity than in the red wine," he said, "with us, that's the custom." At a meal, though, he said, he would likely drink the white wine first. It was full of flavors of fresh, ripe Chenin grapes. It's rare that a malolactic fermentation occurs in the white wine. "It comes from a terroir that is very limestone, which gives a strong natural acidity," Foucault said. Too strong for lactic bacteria to work. "Traditionally, the malo doesn't happen. Schist is less acid." Brézé is an excellent Chenin.

Does anyone nearby ever make sweet wine? I asked. The answer came as a surprise. "We do," Nadi said. That happens only sometimes, when the grapes are very ripe, and it's possible to choose bunches that are 100 percent affected by noble rot, the fungus that concentrates the sugar as well as the flavors, even as it alters them. The goal isn't necessarily to make the same wine every year; the goal is to accept nature.

FIFTEEN

The Slope at the World Center of Sauvignon Wine

Chavignol, Berry

As I approached Sancerre from the west, the mostly flat land-scape of hayfields, pasture, corn, and sunflowers ended abruptly, and the road curved down a steep eroded hillside, passing vines in dull red soil and then in stony tan. These were the vines of the Monts Damnés ("Damned Mountains"), although there are no mountains, just inclines. In the distance, the hilltop town of Sancerre sits on the highest point, around two hundred meters above the Loire River. Halfway down the slope, the vines end and the road slants into the village of Chavignol, whose buildings stretch out along the main street and end on the valley floor, which runs to Sancerre. The flat land each summer is filled with sunflowers; vines are confined to the slopes. Besides wine, the area is known for Crottin de Chavignol, the small, dryish goat's-milk cheese whose taste particularly complements that of white Sancerre wine. Until the 1960s, nearly all the

vignerons kept goats as insurance against the hail that sometimes devastates a vineyard. The wife did the herding, milking,
and cheesemaking, and the husband grew the hay or cut forage.
But when the *vignerons* began to bottle their own wine, they no
longer had time for everything. Goats retreated to farms on the
plateau above; the slopes were too valuable for anything but
grapes.

In the latter part of September, Chavignol was ready for the
harvest. Beside and beneath the village houses, double doors lay
open, revealing barrels, tanks, presses, and hoses. The last were
a reminder of the huge amount of water needed during the harvest to keep all the equipment constantly clean. Here and there
along the street, trailers, rising to eye level or higher, sat empty,
ready to be filled with fruit. Some tractors had been fitted with
harvesting equipment. Other machines were devoted solely to
harvesting, some designed to straddle one row of vines, some two.
In Sancerre, it's exceptional that grapes are cut from the vines
by hand in whole bunches. Most, to save time and money, are
pulled from the vine by the flailing plastic "fingers" of machines,
although that yields a lesser mix of intact grapes, broken ones,
and juice, and good qualities are lost through exposure to air.

Before they retired and ceased to work full-time as *vignerons,*
Edmond and Bernadette Vatan of Clos la Néore in Chavignol
had 4 hectares of vines. They kept a fraction of a hectare of
Pinot Noir and their best 1.6 hectares of Sauvignon. (Now just
1 hectare of Sauvignon remains, in the hands of their daughter
Anne, who married Nadi Foucault, producer of Cabernet Franc
in Saumur.) The Vatan Sauvignon lies in the soil called *terres
blanches* at the center and bottom of the Monts Damnés, where
the grapes are more out of the wind and ripen more fully. "They

are the vines I planted when I was twenty," Edmond Vatan said, "vines of forty-five years." Neither his parents nor grandparents ever kept goats. Edmond and Bernadette were the twelfth generation of Vatans to be *vignerons*. Unlike other producers in the village, they put out no sign; the wine was all spoken for long since.

The house was modern, the last one on the very short stretch of road between the main village street and the vines of the particular section called La Côte des Monts Damnés. Their former house in the village had become too noisy from tourist traffic in summer; they kept it for housing harvesters. Through miscalculating travel times, I arrived very late for my appointment. It was just before noon, but Edmond Vatan graciously and contentedly assured me that it was *"le bon moment"* for tasting wine. He seated me at the dining room table, set down a tray, and poured from a bottle of Clos la Néore, with its small, plain green label high on the neck. Other *vignerons* pour mere tastes of wine into special tasting glasses, leaving plenty of air for capturing aroma. Vatan filled the small stemmed glasses nearly to the rim with his most recent wine, and in a short while he filled the glasses again. He was a self-contained man, not at all the kind of person to offer a stream of fruit and flower names to describe his wine. I don't remember that he described it at all. I liked it very much, as I do whenever I drink it. It's the Sauvignon I've thought about more than any other.

After a moment, Bernadette joined us, in order to be sure, I think, that her more reserved husband would convey what was important about their wine. "We do what we like to do," she explained, "which is to say we do things the way they always used to be done." Everyone used to make wine by long-settled methods. The first change came in the 1950s, when local *vigne-rons* began to clarify their wine with egg whites, which wasn't bad, she noted. But the changes accumulated. "Now all the wines of Sancerre resemble one another, except only a few." Edmond observed, "There is a monotony." His wife stressed that they didn't criticize the present generation and that if they were young, they probably couldn't afford to make their wine in the old way.

It was September 21, the day before the official opening of the year's harvest in Sancerre, and the recent rainy weather had some Loire *vignerons* seriously worried about their crops. The Vatans were unconcerned. "One waits for *good* weather," Edmond said. "Usually, we wait the longest. One risks losing quantity, but to make good wine one must take the risk of losing." The Vatans didn't begin picking until October 5 or later. "We don't work except with the moon," Edmond explained, and he showed me a calendar. "There will be a new moon on October 5. That is important for me—more than tasting the grapes." They picked by hand, nowadays on the weekend with family and friends. I finished my wine and left the Vatans to the midday meal I'd almost interrupted, and I went to find lunch myself in the village. Afterward Edmond would show me the *caves*.

The Loire River is more than a thousand kilometers long, with Sancerre roughly at its midpoint, in the onetime province of Berry in central northern France. The wine appellation is bounded on the east by the river and extends in an irregular shape over fourteen communes. Sancerre was once inexpensive, one of the dry white wines consumed especially with raw shellfish in the bistros of Paris. It's usually drunk young, because with few exceptions it doesn't benefit from age. Especially during the 1990s, Sancerre moved upward in reputation and price, although the price today is still moderate. Anyway, you don't get quality without a price high enough to support it, and throughout the Loire Valley overall the quality of Sauvignon has slowly risen.

Sauvignon has often been considered a second-rank grape, mainly because the wine is not for long keeping, and yet critics grant Sauvignon respect. Its distinctive taste, very unlike that of other varieties, makes it highly useful with food. The axis of the taste is an unmistakable greenness—something grassy or herbaceous. In poorly grown grapes the herbaceousness turns into a distinct smell of cat pee. Walking past one patch of vineyard in the Sancerrois, I smelled it so strongly that I looked around for the cats that I was sure must be close by. Then I tasted a few grapes and realized the smell came from the fruit itself. Some people say a mere hint of cat adds to the complexity of the wine, but it's hard to believe that any detectable amount really gives pleasure. Setting that aside, even within the greenness Sauvignon tends to head in one of two directions—more green or more ripe. The greener examples are more lively with acidity, and the riper ones have more fruit and even flowers.

Apart from greenness or ripeness, New World versions of Sauvignon can be much more forceful than the French. Sauvignon Blanc from California or New Zealand is typically much riper and richer, often markedly herbal, often oaky, too often a little sweet, and with more assertive flavors. Anyone whose impression of Sauvignon was formed by New World versions might be disoriented by the Loire concept—restraint, acidity, dryness, and often something "mineral." That last has become a popular word among lovers of Old World wine, frequently applied, among French wines, to Chablis and Loire Chenin. Those who say "mineral" don't all mean the same thing by it, but usually it describes an utterly dry wine whose marked acidity recalls something stonelike or oceanic.

No one knows where the Sauvignon vine originated. (Unexpectedly, one parent is the minor variety Savagnin, with its curiously similar name, whose origins have their own uncertainties.) Nowhere is the taste of Sauvignon better than in the wines from the *terres blanches* that show up here and there in Sancerre, particularly in Chavignol but also in certain other spots and in other Loire appellations. Geologically, the *terres blanches* are Kimmeridgian marl, a clayey marl that contains sea fossils; it gives richer wine that can improve during a few years in the bottle. *Terres blanches* tend to appear on higher slopes where erosion has exposed the underlying rock. They have the tan color I saw on the Monts Damnés as I first drove into Chavignol. The origin of the name is lost in time, but "damned mountains" could be linked to the hardship of working vines on slopes of up to 30 degrees. In 1921, a storm washed away the vines altogether, and the area wasn't fully replanted until the 1990s.

In his workplaces Edmond Vatan was more serious, more in his element. The bottled wine was in the shallow cellar of an old building set into the hill below the house. Elsewhere in the village was the small *cave,* at approximately ground level, where the wine was fermented. It was built in the sixteenth century as a house, and I could see the remains of a fireplace and tile floor. The Vatans' oak *demi-muids,* common in the Loire Valley and a little more than twice the size of a usual barrel, were a hundred years old, "at least." I put my nose to the opening of one and found a clean smell of concentrated old wine. When the barrels were empty, Vatan periodically burned a sulfur match in them. "One smells and then one looks with a candle and then one washes. One must always smell," he said. To show me, he lowered a candle at the end of a stiff wire into the *demi-muid*. If he saw mold, he knew the barrel needed washing.

Back in 1964 he had installed a new horizontal Mabille wine-press to replace the *click-clack* ratchet of an old vertical turn-screw press. The Mabille also uses the turn-screw principle, and he chose it because it was most like the old kind. Plus it came with a motor. "In the past, it took three or four men to push the bar," Vatan said. He had never checked the temperature of the fermentation with a thermometer. He went by his nose, and if he smelled fruit in the air, he knew that the fermentation was too warm and he must leave a door or window open overnight to cool it. "Also," he said, "one tastes the wine every day during the fermentation."

"If there is a malolactic fermentation," he said, in response to my question about that, "it occurs inside the *demi-muids* and one doesn't perceive it." He racked (decanted the wine from one set of barrels to another, leaving the lees behind) three times during the year, he said, and he bottled when the wine was sufficiently clear, in either May or June or else September— "One doesn't touch wine in summer." First, he would form a single blend from the wine in the *demi-muids*: "One tastes, one tries different combinations, one calls one's friends, and one suc-ceeds." Rejected wine was sold off to a *négociant*. Finally, he gave each filled bottle the traditional airtight seal of hot wax.

Besides the press, Vatan's other innovation was to purchase six enamel-lined steel tanks to hold the blend and if need be to store the wine over the summer. Old hay in a loft overhead provided insulation in cold weather. Vatan didn't clarify the wine using egg whites because, he said, "It's not worth the trouble." And he certainly didn't pump it through a filter. The Vatans had noted earlier that the wine was not absolutely clear. Held to the light, the year-old wine had been very faintly shaded with white.

When I visited *caves* elsewhere in Sancerre, I found that the Vatans were both respected and considered the most old-fashioned. A few other producers, however, follow a related path, notably François and Pascal Cotat, cousins who work separately, and now you can even find a few wines that might be considered eccentric by the standards of the past.

Clos la Néore is full of the green but not at all unripe taste of Sauvignon; it has the concentrated flavor you expect from the *terres blanches*. Among Sancerre's possibilities, it represents the riper, fuller side, but in a way that straddles the racy herbal-acid one. The taste of Clos la Néore and the variations from vintage to vintage have taught me the most about the taste of good Sauvignon. "Enology," another Sancerre *vigneron* once said to me, "is a science that only proved what the generations of old people had always known, what they found with their palates."

SIXTEEN

Parsleyed Ham

Dijon, Burgundy

Early on a Friday morning in summer, the most serious shoppers at the Halles de Dijon, the central market in the Burgundian capital, were carefully coiffed and dressed older women. In the southwest corner of the market, Christian Sabatier smiled at his customers and looked at ease. Some gray showed in his neatly trimmed dark hair, but he looked in his prime as he, his mother, and two sisters briskly filled orders, slicing and wrapping, pausing only occasionally for a short friendly exchange with a customer. The floor on their side of the counter was raised, so customers looked up as they ordered two or three items from the array of charcuterie. In origin, a charcutier is someone who prepares and sells *chair cuite* ("cooked meat"), and over time charcutiers came to specialize in items requiring particular skill—hams, sausages, terrines, pâtés. During the few minutes I waited to be served, the most common request was for *jambon persillé*—"parsleyed ham." It's Sabatier's specialty and Burgundy's favorite and best-known charcuterie. Customers chose a slice either from a long loaf or from the wide hemisphere of a *saladier,* a "salad bowl." In each slice, the green of parsley contrasted appealingly with pieces of pink meat, and there was white fat, including a milky color where the chopped fat had mixed with the meat's jelly. The combination of jelly and meat makes *jambon persillé* a relative of headcheese.

Parsleyed ham isn't strongly salty and intense like dry-cured ham, which must be eaten in paper-thin slices. *Jambon persillé* is sliced thick—you can eat a lot of it. A good one, such as Sabatier's, is particularly tender and moist. A chilled slice is firm and holds together, but eaten outdoors and allowed to warm in the sun, it falls apart. The pieces of ham are more sweet than salty, though there's no more than a touch of sugar in the brine, and at the same time the jelly provides tartness from wine and a little vinegar. There's also a cautious amount of finely chopped raw garlic; some makers add shallots too. The parsley is so plentiful that it's almost a vegetable.

When I later telephoned Sabatier to learn more, he gave helpful answers to my questions in his modest, gravelly voice, but he was confused by my interest. I in turn was confused that he was confused, thinking the quality of his *jambon persillé* was plenty of reason to be calling him up. More than once he asked why I was interested, and the recurring question became a subtheme of our conversation.

I explained that I had heard about him from a friend of mine who had worked in the Burgundy wine trade and lived for two years near Dijon. My friend became interested in *jambon per-*

sillé and began to search for the best, trying far more examples than he can remember. He said to me, "It's like asking, 'How many wines did you taste?' You only remember the good ones." He finally concluded that Christian Sabatier's *jambon persillé* was best beyond doubt. Although my tasting had been much more limited, I could only agree. I told Sabatier all that.

The men in his family have been charcutiers, he said, "from father to son since 1874." He began his apprenticeship at the usual age of fourteen. He works in premises on the Rue de Beaune and has no retail shop. Since the Halles are open on just Tuesday, Friday, and Saturday mornings, on other days Sabatier drives his white truck, the kind that opens on one side to reveal a refrigerated counter, to weekly markets on the outskirts of the city.

He has three children, the youngest of whom was then sixteen, but none had or would become a charcutier. "I didn't show them," he said. At the time, charcutiers all over the country had been struggling, and many had gone out of business. I told him what I had heard from Gilles Verot, the outstanding, leading charcutier in Paris—that people were eating less fat, that they saw charcuterie as old-fashioned, and that good charcuterie is expensive. That's not it, Sabatier responded. The customers in the central and open-air markets are old, and the young shop in supermarkets, he said. Eventually there won't be enough customers. Besides, as with crafts such as breadbaking, no one wanted to be an apprentice. "It's hard. You have to start in the morning at an early hour—the young want to go out at night with their friends." They don't want to get up and go to work in the dark.

Like other old-school charcutiers, Sabatier makes at least a hundred different items, and adds a novelty from time to time. In fact, he said, he had never counted all the things he makes: "It might be two hundred." He also sells a little fresh meat and makes a few prepared dishes, though *boucher* ("butcher") and *traiteur* ("caterer") are separate occupations. He makes *jambon persillé* each week, saying it is as much a part of the patrimony of Burgundy as its wine.

Once, *jambon persillé* was particularly an Easter dish, more or less obligatory in every home in a region running from Dijon south through the top vineyards to the city of Chalon-sur-Saône, seventy kilometers away. But today it's made by charcutiers throughout Burgundy and throughout the year, with only some extra demand at Easter. "One has to reconstruct history, in effect, because we have lost so much," Sabatier said. A few people still make *jambon persillé* at home, buying and cooking the ham and molding it in a *saladier*.

Yet for all its importance, it's not clear that *jambon persillé* is that old. The earliest recipe I've seen that's close appears in the 1901 cookbook *Le Cuisinier Bourguignon*. To make this *"jambon à la bourguignonne,"* the skin and bones are removed from a whole, cooked, dry-cured ham, which is merely covered with a layer of chopped parsley mixed with vinegar—no raw garlic; the skin is replaced, and the ham is accompanied by jelly from the cooking mixed with more parsley and vinegar. Calves' feet, cooked with the ham to make the jelly, are served on the side. But that's a lot of strong-flavored ham, and it sounds like restaurant cooking. The real parent of today's *jambon persillé* might be a much homier version, "obligatory for Easter," for which a recipe appears in the little Burgundy volume, published in 1923, of Curnonsky and Rouff's regional series *La France Gas-tronomique.* A dry-cured ham is soaked, cooked in water (which is changed after an hour to get rid of salt), and then the meat is crushed with a fork. It is pressed into a *saladier* and the rich cooking liquid, mixed with parsley, white wine, and a spoonful of vinegar, is poured over. After all that, the salty meat is surely succulent. The book attributes the recipe to Henri Racouchot, whose restaurant Aux Trois Faisans was the most famous and best place in Dijon. The first recipe I know for the current form of *jambon persillé*—mild ham and jelly all in one—appears in *La Charcuterie Moderne,* a 1924 Dijon professional manual.

For his *jambon persillé,* Christian Sabatier brines his own pork, lightly. These *demi-sel,* or "half-salt," hams used to require a week or ten days in brine, but Sabatier injects the brine, an honest, efficient technique, and the meat is ready in twenty-four to forty-eight hours. He doesn't smoke this mild ham; smoked ham is something else. Like other charcutiers, for *jambon persillé* Sabatier combines the drier meat of the ham, meaning the rear leg, with the more marbled and moist shoulder, brined in the same way.

The hams and shoulders cook together slowly all night in a bouillon of water, white wine, carrots, onion, bay leaf, clove—"everything needed to supply the seasoning"—along with calves' feet and extra pork skins for gelatin. Afterward Sabatier separates the meat into its natural small sections, discarding the bones. He layers the meat with lots of chopped raw parsley mixed with some finely chopped garlic and a little vinegar. The key with the garlic, he said, is restraint. He moistens everything with the rich broth from cooking, and places the long-cooked, tender skin on top, pressing the *jambon persillé* a little and chilling it.

At different charcuteries, the *jambon persillé* on display behind the glass counter looks somewhat different, and it varies in tenderness and seasoning. Some versions taste cheap, and in the least appealing the parsley is a lurid green. Sabatier thought that the parsley in those might have come already prepared. Fresh parsley, after it's mixed with the jelly, turns olive drab. "Some people work with fresh parsley," he commented, "and some work with dehydrated."

Jambon persillé, as he said, is eaten with cornichons and mustard for their acidity. There's bread, of course, and "a glass of Aligoté—the same as used for the kir, mixed with the cassis of the region." Aligoté wine comes from the productive Aligoté grape, a variety that's almost certainly native to Burgundy and is the region's second most common white grape, though a long way behind Chardonnay. A glass of good Aligoté wine is slightly acid, clean, and fresh, made for drinking young—perfect with charcuterie.

Toward the end of our second conversation, Sabatier was still not sure why I was interested. But it came out that, with some of his colleagues, not everything purported to be made in-house is in fact made in-house. "There is '*jambon maison*' that is not *jambon maison* but is bought from a factory." Some charcutiers, he offered, sell their personalities and not the product. Finally a thought came to him that he seemed never to have had before. Still in his modest, deep voice, he said, "*Moi, je suis pur moi*"— "I'm pure."

SEVENTEEN

A Spice Cake
Lost in Time

Dijon, Burgundy

Pain *d'épices* is "spice bread" or, loosely, gingerbread. It's tra-ditionally dense, though not heavy, and smooth with a fine crumb. You can taste honey, but it's usually impossible to pin down what the spices are. Recipes show that the key ingredients are aniseed and honey, so unlike the ginger and molasses of English and American gingerbread. A typical French mix might also include cloves, cinnamon, coriander, and some form of or-ange. Probably because of the anise, not everyone likes *pain d'épices.* (Somewhat ironically, aniseed isn't strictly a spice, in the sense of being obtained by trade from the East; it comes from a Mediterranean plant.) In the Burgundian capital of Dijon, Mulot et Petitjean is the last of the city's old makers of *pain d'épices,* the descendant of a business that opened in 1796. The shop on Place Bossuet with half timbering on its two upper sto-ries is located behind a neo-Gothic storefront from 1919; the highly decorative interior from the same year is even more hand-some. At the time of those renovations, the baking had already been moved from the cellar to a separate facility, and today there are five shops altogether. In France, you can buy industrial ver-sions of *pain d'épices,* and in Dijon, besides Mulot et Petitjean, a few other, newer businesses also make some spice bread. Scat-tered throughout the country, certain beekeepers make it and sell it alongside their honey at open-air markets; theirs is like some sort of heavy conventional cake with spices. Real *pain d'épices* has a particular texture from a specific technique.

It was surely inevitable that long ago honey would be com-bined with spice and flour to make a cake. It might have been first done by Arabs, who might have brought the cake to France at the end of the first millennium. Even within France, it's im-possible to specify a place or period of origin. Spices were in widespread use in medieval cuisine, when the normal sweetening was either honey or, in wine regions, *sapa,* which is the boiled-down juice of sweet grapes. Only in the 1500s did sugar become available in Europe in sufficient quantity and at a low-enough price to be commonly used. *Pain d'épices* may be related to the medieval spice breads still made in Italy: *panpepato* ("peppered bread," with heat from black pepper) and its offspring *panforte* ("strong bread," strong with the acidity of the fruit). They're wonderfully dense disks of dried or candied fruit, almonds, spices, and honey, but they've lost all or nearly all the flour they once had. French *pain d'épices* often contains some candied fruit and nuts, but flour and sweetening dominate, and there's no heat. The shapes are varied; some loaves are enormous.

When I asked Catherine Petitjean, the highly capable director of the business, whether *pain d'épices* is more bread or more pastry, she answered, "For me, it's bread—it's between the two, but there's less than 3 percent fat, so it's closer to bread."

The oldest French formula calls for equal proportions, by weight, of flour and honey. No other liquid and no eggs lighten the dough or cut the taste. These days, since honey costs so much more than sugar, it's rare to find *pain d'épices* sweetened purely with honey, apart from loaves made by beekeepers. Once baked, *pain d'épices* keeps indefinitely. The honey absorbs humidity from the air and keeps the cake moist.

Pain d'épices used to be made in a number of cities of northern France, including Paris, but its strongest links were with Dijon in Burgundy and Reims in Champagne. Until a hundred years ago, Reims had the leading reputation. The makers there, like those in Paris, used not wheat flour but only rye. The honey was sometimes dark, intense buckwheat honey (eventually some makers in France switched to cheaper molasses).

But toward the end of the nineteenth century, the makers in Dijon replaced the heavy rye-flour version with a lighter white flour one containing egg yolks. That seems to have given them a new success, and their reputation eclipsed all others. Then after the Second World War, everywhere in France, nearly all the old *pain d'épices* businesses, whatever sort of cake they had made, collapsed. Catherine Petitjean blames the use of poor ingredients, including rice flour, which were all that were available during those difficult years. And maybe spice cake seemed too much of a luxury, or simply old-fashioned. In Reims by the 1990s, the last of the former makers was ordering its *pain d'épices* from an outside mass producer. In Dijon, of the dozen longtime houses, only Mulot et Petitjean survives.

Out of curiosity, at home I once mixed three doughs containing equal proportions of flour and honey, nothing else, on the model of the original. One dough was made of white flour, and the other two of whole organic rye flour. I left the stiff mixes covered on the kitchen counter. After three weeks, two were unchanged, but one of the rye-flour doughs had acquired a spicy, peppery aftertaste. Long ago, some makers exploited that effect by omitting spices altogether. *Pain d'épices* was so popular that there were many cheap versions. I added spices and baked my doughs, and the loaves were good, though it would take many trials to master the technique.

You may be wondering what possibly makes the dough light. And if you try to penetrate to the essence of *pain d'épices,* the leavening is the murkiest subject. The makers of *pain d'épices* were among the first French to embrace baking powders, about the same time the Dijonnais makers began to use white flour. Baking powder gives a softer, more cakelike texture. But what was the leavening before that? A few organic makers today employ *levain,* and I've had good *pain d'épices* leavened with commercial baker's yeast, but neither of those, as far as I can tell, is traditional. Those who use them must reduce the sweetening, because yeasts struggle to work in a very sugary environment. I suspect that in France there was originally no added leavening at all, just as in Italy the surviving medieval spice breads have none. And yet something made the bread a little light—a brick of a loaf wouldn't have been popular.

For sure some lightness comes from the main mixing, called *braquage.* First, the flour is simply mixed with the sweetening, both honey and sugar. The next step, incredibly, is to set aside that simple dough to mature for days or months. At Mulot et Petitjean, the time was once more than a year. But it's expensive to store a year's worth of dough, and most recipes today don't even mention the aging. At Mulot et Petitjean, the current time is fifteen days to three weeks, sometimes longer. "The older it is," Petitjean said, "the better it will keep, and the more beautiful it will be." Next the egg yolks typical of Dijon go in, along with baking powder and spices. Petitjean hasn't changed the recipe; it's just as she has always known it. Once all the ingredients are in, the *braquage* takes place with the specific purpose of softening the dough and adding more air.

When I asked a researcher at the Institut National de la Recherche Agronomique about what occurs in the dough during the aging, he said there has been no scientific study, but he confirmed that after the dough has matured for several months, the spice cakes rise more in baking and have smaller, more consistent holes.

Mulot et Petitjean thrives under its director, making about five hundred tonnes of *pain d'épices* each year. That's partly because about twenty years ago the *sucré-salé*—"sweet-salty"—taste came into fashion and chefs began to incorporate *pain d'épices* into savory recipes, including for foie gras. Now Mulot et Petitjean makes the cake in many variations and sizes, but the standard loaf still weighs, as ever, just over six kilos, and is cut to order in the shops into about 500-gram squares. *Pain d'épices* is a very particular food, whose origins are lost in a complex, elemental past.

EIGHTEEN

The Goal of a Gulpable Wine

Villié-Morgon, Beaujolais

Once upon a time, Beaujolais was a red wine with nearly mythical qualities of thirst-quenching goodness. It was "tender, full of fruit, fond, gulpable, and the rest," and it went "with any dish." Georges Rozet wrote that in 1949 in *La Bourgogne Tastevin en Main.* The wine was low in alcohol, light, refreshing, sometimes cloudy when young, and slightly fizzy with carbon dioxide, and most of all it had a strong perfume of fresh fruit. In the recurring French description, Beaujolais was *gouleyant*— "gulpable." It was an inexpensive wine for every day, meant to be drunk within a year of the harvest, and an outstanding complement to food. Beaujolais has a sweetness, or gentleness, because the Gamay grape, the sole variety in Beaujolais, is low in tannin. (In most red wines, it's the tannin, sometimes bitter and astringent, that tastes unpleasant with fish and erases the best flavors of vegetables and cheese.) Gamay also has less acidity than many varieties, although, without much tannin to hide it, the acidity is apparent and helps the wine taste fresh. And while Gamay has specific aromas, of cherry or strawberry, for instance, depending on where it's grown, nothing about the wine calls for finicky matching with dishes. Reading the old praise you can hardly believe such a wonderful wine ever existed. It probably stood out because at the time few other wines combined strong fruit with such easy drinking and a modest price. But then during the 1960s, the old Beaujolais seemed to disappear, and it didn't reappear in any quantity for almost forty years.

The producers had begun using chemicals to push yields higher, which prevented the grapes from becoming as ripe as before, and they picked early to avoid the risk of bad weather and because more acidity from less ripe grapes makes winemaking easier. In compensation they added sugar to the fermentation, pumping up the alcohol. The red grapes were still picked by hand, as required under the rules. And they were put into the fermentation vats still whole in their bunches, which was the old way. But the producers began to add selected yeasts to obtain particular flavors—banana is always cited. And where the vessels had been wooden and open at the top, now nearly all Beaujolais producers switched to *closed* vessels of fiberglass, concrete, or stainless steel. After two or three days the fermentation produced enough carbon dioxide to eliminate air and oxygen. The carbon dioxide protects flavors that would otherwise be lost to oxidation. (A few makers didn't and don't wait for the gas to bubble up from the fermenting juice; they add carbon dioxide from a tank to keep out oxygen from the start.) Like many other wines of the time, this Beaujolais was heavily filtered to make it perfectly clear and to prevent sediment from forming, at the cost of flavor. Every fall, a flood of cheap Beaujolais Nouveau appeared, a third of the region's wine. All Beaujolais began to be seen as beginners' wine, and among many wine drinkers it fell far out of favor.

Whole-grape fermentation partly protected by carbon dioxide always set most Beaujolais apart, although the closed vessel exaggerated the effects. The method, called semi-carbonic maceration, takes place in three horizontal zones. The grapes at the bottom burst from the weight of the grapes above, and there the juice ferments in the usual way. At the top of the vat is the carbonic zone, where the whole grapes surrounded by carbon dioxide undergo an intracellular fermentation without the action of yeasts. That gives a little alcohol as well as brighter color, less tannin, reduced acidity, and certain characteristic aromas. In the middle zone, whole grapes immersed in juice undergo a smaller amount of the same transformation. The presence of the stems, inherent with whole grapes, can give a bit of green taste to the wine. The maceration lasts eight days or longer, before the wine is run off and the grapes, many still whole, are pressed. Their sugar-filled wine, called *le paradis,* is combined with the rest and then the fermentation continues until the sugar is used up.

More than 130 million bottles of Beaujolais are produced each year. As in Burgundy, the properties are still mostly small. The three thousand *vignerons* own an average of just nine hectares each. Most of the Beaujolais growers by far sell wine or grapes to *négociants,* who handle almost 70 percent of the wine, or they belong to a co-op rather than bottle and market on their own. Probably the large number of growers and the great quantity of modest wine caused the market to be dominated by middlemen. Although the character of individual vineyards doesn't always appear in a wine or is lost in a blend, the *vignerons* know what each spot is capable of—each has its name, or *lieu-dit*.

Beaujolais, the region, lies just south of Burgundy, between it and the city of Lyon, which is just a short distance down the Saône River and was the wine's first big market. The second big market, after canals and then railroads made transport easier, was the bistros of Paris. Although Beaujolais is often placed with Burgundy, the region stands largely apart. Philip the Bold, king of France, in 1395 in his charter in defense of Burgundian wine, recommended Pinot Noir and ordered the uprooting of the "very bad and very disloyal plant named Gamay." It grew too vigorously in the limestone soils of Burgundy, producing high yields of thin wine. But in Upper Beaujolais the meager, sandy soil over granite checked Gamay's lushness, and it continued to be raised there. (A few white grapes have always been grown in Beaujolais as well; Chardonnay goes into the small production of Beaujolais Blanc.) Compared with Burgundy, the Beaujolais climate is warmer, and the area begins to feel southern. The houses aren't all concentrated in villages; many are scattered among the vines. Shallow-pitched roofs are covered with curved clay tiles. A number of the roofs, however, now have flat factory tiles, and a number of houses have been renovated to the point that they look new.

Beaujolais's poor soils don't hold moisture, so the vine roots drive deep to find it. Most plantings are old. On a Beaujolais label, the phrase *vieilles vignes* ("old vines") commonly means fifty to one hundred years. The official minimum density for the better wines is six thousand vines per hectare, but in Beaujolais, as in many regions, the traditional density is far greater, from nine to thirteen thousand vines per hectare. Today, because so many of the Beaujolais vines are old, the average density remains high. Training the vines in a short fan is permitted, but the traditional shape is the ancient, low goblet dominant in southern France and around the Mediterranean. Several craggy arms, pruned close, surround an open middle. Each summer after the shoots have grown long, they are gathered on top of the goblet and tied together in a bunch (once with a willow shoot), or they're supported by wires running along the rows.

Upper Beaujolais, the northern half of the region, is the source of Beaujolais-Villages and of the ten Beaujolais *crus,* each of which has its own appellation. Almost all the best Beaujolais *vignerons* are located in the *crus,* with their pretty village names: Saint-Amour, Juliénas, Chénas, Moulin-à-Vent, Fleurie, Chiroubles, Morgon, Régnié, Brouilly, and Côte de Brouilly (going from north to south). The names are important because *cru* labels rarely mention "Beaujolais," as if to say that their wine is not to be confused with the mass of Beaujolais. *Cru* Beaujolais has more fresh-fruit aroma, lighter body, slightly lower alcohol, and less tannin, which together add up to more refreshment.

Nearly all of Upper Beaujolais lies on pink granite, which erodes evenly to form rounded hills with light brown soil. But the minerals mixed with the granite vary, and they're probably responsible for most of the differences in taste. Among the lighter, fruitier *crus,* the best and most elegant wines overall come from Fleurie, whose taste, as the name suggests, is typically flowery. Among the *crus* with somewhat more substantial flavor and a little more tannin to allow the wines to last, the most prestigious, longest-lasting wines come from Moulin-à-Vent, whose granite contains seams of manganese. More affordable and more typical of Beaujolais is Morgon, which has schist, a layered rock that breaks down to give a soil called *morgon* or *roches pourries* ("rotten rocks"). The wine's characteristic aromas are cherry or wild cherry. Morgon happened to become the center of the revival of Beaujolais.

Marcel Lapierre, who died, at sixty years old, just after the 2010 harvest, lived outside the village of Villié-Morgon. A bearded, outgoing man, he was the driving, influential force behind the new wave of old-style Beaujolais and a major force behind "natural wine" in general. His son, Mathieu, had already been working with him, and since Marcel's death there has been no break in style and no loss of quality. The Lapierres have thirteen hectares, two on the Côte du Py, which is the gentle, enormous hill that is the best location in Morgon.

Now an old story. Marcel Lapierre was just another conventional grower until 1980. In that year a sculptor friend sent him to see Jules Chauvet, a Beaujolais *négociant* who was active from the 1930s until he died in 1989. He was also a biochemist and a respected taster, not widely known in France but not a marginal figure either. According to the profoundly influential Bordeaux enologist Émile Peynaud, Chauvet was responsible for modern analytical tasting for aromas, such as those of particular fruits and flowers (an approach some critics have pursued to a fault). Starting in 1951 in his *négociant* business, Chauvet began to vinify a part of the wine without sulfur, convinced the aromas were superior. He also found that the taste of a wine was finer when it was made with indigenous yeasts and without added sugar. Similarly, he was attracted to semi-carbonic maceration for Beaujolais, a technique that others had already begun to look at. And he believed a cooler fermentation produced finer aromas.

For winemakers, sulfur is a blessing, but a mixed one. It's an extremely useful antiseptic and antioxidant that had at least some use in ancient winemaking and has been commonly used for at least two hundred years. It's essential for sterilizing barrels and other equipment that can harbor undesirable microorganisms, and, added to wine or to the grapes when they arrive at the *cave*, it reduces the loss of flavor to oxidation and the possibility of bacterial spoilage. It's risky to make wine without sulfur, and still more so not to add any at bottling. But in recent years, first in France under the influence of Chauvet, and then in other countries, a limited but growing number of small producers have partly or totally rejected adding sulfur to wine, and they've attracted sympathetic, enthusiastic customers.

Lapierre abandoned the use of chemicals in the vineyard and became a strong believer in semi-carbonic maceration. Following Chauvet's advice, at first he simply picked in the cool of the morning. Later he used refrigeration to keep the temperature of the grapes between 10 and 15 degrees C (50 to 60 degrees F). All wines used to ferment at uncontrolled temperatures that sometimes rose high enough to cook some of the good aromas. Lapierre, like nearly all winemakers now, limited the rise through refrigeration, aiming to go no higher than 28 to 30 degrees C (82 to 86 degrees F).

He attracted a small group of like-minded *vignerons*, all friends, who began to work in the same way. They added no sulfur except for a very small amount at bottling and sometimes none at all. (Those who added none in those early years, when producers hadn't mastered no-sulfur techniques, took a big risk. Out of a case of twelve zero-added-sulfur bottles, shipped overseas through the usual channels, all but three could be disappointing. For one thing, the bottles had to be kept continuously cool, something importers now pay attention to.) Lapierre and his friends were strongly influenced by Chauvet and his belief in mainly traditional methods. "The old people, when they had a problem," said Lapierre, "didn't know why." Chauvet did, or he tried to find out, saying, "You must understand chemistry perfectly in order to avoid the use of chemicals." He saw himself not as a traditionalist but as a scientist, objective and skeptical. "It's complicated—he was a little of both," said Lapierre. "It was a very scientific approach, and he was very prudent in his advice. He always said, 'I'm not the one who pays.' He was modest. He was exactly the opposite of a guru."

Some tasters have for years noted in Beaujolais aromas of banana, hard candy (*bonbon anglais* in the French taster's language), and sometimes kirsch. The last can be considered positive, but I take it to be negative, meaning cherry allied with something like nail-polish remover, which might be left over from carbonic maceration. The banana (specifically it's isoamyl acetate) may have some of the same nail polish. Beaujolais didn't always taste like that. When Chauvet compared sixteen fermentations for a research paper in the 1950s, the tasters found no banana and only faint candy aromas in wine from two wild yeasts from particular vineyards, but clear aromas of banana or candy showed up in most fermentations from two selected yeasts. Apparently plenty of consumers like banana, because yeasts giving banana were identified, put into commercial production, and became popular among Beaujolais producers. But in the French press a banana-generating yeast called 71B was so much criticized that its use diminished. Carbonic maceration increases both the banana and the candy.

Unlike conventional winemakers, none of the resurgent Beaujolais producers add sulfur at the start of fermentation, so as not to harm the wild yeasts that give finer, more complex aromas, and that they believe are an essential part of the taste of each terroir. Besides, Lapierre said, the sulfur in the wine "modifies the aromas, makes the wine much less fine." (And the free sulfur contributes to a headache if you drink too much wine.) The catch is that without sulfur unwanted biological activity may spoil the wine, so for those who don't use it from the start, monitoring bacterial counts is key.

Lapierre asserted that until 1960, all the Beaujolais *vignerons* made wine in the way his group did, adding no sulfur dioxide to the fermentation and using no commercial yeast. To me he said, "That was progressively abandoned until now the number who do it is 1 percent—to give a figure. There was a generation in between that didn't ask questions." The alcohol had ranged from 9 to 11 percent (rising to 12 or exceptionally 13 percent, in a very warm year), and now, with chaptalization, or "sugaring," it was 13, 14 percent, or more every year. (The alcohol then settled back to 12 to 13 percent, with some producers' bottlings even less, but the warming climate is driving it back up again.)

Within Beaujolais, winemaking methods were always a little diverse. During fermentation, for instance, the bubbling carbon dioxide carries the whole grapes and broken grape skins upward until they form a dense cap on top of the juice. Lapierre's father and many other winemakers sometimes used a wooden grille to push the cap back down into the juice, crushing many more grapes. The immersed broken skins gave the wine more tannin, aroma, and color. Marcel and now Mathieu normally allow eight to twelve days of maceration, though much longer for the very best grapes. Eventually, the cap of grapes and skins is submerged using an oak grille. "At the end it's like Burgundy," Marcel said. There may be a *pigeage* in which the cap is punched down in the traditional way with the feet. The wine is matured for ten to twelve months in old barrels and casks. Lapierre said his wine was at its peak after three to four years.

In most years his alcohol was then around 12 percent, higher than the traditional figure, and the reason may be that the grapes were already becoming riper and sweeter (now the Lapierre alcohol is at least 13 percent). Lapierre, speaking of the past, said to me, "They always picked ripe." I asked him whether a riper crop is always better or whether there is a moment when aromas become less attractive or start to be lost. "For me, it's never too ripe," he said. The Lapierres' Morgon was and is fruity, a little grapy, and reliably delicious. It isn't the most cherrylike Morgon, but it's full of mixed red fruits and berries. Are you looking for a wine that is *gouleyant*? I asked. Lapierre answered, "Me, I look for wines that are *gouleyant* and silky in the mouth."

Led above all by Marcel Lapierre, during the early 2000s, bottles of delicious Beaujolais began to be widely exported and became highly influential examples of "natural wine." The semi-carbonic and carbonic maceration methods also began to be practiced by some producers of Gamay in the Loire Valley and other places.

But the cool carbonic maceration was sometimes criticized for producing too-predictable aromas, including those of fresh unfermented fruit, that would override the individual character of a wine with a sort of generalized tastiness. Sometimes the wines were said to be too light, not winey enough. The Morgon of Lapierre and his friends, some said, didn't taste enough like Morgon. The low acidity gives the wines a softness and freshness that is surely less winey. But there are also flavors from fermentation, and there is compensation in the form of more of those captured fresh aromas.

Today many people look to Beaujolais for satisfying, moderately priced red wines. Prices have risen somewhat, but the better Beaujolais has a bit of a reputation as "affordable Burgundy." The number of good producers has swelled and overall quality is still rising, with the wines becoming more substantial, moving away from the old simple, light deliciousness. Critics like the wines, though a few have started to wonder just how serious Beaujolais should be. You wouldn't want to lose the ideal of a wholly gulpable wine.

But some Beaujolais had always been more substantial, more than just gulpable, even in Morgon. On a street at the edge of Villié-Morgon, a solid line of houses directly abuts the street. Through an arch with heavy wooden doors is a courtyard and a handsome seventeenth-century house with a wide overhanging roof, an outdoor staircase, and a balcony. Unlike so many in Beaujolais, this house hasn't been modernized. I entered the *cave* beneath it. Black-haired Louis-Claude Desvignes, when I first met him in 2004, seemed far too young and energetic to think of retiring, but in a year his daughter, Claude-Emmanuelle, would take over. She had an air of competence, though she had worked with her father for only two years. Louis-Claude said he looked forward to retirement, and then he said he wouldn't ever retire really. When I spoke with Claude-Emmanuelle not long ago, she said her father is seventy-seven now and still working. At the time he said, "She'll continue to do exactly what we have always done. There's no reason to do anything different. It's only nature that may change." That is close to what happened.

Most of the Desvigneses' wine is sold directly to retail customers who come to the *cave*. On my first visit I stood with the father and daughter among bottles and barrels, and Louis-Claude spoke quickly and with assurance. He sounded as though he had said the same thing over and over for so many years that he had distilled the information to a tight formula. I must have caught him in a serious mood that time, because when I telephoned six months later to make an appointment for another visit, he seemed happy and almost hyperactive. When I arrived, Claude-Emmanuelle, equally assured, was calm and contributed more than she had before, the two seeming in perfect accord. My notes don't always make clear who was speaking. As many questions as I could ask were answered in full, and I realized Louis-Claude had a strong sense of fun. When he was young, his family raised a little Chardonnay to have white wine for the family table, only one or two hundred liters. "Not a few had that," he said. He confirmed that in Beaujolais the practice had always been to ferment whole grapes in open wooden vessels. The bunches were lightly rolled into place, he said, to keep from breaking the grapes.

I was such a believer in semi-carbonic "natural" wines that at first I was a little confused by what I heard and tasted. The Desvigneses' wines were more conventionally French, and I was having trouble reconciling two different versions of Beaujolais, both said to be traditional. Morgon in the past, father and daughter agreed, was drunk after ten years, and that's the kind of wine they want. They're backed up by old accounts that say the better *crus* could age for five, ten, or fifteen years. The Desvigneses were emphatic; they spoke of sometimes twenty years. Louis-Claude said, "The 1961 is still superb," adding judiciously, "I haven't tasted it for three or four years." Just two bottles were left. Now, Claude-Emmanuelle says, there's just one. And was the last bottle you opened still good? *"Ah oui, oui, très très bon, très en finesse"* ("Oh yes, very very good, and very delicate").

The Desvigneses' eleven hectares include two and a half on the Côte du Py and three just below that in the *lieu-dit* Javernières, made into separate wines. The Côte du Py vines average at least ninety years old—there's no record of the date of planting. The Javernières are one hundred. And there are two more good, though lesser bottlings from younger vines. (For those, the grapes aren't fermented whole; rather, they're destemmed.) The grapes, Louis-Claude told me, are much riper than in the past. "The time between flowering and maturity is shorter," he said. He didn't attribute any of that to better vineyard tactics, because he didn't think they were better. To him, it goes without saying that the whole cause is *le réchauffement climatique*—"global warming." "Soon they'll be growing Gamay in Alsace," he said.

Recently, his daughter emphatically agreed, saying that in 2015, they harvested on August 29, ten days earlier than usual, and when her father was young, he harvested in October. Her younger brother, Louis-Benoît, has joined her in the business. Each does a little of everything.

"The fermentation is as one has always done," Louis-Claude told me. And yet in the mid-1960s, he explained, the last of their wooden fermentation tanks were replaced with closed, unlined concrete tanks. The *cave* has since held no wooden containers: "Absolutely not," Claude-Emmanuelle confirms. The Desvigneses, so the fermentation takes off quickly before undesirable creatures can multiply, add a commercial yeast chosen as a starter because of its neutral effect on aroma. Claude-Emmanuelle suspects that native yeasts do an important part of the work. The Côte du Py and Javernières are fermented in whole bunches. There's no chilling. Claude-Emmanuelle also adds some sulfur at the start, which her father said was always done, for more color, less oxidation, fewer bacteria, and a better selection of favorable yeasts.

The temperature of the fermentation is held to a maximum of 30 to 35 degrees C (86 to 95 degrees F). There's refrigeration to ensure that, but long ago that was the usual range. The family has never employed a wooden grille, but with the younger vines for the two lesser wines, Claude-Emmanuelle stems the grapes and crushes some to begin with. Louis-Claude would sometimes punch down the cap of skins and grapes ("with the feet, of course—it's not automatic as in Burgundy," he said). Claude-Emmanuelle, because the *pigeage* affected just the surface, introduced *délestages* to increase the maceration: two or three times during the fermentation the liquid is all drawn off and then reincorporated, with the effect of crushing the grapes and extracting more sugar and color. "It's a little brutal," she says.

Louis-Claude had acknowledged that the neighbor's chilling gave their wine more fruit. His comment appeared to be neutral. Extra fruit isn't what the Desvigneses look for, and yet their wines don't lack fruit. His old partly wooden Vaslin press, the motorized kind that French *vignerons* first bought, and which he was happy with, has been replaced with a more gentle, pneumatic stainless-steel one, which Claude-Emmanuelle says gives a notably better result.

Louis-Claude had said, "Twelve and a half to 13 percent alcohol is truly ideal." Claude-Emmanuelle comments now, "It's true that 12.7, 12.8 is very digestible, very agreeable—but now it's rare." Thanks to the warmer climate.

The Desvigneses' Côte du Py vines have a northeastern exposure and lie in granite and schist; the Javernières vines have a southeastern exposure and lie in clay with iron oxide, and the wine they produce will last longer. The two wines have well-blended tannin and more body than most Beaujolais. They are close to each other in price and to me not far apart in taste. They have less fresh fruit than much Beaujolais. They are in truth winier wines, with flavors of red berries and what might be black currant. On my first visit I found more fruit in the Javernières, and on my second visit I preferred the Côte du Py. In subsequent tastings elsewhere, these wines have stood out as a different form of excellent Morgon.

In taste, Claude-Emmanuelle says, her wine is approximately the same as the wine of her father and grandfather. She has turned to organic methods, though she doesn't seek certification. She says of her father, "He knew the era of working with horses. He saw the first tractors, the first use of herbicides." When he saw the changes Claude-Emmanuelle was making, "at first he was a little reticent. Now he's very happy."

NINETEEN

Lyon and a Cook
I Never Met

Lyon, Lyonnais

T he city of Lyon is on the Rhone River four hundred kilometers southeast of Paris. Founded as a Roman settlement in BC 43, Lyon became the capital of Gaul under the Empire. Much more recently, in 1925, the critics Curnonsky and Rouff went so far as to call Lyon *"la capitale gastronomique du monde"*—the gastronomic capital not just of France but the entire world! They made that assertion in the pair of Lyon volumes in their series of little paperbacks—restaurant guides of their day—describing the "culinary marvels" of France. The authors knew they would have to defend their judgment. To back it up, they cited the quality of the city's raw materials and the number of restaurants, "enough to make the glory of three French provinces plus the rest of the world." Lyon is the third-largest city in France (after Paris and Marseille), and they said Lyon's relatively small size was an advantage. It wasn't too big or too hurried, so chefs could take the time they needed to do their best work. And Lyon didn't have a lot of foreigners, whose ignorance and lack of appreciation would discourage the chefs. In Paris, "it is beyond doubt that foreign customers, with little or no education in the art of eating, are ruining the best tables." To underline the point, a drawing shows a cowboy pouring salt on his food and washing it down with gin, while in the background stands a very sad-looking chef. Curnonsky and Rouff named four top places in Lyon that had open kitchens where you could be assured of the quality by watching the cooks at work. Some other writers too, through the mid-twentieth century, called Lyon the most gourmand of French cities.

It straddles the meeting of the broad Rhone and the lesser Saône. The water divides the city into three parts, tied by two dozen bridges. It used to be said that flowing through the city was a third river, of Beaujolais wine, produced a short distance to the north. According to Curnonsky and Rouff, "The Lyonnais—the real ones, the pure—drink it all day long at any occasion, each time they meet and until very late at night." Less wine is drunk today and Beaujolais shares the focus with other wines, but in many of the city's restaurants you can still order it by the *pot,* an old measure of a little less than half a liter.

Central Lyon, with its wide urban spaces and blocks of six-story buildings in light gray stone, suggests a bright, confident nineteenth-century affluence. The city is busy, and yet like most provincial French cities today, it feels second tier—very much *not* Paris. Even before the internet transformed commerce, easy communication and travel led the French to look past the closest big city to more important cities beyond. Which may explain why the gastronomic reputation of Lyon no longer looms as large. Still, there are very good things to eat.

One summer morning I had been too rushed to have coffee, and I felt my day hadn't properly begun. I'd hurried even to get to the restaurant where I'd reserved for lunch and then found I was the first customer to arrive. As soon as I was seated, I ordered a cup of coffee, something that in France is never done. I made explanations and apologies. The waiter was friendly and he brought the coffee, but he showed no glimmer of understanding why anyone would begin a meal by drinking coffee. I'd been spending a lot of time in France, enough so that I had the confidence and skill to defy convention in that small way. In a fancier place, I wouldn't have done it, but I was at Café des Fédérations in Lyon, the best known of the city's *bouchons*. That old French word means "cabaret" or "little restaurant," and in use it survives almost exclusively in Lyon. The *bouchons* are always simple places, but their food shares qualities with the food even in luxury places.

Old and new places calling themselves *bouchons* are scattered around the city. The dishes in the real ones are almost uncanny replicas of those of decades and more ago. The Café des Fédérations, on a side street not far from the Hôtel de Ville, has about it a hint of both raffishness and the museum. But it and other *bouchons* are alive, often loud. When you go, every table may be filled, or you happen to pass by and, seeing the glow and hearing the voices, you wish you could get a table.

Until the end of the nineteenth century, the city's main industry was silk weaving, and the cooking was shaped in part by the *canuts* ("silk workers"), who often ate alongside their employers and the middle class in the *bouchons*. Everywhere today you find inexpensive and highly flavorful *cervelle de canut* ("brain of a *canut*"), which the *canuts* themselves sometimes ate daily, as the center of their diet. To make it, you beat fresh cheese and mix in chopped fresh herbs (chives, sometimes parsley, sometimes chervil, sometimes shallots—always black pepper), and you thin the mixture with some combination of vinegar, white wine, olive oil, and cream. The result is so extremely flavorful and good that you can imagine eating it every day.

At lunch, the Café des Fédérations grew busy. I ordered a harmless, very easy to drink Beaujolais. Then came little plates— of sliced sausage, lentils with mustardy vinaigrette, slices of fish loaf with tomato sauce. The main plate was *tête de veau* with rémoulade. Instead of dessert, I chose *cervelle de canut*. The coffee, the first cup as well as a final one, was okay, which for a modest place in France can be high praise. I've had better meals in Lyon, but none more firmly anchored in place.

Another typical opening to a Lyonnais meal might be *saladier lyonnais*, which contains boned sheep's feet, sautéed chicken livers, hard-cooked eggs, marinated herring, fines herbes, and a highly flavored vinaigrette. You can follow that with a *tablier de sapeur*, or "fireman's apron," which is a large section of tripe, breaded and fried. The outer crispness contrasts wonderfully with the firm, slippery inside; it's served with a rich sauce, which one time was *ravigote* (a variable sauce, in this case a vinaigrette with shallots and fines herbes). Tripe also appears as *gras-double à la lyonnaise*, long, thin slices sautéed with onions and flavored with a little vinegar. *Gâteau de foies de volaille* is a flan of chicken livers with garlic, frequently served with a fresh tomato sauce, an especially good combination. There are breaded pig's feet and potato pancakes. Eel and river fish, as in other regions, are stewed in red wine to make *matelotes*.

Restaurants, high to low, offer *quenelles de brochet*—long pike dumplings that swell in poaching. To bind the fish, the typical Lyon version contains flour, and cheap versions have enough flour to make the smooth white interior dull and heavy. But the lightest are airy and delicate—like a soufflé, once cooked they shouldn't wait. Quenelles served au gratin may be covered with a classic *sauce Nantua,* which is pink with crayfish butter.

The city's wealth of raw materials comes from the surrounding regions, including Bresse with its famous fat chickens. Dishes too are borrowed from those regions, and Lyon embraces others that occur widely in France—gratins, coq au vin, *poulet au vinaigre,* onion soup. Prime characteristics of the cooking are richness and the simplicity of the recipes. Fresh and cured pork are important, notably the sweet, mahogany *rosette de Lyon* and the briefly aged pink *cervelas de Lyon,* which often contains pistachios and sometimes truffles (the place to buy it is the charcuterie Reynon). There's an appreciation for marrow and innards. Lightly browned onions, vinegar, and accompaniments of mustard and cornichons frequently point up whatever's on the plate. The food is unmistakably flavorful. Even in luxury Lyonnais restaurants, the food was always at bottom home cooking, produced with the care and skills of a chef. The result, at its best, was precise, balanced, elegant, but not showy.

And yet of the foreigners who cared deeply about food and came to eat in Lyon when the traditional cuisine was at its peak, neither the famous English cookbook writer Elizabeth David nor the American newspaperman (and author of *The Food of*

France) Waverley Root wholly admired it. David didn't explain why, and she did *love* the food of one particular restaurant. Root offered almost a warning, "My personal experience has been never to have eaten a really good meal in Lyon." The food, he said, is "hearty rather than graceful, and is apt to leave you with an overstuffed feeling." But he too found a restaurant to admire. He very much liked the rich food prepared thirty kilometers away in Vienne at Fernand Point's restaurant La Pyramide, which was by every account the best restaurant in all of mid-twentieth-century France. Its food to him was "Lyonnaise cooking at its best."

The chefs who made the city's reputation were especially the *mères,* the "mothers," who owned some of the best restaurants. Their influence still echoes, though their line came to an end about the time of the Nouvelle Cuisine upheaval. Perhaps the most important "mother" of all was Eugénie Brazier. A well-known photograph looks up at her from the waist, and her girth is apparent. She is dressed in spotless white, her mouth is open in an ambiguous smile, and her eyes are nearly closed, as she stirs a big steaming pot. She left her kitchen in 1974, at the age of seventy-eight, before I ever visited Lyon, and she died a few years later. (Her restaurant on the Rue Royal, still called La Mère Brazier, continues in the hands of the chef Mathieu Viannay, who has two Michelin stars and still prepares her most important dish.)

Brazier didn't come from a family of *canuts;* she grew up just outside the city on a farm. She became a cook for a well-to-do Lyon family, and then for a crucial few years after the First World War she worked for Mère Fillioux, whose restaurant was known for its menu of three fine dishes: artichokes with foie gras, quenelles, and *poularde demi-deuil*—poached chicken "in half mourning." Mère Fillioux hardly went beyond perfecting and proudly repeating those dishes and one or two others.

Brazier went on to a second restaurant, and then in 1921 she started out on her own, taking over a grocery with a bar at no. 12 on the Rue Royale. She immediately eliminated the bar and transformed the business into a restaurant, aiming steadily upward. The principal menu was the one she had learned from Mère Fillioux, centered on *poularde de Bresse demi-deuil*. But she applied her own taste, making the artichokes into a cold dish, for instance, so as not to ruin the foie gras with heat. She took care with every detail, and everything possible was made from scratch.

Her essential dish, *poularde de Bresse demi-deuil,* is made by slicing black truffles very thin and placing the circles under the skin of a young Bresse hen; the black and white constitute the "half mourning." Brazier wrapped and tied the chickens in muslin and poached them with carrots and leeks in white chicken stock. Before they were done, the pot was taken from the heat and the birds finished cooking in the hot liquid. Mère Fillioux had carved the chicken herself at each table in the dining room, using only a small kitchen knife, to show off the tenderness. Mère Brazier didn't do the carving herself, but she too had her chickens cut in the dining room with a small knife. At other top Lyonnais restaurants, poached chicken was rich with foie gras stuffing, covered with a flour-thickened *sauce velouté,* and garnished with sweetbreads on croûtons. Brazier's accompaniments were instead the simplest—carrots, leeks, and turnips; some of the cooking liquid; coarse salt, cornichons, sour cherries in vinegar, and mustard. All of them impeccable. In 1933, she became the first woman to receive three Michelin stars.

At the same time as her city restaurant, Mère Brazier opened a second restaurant, just during the summer, outside the city high on the Col de la Luère. The menu was again artichokes with foie gras, quenelles, and *poularde demi-deuil,* with the further choice of Langouste Belle Aurore. (This was less praised—lobster with a heavy, old-school cream sauce, bound with flour and flavored with Cognac.) The Col de la Luère restaurant also earned three stars.

Twenty-year-old Paul Bocuse arrived there on a bicycle in 1946, straight from the army, and was taken on as a *commis,* the lowest level of cook. He too was from a small village outside Lyon, and at the restaurant his tasks included milking cows, chopping wood, doing laundry, and ironing. He didn't object, and he wrote long afterward, "You had to know how to do everything and do it well." About Brazier, he remembered especially "the intensity of her look." And of her cooking, he observed, "Simple is not the same as easy." (Bocuse went on to work for Fernand Point at the same time that the Troisgros brothers did. Point set the three of them on the path that led eventually to Nouvelle Cuisine. Bocuse and his celebrated restaurant, L'Auberge du Pont de Collonges, just north of Lyon, have had three stars for fifty years.) It seems unimaginable today that any chef as important as Brazier could forgo invention and focus her drive on repetition and rigor, on maintaining and enhancing a culinary inheritance.

Of the Col de la Luère, Elizabeth David remembered, "This was for a time my favourite restaurant in all France. . . . With the exception of one dish of fish quenelles with a rather rich sauce, the food was all comparatively plain." She said, "The Mère Brazier's wines were the young Chiroubles and Brouillys of the Beaujolais region, and their white equivalents from Mâcon and Pouilly Fuissé. To my mind nothing could be more felicitous, in combination with the food and the surroundings and the general mood of the place, than those fresh, youthful, grapey wines." She summed up: "There was a gaiety and grace about the lunches at the Col de la Luère which seemed to me to be most essentially French. The restaurant could have been in no country but France, the cooking practised by Madame Brazier and her brigade was the cooking of the French provinces at its best and also its most traditional."

TWENTY

———◆———

Sea Salt

Ars-en-Ré, Aunis

At the edge of the small town of Ars-en-Ré, right next to the road, a giant Quonset hut holds huge mounds of coarse gray salt as well as a shipping area and a small office. I watched as vacationers bought ten-kilo sacks of salt to take home. Jacky Meneteau, who was then president of the salt-makers' co-op, drove up in an old black car made rusty by salt. Gray-haired, well tanned, and unshaven, he was wearing a T-shirt, running pants, and espadrilles.

The president of the Coopérative des Sauniers de l'Île de Ré must be a *saunier*, a "salt-maker," and Meneteau owns, he said, at least fifty of the *carreaux* from which salt is gathered. They're square ponds, five or six meters on a side, dug about a hand's length into the earth. A fifth of the long, irregularly shaped island has been sculpted in this way, although only about a third of the *carreaux* are in use. Meneteau pointed to a chart on the office wall showing that production in 1911 totaled thirty-three tonnes. In the last dozen years, the average had been only about two tonnes.

Ars is one of about ten small towns and villages on the Île de Ré, which in 1988 was connected to the mainland port of La Rochelle by a long, high bridge. Parts of the island in summer are crowded by vacationers. Besides making salt, the islanders raise a few crops as well as mussels and oysters, and they fish. The upper half of the sharp steeple of the Ars church is painted black and the lower half white, to guide boats.

Written evidence of salt making elsewhere on France's Atlantic coast goes back as far as 634, but salt-making on Ré began much more recently, in the fifteenth century. On the leeward side of the island, where alluvial material had accumulated, large areas were claimed from the sea and protected by dikes. Each of these areas is a *prise,* a "taking." The *sauniers* continue to work by hand, and only in summer, when long warm days bring little rain and few clouds, and the winds are steady.

The co-op, Meneteau said, had a little more than sixty members and their average age was over sixty-five. If nothing was done, in ten years, salt-making on the island would cease. But the government had set up a training program for the young of all three of France's Atlantic salt-making regions, and the average age of Ré *sauniers* was starting to fall. More of the *carreaux* were being put back into use. The *sauniers* typically coordinate their work with that of raising potatoes and grapes and making wine. Besides, they maintain the dikes and the network of reservoirs, channels, and *carreaux,* repairing the continual damage by the sea and weather.

There's no such thing as a normal amount of salt produced

each year from a *carreau*. "The amount of production is a function of climate," Meneteau said, "because it relies on evaporation of water." Everything depends on the weather. Still, he estimated, over the course of a decade a family averages one tonne a year per *carreau*. "Why do the *sauniers* work in bare feet?" I asked, looking at a big color poster on the wall showing just that. "You go too fast in shoes," Meneteau said. With bare feet, you don't knock particles of dirt into the *carreaux*. "That's the only reason."

In Mediterranean France, where the tides are insignificant and a much larger geographic area is available for salt-making, the work is mechanized. On the Île de Ré, the only machines are the tractors used to gather the many small piles of salt into big ones and transport them from the marshes. "Generally," said Meneteau, "it is the work of a family, although one person can do it. If the young work, then a family can earn enough. The price of salt must be high enough for the young to continue."

With feeling, he asserted, "It's very *recent* that the workers took over their own institution." Before the French Revolution, the marshes were owned by the *seigneurs,* and afterward, he explained, by their descendants, who lived at the end of the island closest to the mainland. Only between the two world wars did most *sauniers* for the first time own the land they worked. "The families worked for generations in the marsh." Now they own their *carreaux*. "They don't want to sell even if they don't produce."

Every fourteen days, the tide is unusually high and seawater is let in past the dikes to fill large holding ponds. From there the water flows into smaller reservoirs and ever smaller channels, moving by gravity, proceeding slowly downward. All the while it's evaporating; it's a concentrated brine by the time it finally enters the few-inch depth of the *carreaux*.

Jacky Meneteau drove me into the marsh in late afternoon to see if we could find someone at work. The *sauniers* work in the morning and evening, avoiding the midday heat. In the neat geometry of one set of squares, we spotted Jean-Yves Beau, a man in his thirties, looking like a vacationer in shorts, sunglasses, light sneakers, and a baseball cap.

When the sun shines continuously and the wind comes from the northwest, a thin sheet of salt forms on the surface of the *carreaux,* like the thinnest crust of ice. That's the *fleur de sel,* the finest, whitest salt. On the days when it appears, the first work is to rake it off. But that afternoon there was too little to bother with. Beau wielded his extremely long-handled *simoussi,* a tool with a wooden crosspiece at the far end. He worked gracefully and methodically, with the economical movements that come from endless repetition. Starting in one corner of the *carreau,* he gradually pulled the crystals from the bottom into a neat pyramid.

The wet salt was faintly pink from an alga that inhabits the brine. Dried *fleur de sel* is white, but most of the salt remains dirty gray from a trace of the alluvial clay. That's the natural material of the marsh; it lines the bottom of the squares, allowing them to hold water. *Fleur de sel* costs more, and chefs often prefer it, but it doesn't taste very different from the gray, only a little gentler and clearer.

I asked Meneteau how Île de Ré salt compared with the salt made farther north on the island of Noirmoutier in Poitou and on the coast near Guérande in Brittany. "Maybe the odor is a little slow to show itself and the taste is not quite the same," he said. "But if you analyze it, there's not much difference."

If you open a package of coarse gray sea salt and look closely at the big crystals, you see they're amalgamations of many small square ones. *Fine* gray sea salt is just coarse salt ground up, which does no harm, is easier to disperse, and dissolves more quickly.

Salt adds to the pleasure of almost everything we eat. Like a few drops of lemon, it intensifies the flavor. And in quantity it preserves, making possible aged hams and sausages, cured anchovies, caviar, and cheeses. Salt's highest contribution is to protect these foods as they mature over time and undergo their complex transformations. When a small amount of salt is used in cooking, it's impossible to identify any particular origin, but good salt is one of the many details of good cooking that taken together produce a transcendent taste.

The unrefined sea salt from the Île de Ré has depth; evaporation is all that has taken place. In contrast, the rock salt commonly sold in North American supermarkets has only a plain saltiness. And the mechanically gathered salt from the French Mediterranean is sour, sometimes metallic tasting. Île de Ré salt is distinctly superior, because it contains not only sodium chloride but magnesium, iron, manganese, zinc, and other minerals. It tastes like the ocean.

TWENTY-ONE

Snails

Champagnolles, Saintonge

When I met soft-spoken Louis-Marie Guédon, he was in his early thirties and already head of the *groupement* of Charentes snail producers. He lives in the hamlet of Chez Marchand, near the village of Champagnolles, in the broad flat plain that runs to the Gironde Estuary, southwest of Cognac. "Thirty years ago all the families had cows," Guédon said. Then the small farms were combined into fewer big ones. Louis-Marie's grandfather farmed, but his father was the *maître de chai,* the master taster and person in charge, of the common *cave* of five village co-ops that produce Cognac.

The people of the twin Charente departments (Charente and Charente-Maritime), largely rural, have long been called *cagouillards* ("snails"), more or less for their supposed slowness. Perhaps because many people in the Charentes were once poor, the region hasn't produced a famous cuisine. A few dishes are well known, such as *mouclade* (mussels in a cream sauce, often with saffron), the fish dish *la chaudrée* (often called the bouillabaisse of the Charentes), and snail preparations. In this area, snails are called not *escargots* but *cagouilles;* a little farther north, in the former province of Aunis, they are *lumas.* Guédon's area is Saintonge. I asked him if he spoke the dialect. "I understand it," he said, "but I don't speak it. They speak with what we call 'a full mouth.'"

Each year the French eat some forty thousand tonnes of snails. A quarter of those are estimated to be wild and consumed by the gatherers. Another twenty-five thousand tonnes are gathered in Eastern Europe and elsewhere and exported to France. And about sixteen thousand tonnes are raised in France, mainly in the Charente-Maritime, which is much better known gastronomically for its other mollusks, mussels and oysters—the first cultivated just offshore and the second in vast flooded sections along the coast. Snail cultivation began only in 1983, after researchers found ways to get snails to reproduce under the conditions of a snail farm.

Across the road from Guédon's house, the outdoor snail "parks" were enclosed on all sides and overhead in green netting, which cast a light shade. Around the bottom, an electrified metal band kept the snails from climbing the nets in the night and then falling down and breaking their shells during the day. Next to the parks was Guédon's father's garden, made of beautifully interwoven vegetables, vines, and fruit trees.

In the parks, the snails eat grass and weeds, along with grain supplied by Guédon. He raises two kinds of snail, the native *petit gris* ("little gray," or *Cornu aspersa*), and the nonnative subspecies *gros gris* ("big gray," or *C. aspersa maxima*). The *petit gris* weighs ten grams and the *gros gris,* twice that. They taste the same. The French who live along the Atlantic coast prefer small snails, but three-quarters of the French prefer large ones.

A *vigneron* in the Loire Valley once told me that he and his neighbors used to gather the snails that lived in the openings in the stone walls surrounding all the vineyards, but then the walls were pulled down to make the vineyards continuous and easy to work by machine. This traditionalist was appalled that snails would be farmed and would eat anything other than a wholly wild diet. But what do you do when the walls are gone?

Wild snails must be "starved" before they can be eaten, in case they've ingested some plant or mushroom that's toxic to humans. Farmed snails require no such cleansing, and because they grow quickly under the easy conditions, they're more tender. The old cooking times were two hours or more ("three to four hours," instructed Raymond Oliver, one of the great chefs of the 1960s, and France's first TV chef), but farmed snails take just an hour.

Naturally, I wanted to know from Guédon the desirable taste of a snail. "Snails have no taste," he responded. Chefs provide the flavor, and they want "a product as fresh and neutral as possible." So why have gourmets been attracted to snails since Roman times? "I have no idea at all," he said, in a way that made us both laugh. He has eaten so many snails himself that now he doesn't eat them often.

I thought later that farmed snails probably have less flavor. Twice I've faced a large bowl of dozens of snails, not in France but in southern Italy, once cooked with minimal flavoring and once with nothing at all. You picked them out of the shell with a large pin. These snails were likely wild Mediterranean *Theba pisana,*

and they did have a distinct taste. It was what with snails is sometimes described as an "earth" taste, and it's not immediately, obviously seductive. Butter, parsley, and garlic give any snails much
more appeal, and some Charentais like a garlic-butter sauce,
which may be borrowed from national French cooking.

One common Charentais snail dish, which I enjoyed in a restaurant, involves lengthy cooking in a combination of several
herbs and spices, onions or shallots, and red or white wine, with
sometimes a thickening of breadcrumbs, sometimes an addition
of sausage. One or two recipes call for flavoring with a fig leaf.
As you can probably tell, that range of variation comes from
reading cookbooks, which with any dish tend to diverge in the
details (and sometimes the essentials).

In the hamlet of Chez Marchand, the old local ways of cooking snails were still the current ones, Guédon said, and there
were just two of them. They were "very simple," he added, in
case I had grand expectations. One is: you take the meats from
the shells (having first cooked the snails in a court bouillon),
heat a combination of red wine and breadcrumbs, add the snail
meats, and cook for one hour, seasoning with salt and pepper.
Only five ingredients? "Yes." The second preparation is even
simpler: you grill the snails in their shells for five to ten minutes,
and remove them from the shell, as you go, with a *fourchette à
escargot* ("snail fork"), seasoning with salt and pepper. That's
far simpler and more rustic than anything conjured up by
"French food."

TWENTY-TWO

Blackened Cheesecake

Saint-Estèphe, Angoumois, and La Mothe-Saint-Héray, Poitou

The discriminating Cognac producer Jean-Louis Brillet started me down a path by assuring me that the best Charentais cheeses came from a farm not far away, near the little village of Saint-Estèphe. I followed his clearly sketched map to Fromagerie Jousseaume, which was right beside the N10 highway with its fast trucks and anonymous traffic. But the house and other buildings were set back and had a feeling of farm and home. The ensemble was U-shaped, taller and more formal than the buildings of most of the region's farms. To the right of a small courtyard, a sign pointed to the goats in barns; to the left, another sign pointed to the *fromagerie.*

Indoors, there was no one to be seen. Half a dozen or more different kinds of cheese were displayed in a refrigerated cabinet; on a sideboard were bottles of the family's Pineau des Charentes, the regional apéritif fortified with Cognac. Beyond, the work areas were visible, and after a few minutes, Christiane Jousseaume appeared. She was a warm, assured person who had learned some of her cheesemaking from her mother, who made fresh cheese, but mostly Jousseaume had taught herself, she explained. I bought two of her briefly ripened cheeses, specialties that she had more or less invented using traditional techniques, and later when I tried them they were superb. The surface of the hemispherical *taupinière charentaise* was peppered with the wild molds—white, pale yellow, blue-green, and blue—that appear in succession during about two weeks of ripening. The *taupinière* was soft, creamy in color and texture, with the delicacy that comes from hand ladling the curd into molds, breaking it as little as possible. The flat rectangular orangey *briquette de l'Angoumois* was firmer, more piquant and flavorful. Both cheeses were precisely as they should be.

Before I left, Jousseaume said she would like to introduce me to something else. She fetched an item that was about six inches in diameter, shaped like a paunchy flying saucer, and burnt entirely black on top. It was a *tourteau fromagé*. A thin bottom crust held an airy combination of flour, sugar, eggs, and fresh cheese: "That's all." The eggs had been separated and the whites whipped to a foam. Of the blackened top, she assured me, *"Ce n'est pas brûlé"* ("It's not burnt").

It was a pastry, and she cut me a slice. The *tourteau fromagé* was tender, light yet substantial. The black scarcely penetrated the surface, and the *tourteau* did not in fact taste burnt. The fresh goat's-milk cheese gave no goaty flavor; it contributed a tartness, as if lemon had been added.

The farm was in the area of Charente called the Angoumois,

a county in pre-Napoleonic days, but *tourteaux fromagés* don't belong there at all. They originated in southern Poitou, the old province that adjoins to the north. Although Jousseaume is Charentaise, her husband was from Poitou, and so she made *tourteaux* for the family, before she began to sell them. By tradition, the cheese used is goat.

A few days after I met Jousseaume, I set out to find *tourteaux fromagés* on their native ground. I started at the town of Cognac and drove northeast, passing occasional blocks of vines interspersed with wheat, hay, corn, sunflowers, and woods, and soon crossed into Poitou. In a half dozen towns large enough to have a bakery, I stopped and bought *tourteaux*.

It was important that they be fresh, taken that day from the oven, and as a rule they were. A few times, when I asked the person behind the counter, she would tell me that the fresh cheese was cow and not goat. If I asked why, I was told that goat's milk cost too much or that nearby farms no longer kept goats. In a bakery at Prahecq, a sign on the counter announced that *tourteaux fromagés* had just been baked; the efficient young proprietress said the cheese was cow, but she assured me, "You will not be disappointed." In fact her *tourteau fromagé* was perfectly fresh and light, yet without the goat piquancy, the taste was somewhat plain and sweet.

I arrived in the town of La Mothe-Saint-Héray during the quiet midafternoon hour when shops begin to reopen. La Mothe is at the heart of the area where *tourteaux fromagés* originated, and when I asked a few questions, including at one bakery that didn't make *tourteaux,* I was directed to the pâtisserie of Daniel Favreau.

I should say that one regional product exists in the context of others, and La Mothe-Saint-Héray and the Daniel Favreau pâtisserie are even better known for a more usual baked item, the *fouace,* one of France's scattered regional *fouaces.* Those are enriched breads that share their ancient origin and etymology with the Provençal *fougasse* and Italian *focaccia*—usually they're flat to very flat in shape and baked directly on a hearth. Favreau claims to be the only true maker of the Poitevin *fouace,* having inherited the secret recipe of the previous commercial baker. One of the low but swollen disks, not quite a foot in diameter, was sliced on the counter for tasting. I tried a piece. It was a sort of proto-brioche, made with butter but without eggs and a little sweet. The top was deeply browned. "It was a very popular cake," according to Jeanne Philippe-Levatois in her excellent 1968 cookbook *Cuisine de Poitou & de Vendée,* "a little bland but very good, eaten by dipping it in good red *vin de pays.*" The *fouace* was produced in bakeries and in homes: "When the dough was kneaded, one enriched a piece of it, which one had set aside, with a little butter, some nuts and raisins, and one made this into a ball which one set in the oven at the same time as the bread." The version I tasted had neither nuts nor raisins; they're not part of what defines the cake. It was nothing dramatic, and yet it was a small discovery, simple and honest—not an overlight, little-flavored, quickly staling modern bread.

At Favreau, the woman in charge—in middle age, the kind of person who reminds you that France is not the home of customer service—said that the cheese was cow. She made a mild expression of distaste at the idea of goat. Outside, I broke into the *tourteau.* Sadly, it wasn't more special at the source, although it was good.

I took my collection of *tourteaux fromagés* back to the group of vacationing friends I was staying with, and they liked them all, even the next day when the *tourteaux* weren't fresh. I was the only one who wasn't completely enthusiastic, wanting them all to taste like Mme. Jousseaume's with its edge of goat acidity.

The *tourteau fromagé,* for all its odd appearance, is a kind of cheesecake. Some old recipes, perhaps the oldest, don't call for separating the eggs and beating the whites, so the texture is dense, more like that of familiar solid American cheesecake. The airy, creamy version of *tourteau fromagé* extracts maximum effect from a handful of ingredients: a fresh goat's-milk cheese, a few eggs, a little flour, and a little sugar. The goat's-milk cheese gives moisture, substance, and piquancy. The egg yolks bind and strengthen, the whites lighten, the flour adds a little structure, and the sugar contrasts with the cheese's tartness. Inevitably, when the delicate, sweet filling is exposed to a very hot oven, the top blackens, to make a surprisingly gentle, essential counterpoint.

—◆—

TWENTY-THREE

If You Aren't Worried, Then Maybe the Cheeses Could Be Better

Roquefort-sur-Soulzon, Rouergue

The village of Roquefort-sur-Soulzon, in the sparsely inhabited former province of Rouergue in southern France, lies above the valley of the small Soulzon River, at the top of rocky slopes, from which further rise the cliffs of the Combalou Plateau. Beneath the village are the caves filled with the famous blue cheese. Billboards along main roads announce the names of the biggest producers: Société, then Papillon and Gabriel Coulet. In the village, there is almost nothing but cheese, and yet none of the cheese is made there. The eight cheesemaking dairies are off among the farms that raise the sheep that give the milk. Some of the farms are in the Causse du Larzac, which covers almost a thousand square kilometers; it's the largest of the Grands Causses and the place where Roquefort cheese was first produced. The rugged *causses* are limestone plateaus ringed with cliffs. The Combalou by Roquefort is a small one. The edges of some fall spectacularly to gorges, such as those that dwarf long sections of the river Tarn. In the *causses,* almost the only human activity is raising sheep.

The very large Roquefort appellation embraces not only the Causse du Larzac but other *causses* to the east and hills and mountains to the west. Much of the landscape has a grandeur, from the wide horizons and the dominance of nature. You see the scale and beauty from the A75 autoroute as it crosses the rocky, inhospitable Causse du Larzac. You feel them more keenly on high, empty back roads. In valleys and on rounded hills, some fields are giant rectangles, but often the fields are strangely irregular, and occasionally they are very small, rising up inclines until they can go no farther. The stone-walled terraces that endure in places were once farmed, but they are nearly all abandoned. Sheep, of the Lacaune breed, are visible only occasionally, scattered in a pasture or driven by a shepherd, the flock winding around obstacles like a single animal.

The Rouergue is one of the places where you may still hear Occitan, the langue d'oc, the old language of southern France. Even when they speak French, many Occitan speakers roll their *r*'s and tend to pronounce all the letters of a word, so unlike usual French. Roquefort has three syllables: "roh-keh-FORT." Provençal, the best-known Occitan dialect, has nearly disappeared, but in the Rouergat countryside (and the Rouergue is nearly all countryside), a number of older people speak Occitan and some younger ones understand it. When you thank someone, the response isn't the usual French *"De rien"* ("It's nothing"). The Rouergats say, *"Avec plaisir"* ("With pleasure"), a direct translation from Occitan. And they say it with feeling, as if they were the ones thanking you. The people seem to have a special kindness.

When I first visited the region, some years ago, I was there for a week to learn about Roquefort. I entered the tranquil village of Martrin, where just forty or fifty people live, driving slowly, looking for the dairy of Roquefort Carles, which is the second to smallest of the seven Roquefort producers, making just 1 percent of all Roquefort. There was no sign, but behind a tall house, which was a sort of island surrounded by village streets, several milk cans were hanging. I drove around to the front, and immediately a young man came up to my car, smiling and without hesitation. He expected me, and in Martrin a stranger was obvious. He was Serge Condamines, the Carles cheesemaker.

Twenty-eight farms, he said, all around Martrin, produce for Carles. The area is west of the village of Roquefort among strongly rolling hills. Condamines drove me to the hamlet of La Cloutarié, which comprises three farms close together. René Barthe and his son, Jean-Marie, had delayed their afternoon milking until we arrived. Jean-Marie was in his thirties. René was white-haired and much older, although when you spend your life outdoors, your face can look older than it is.

Inside a big metal barn, the two men worked quickly. René opened the door to the adjoining stable and the first ewes pushed in, rushing to the stanchions. They were aggressive and at the same time skittish—sheep frighten easily at almost anything, an instinct that protects them from predators. The Barthes filled the two rows of stanchions alternately and moved the machines quickly from the teats of one ewe to the next. Milking takes one minute and forty seconds per ewe, Jean-Marie said.

The Barthes were milking 192 ewes that day in mid-June, near the end of the milking season. No Roquefort is made during almost five months of the year, when the weather is warmest, and the ewes would soon be bred. The Barthes kept 20 to 25 rams and introduced new stock through artificial insemination. The ewes begin to give birth each year in November, restarting the dairy cycle. Ewe's milk is much richer than cow's, but there is much less of it. To make a kilo of Roquefort requires about 4.3 liters of milk, and an average ewe on an average day gives only a quarter to a third of that.

René Barthe spoke quickly, and at first his strong accent was hard for me to understand. He had milked by hand until 1973. Without a machine, one person can milk just 30 ewes, which limits the size of a flock. He said that it used to take two people two and a half hours to get just 80 liters of milk. (I had wanted to visit a farm milking by hand, and Condamines had telephoned the last Carles farm still without machines, but the family was embarrassed to be so old-fashioned and said no.) Now farmers have bred their ewes for a higher yield, to the point that the Roquefort dairies have set a milk quota for each farm.

When the milking was over, we stood behind the barn taking in the panorama and the quiet. "Here there is nothing but sky and earth," René said. He seemed to mean not just the beauty of the situation but also its limits—the extent to which life depended on what you could accomplish between sky and earth. In a modern economy, those limits no longer apply, but to René Barthe they remained real.

The Barthes harvest their own grain for the sheep. To feed them, Jean-Marie said, "we buy virtually nothing; the goal is to buy nothing." Besides producing milk, they sell lambs to other farmers who raise them for meat. For themselves, the Barthes keep chickens, ducks, several cows, and two pigs for charcuterie. The pigs were in the small stone building that was once the *bergerie* ("sheep barn"). It formed part of a courtyard beside the house, where the date 1819 was carved over a door. But the farm is older than that. "It was always here," Jean-Marie said.

Bread is the essential accompaniment to cheese, and I asked René about the local kind. The first village baker opened in Martrin only after the Second World War. Before that, everyone baked bread at home twice a month. The loaves were white and weighed three kilos. Today the common loaf in the Rouergue is a *flûte,* shaped nothing like the instrument, being at least twice as wide as a baguette, shorter, very white, and full of air. "It goes too quickly at each meal," said René Barthe. The family buys round two-kilo loaves instead.

What else did people eat back when they baked their own bread? "They ate chicken and pork; meat from a butcher was too expensive. They ate Roquefort that came back from the *caves.* A little they ate *pérail*"—the small, white, disk-shaped ewe's-milk cheese of the region that is still made on certain farms as well as in dairies. "They ate a lot of chestnuts, in porridge or roasted," René said. "They ate what they had." Everyone grew grapes then and made wine, but no one has grapes now.

Just before we left, René Barthe slid open a barn door to release the sheep. He rushed with his long stick to get to their head and lead them to pasture.

I returned to Martrin with Serge Condamines to see the house where he makes Roquefort. Wisteria bloomed over the front door. Fifty years ago, the house had belonged to a doctor, and the faintly elegant rail of the sagging main staircase recalled that time. Now the rooms were full of cheesemaking equipment, and there was a small lab for testing milk and cheese. Roquefort is as good as it is because it is made from whole raw milk with all its natural microflora and aromas intact. Morning and evening milk are combined and made into cheese promptly each morning. The process is essentially the same at every producer, except that at all the others (but the very tiniest, Le Vieux Berger of the Combes family) the methods and equipment are industrial.

Condamines stirred rennet and a starter of acid-producing bacteria by hand into milk at 33 degrees C (91 degrees F). Some of the bacteria produce more acid, which is essential to cheese, while others produce more carbon dioxide gas to slightly swell the small craggy holes where the blue mold will grow. In two and a half hours the milk has formed a tender curd, which is cut into small cubes by the wires strung on the *lyre*. That releases much of the whey, and the cubes are stirred in it for two more hours to keep them from sticking as they shrink, releasing more whey and each cube forming a skin in the slowly mounting acidity.

A powder of spores of blue mold—*Penicillium roqueforti*—is shaken onto the curd, by eye, from a container like a big kitchen saltshaker. The cubes of curd are scooped into tinned steel molds with drainage holes. The curd remains loose enough to leave tiny openings, air spaces, between the fragments. Two full molds are put together to make each three-kilo cheese. The cheeses dry in their molds for three days, and then they are taken out and rubbed with salt. They are turned twice a day, as they dry, for five more days.

The whey from cheesemaking was pumped across the road, through a pipe laid in the street, to a tiny cheesemaking business that was not part of Carles and made only ricotta, *recuite* in French, or *recuèja* in local Occitan—all three words meaning "recooked." Next door to that, a butter-smelling, equally small bakery produced the ricotta tart called *la flaune* and the sweet Rouergat bread called *la fouace,* which is rich with butter and eggs. Both *flaune* and *fouace,* whoever makes them, are typically flavored with orange-flower water, which until two or three generations ago was the typical flavoring of sweet baked items throughout the South. When a *fouace* is raised with a *levain* (a sour starter), as this one was, it can be excellent; it's an old-fashioned cake that might be eaten before Sunday dinner accompanied by an apéritif.

A short distance away through an archway and a garden was the village's combination grocery-bar-*tabac,* set up in the house where the curé once lived. As I sat at a table with Condamines eating freshly baked *fouace,* a smiling farmer in boots stopped to speak and threw in a sentence I didn't understand. Condamines turned to me and said, "That was Occitan." The farmer was surprised to discover that anyone in the village was not French.

Eight-day-old Roquefort cheeses are trucked from Martrin, and all the Roquefort dairies, to the *caves* in prosperous Roquefort, where many more people work than live. Buildings rise two and three stories on either side of the narrow, sloping main street. Big refrigerated trucks are parked here and there, the front wheels of some being driven onto wedges to level the beds for loading.

Roquefort means "strong rock," but the Combalou Plateau is fractured. In prehistoric times, the limestone cliff extended farther out, and the village rests on a mass of rock from its collapse. The *caves* are built into openings in the tumbled stone. Some retain irregular walls, but all have been enlarged and squared off. Some of the biggest, handsomest *caves* are vaulted and seem entirely human creations. What makes the *caves* exceptional is the humidity that arrives steadily through natural fissures called *fleurines*. The air is so slow that you can't feel the current, but if you hold a match in the entrance to a *fleurine* you can see the flame move. Behind the village and below the present cliffs is a sunken area where rain and melted snow penetrate and raise the humidity in the *caves* to more than 90 percent.

The head of Roquefort Carles today is Delphine Carles, but at the time I first visited it was still her father, the gentlemanly Jacques Carles. His father had started the company in 1927, but Jacques was as earnest about the cheese as if he had just launched the business himself. He entered and left the narrow building not by the main door leading to the office but by a door that opened directly onto the room where cheese was being prepared and shipped. He didn't seem to be checking on the few employees, who were relaxed around him, but only on the cheese.

The single Carles *cave* descends four stories into the stone. We entered the cool and damp space with the *maître de cave*, Robert Migairou. The floors, which once were wooden, now are poured concrete. As in other Roquefort *caves*, the small caged elevator is for cheese; people use stairs. Fresh air, Carles said, rises or falls in his *cave* mainly according to the direction of the prevailing wind.

The squat cylinders of cheese sat on oak and chestnut shelves that had been saturated with the salt and moisture of countless cheeses. The gorged air allows little evaporation, and small puddles of whey from the cheeses remained on the wood. The cheeses were placed on edge, to expose both of their wide, flat sides to the air. Most producers now insert plastic sheets between the cheese and wood, or they put their cheeses first into slotted plastic crates. But in fact the salt and acidity in the wood, the cheeses' own chemistry, and the producers' stringent tests of milk and cheese provide the best protection against any pathogens.

Up in his office, Jacques Carles had given me his full attention as he answered questions, but in the *cave* he seemed to half forget me. He was more in his element, completely assured, intimate in his knowledge of the ripening. Using his stainless-steel trier, the essential tool of the cheese ripener, he drew out and smelled a tapering cylinder of cheese, riven with blue. He showed it to me only as an afterthought.

Carles and Migairou worried about the cheeses from habit. "He makes me afraid," Carles said. Among the callow white cheeses, Migairou was concerned about a small group he had set aside from one batch. From standing on edge, under pressure of their own weight they had begun to turn oval. "I'm afraid," Carles said again. "It's a métier that makes you afraid." He was certain these cheeses were unusually moist and delicious, but he was concerned that the market wouldn't accept them because they weren't perfectly round like the rest.

On a far shelf sat big round loaves of bread, placed in the cave to mold and supply spores for future cheese. They were made of rye, the better to hold moisture and become moldy. In the past, the bread captured wild molds, but the results were unpredictable, and not all the molds were good. Now each loaf had been punctured with a dozen holes, narrower than pencil size, and a pure strain of *Penicillium roqueforti* had been inserted. Then the holes had been plugged with homely pieces of tinfoil. The bread turns completely moldy in just ten to fifteen days, Carles said. He broke open a loaf to reveal a solid green interior. It smelled clean, not moldy. The crust would be pulled off, the rest of the loaf crumbled, dried, ground, and passed through a screen to make a powder. Only one other producer, Papillon, still relies on rye bread.

Carles explained, "It's much easier to raise penicillium on a gelatin medium rather than inside a loaf of bread. But the medium makes a difference that is unquestionable." He was especially convinced of the superiority of the handwork in his cheesemaking. "The stirring is less violent. When you have your hands in the curd, you can tell whether it is one time too soft or another time too hard. Only those who have their hands in it have the amount exactly right." He further said, "There are differences in the milk from different areas of production, differences that come from the process of cheesemaking, that come from the strains of penicillium, a million parameters. One finds differences in the cheese from one day to the next."

The making of Roquefort sounds charming and traditional, and at Carles it is, but at every producer part of the aging is strikingly modern. Because Roquefort is sold year-round, while being made during just the cooler months of the year so as to avoid the problems that come with making cheese in the summer heat, most cheeses spend no more than two to three weeks in the *caves*. After that, each is wrapped in a pliable sheet of tin, which prevents drying and, more important, allows in very little air. The lack of oxygen slows the blue mold and prevents it from taking over. Then the cheeses go into storage at about freezing temperature, again to hold back ripening. The producers embraced refrigeration as early as 1900, and the deep chill isn't tragic, but refrigerating a cheese is never ideal. It suppresses the life within and somewhat alters the taste.

With Roquefort, as with other food and drink, there's a relationship between quality and risk. "In the past, customers accepted variations in taste," Jacques Carles said. "At the table, they discussed: 'This was good, that was less good.'" Are the best cheeses of today the same as the best of the past? "No," he answered immediately. "If you want to have very, very good cheese, you have to take risks in production. There are strains of penicillium that are excellent but are dangerous because they also accentuate defects. With a strain like that, according to the quality of the milk, one day you can have an excellent cheese that supports aging for a year and a half. Or you can have a cheese that ages too fast and has a powerful taste that is only for more knowledgeable cheese lovers."

Roquefort Carles accepts a degree of risk, not all. It takes a chance, for instance, that a cheese might turn out too moist or without enough acid. That's not to say that Carles Roquefort is remarkably different from that of other producers, but a careful taster might find that it more often stands out.

Among all cheeses, Roquefort is one of the more sensitive—vulnerable—especially after it leaves cold storage. The producers, I found at several *caves,* can be harsh critics of their own work. When you cut a slice, Roquefort should be moist enough to glisten, and if you're familiar with the particular brand, then the holes should be just the right shade of blue or blue-gray for the particular strain of mold. At its peak, the mold has a look I can only call fresh. In your mouth, a sensation of luscious moisture should accompany a refined intensity. The blue flavor almost recalls anise and ends on a spicy black pepper note. Usually, there's a touch of something like nail-polish remover (a hint of it is characteristic and adds to the complexity). The blue is balanced by white, so the taste goes back and forth a little. And when everything is right, the tang, salt, and marked flavors are set off by a dairy sweetness.

TWENTY-FOUR

Guy Gedda and Real Provençal Cooking

Bormes-les-Mimosas, Provence

In the heavily built-up hillside town of Bormes-les-Mimosas, between Toulon and Saint-Tropez, on a midmorning in June, Guy Gedda met me on his wide terrace with a distant view of the sea. The same terrace served as the dining room of his last, somewhat luxurious restaurant. In the South of France, people don't use air-conditioning except in their cars; at night, the air cools comfortably. Gedda had white hair and a gray mustache; he was relaxed, dressed in T-shirt, shorts, and sandals. His last name, he said, pronounced with a soft *g* and an accent on the final "ah," is almost certainly Niçois in origin. After a lifetime spent in the kitchen, Gedda had retired two years before. Since then he had been serving as a consultant on Provençal cooking and he had been donating his time to such things as judging serious bouillabaisse contests. Gedda was born to the west in Vieux Marseille, in the same room where his great-grandmother had given birth to fourteen children. His grandparents and then his parents ran the Bar Magnifique, a restaurant on the Quai de Rive Neuve in the old port.

"The cooking was Marseillais and Provençal," he explained in his sweet-tempered way, "*pieds et paquets, soupe de poissons, daube provençale,* and all the products of the sea, of course." The first dish is sheep's feet braised for hours with small "packages" of sheep tripe; next, the rich, brown fish soup is made with small, oily, bony fish caught among the rocks and suited for little else; this particular daube was a stew of lamb with white wine; and many of the shellfish were served raw. The cooking was the same as the Provençal customers might have eaten at home, except that the restaurant emphasized large servings of meat and fish.

"In Provence, it's the vegetables that count—meat is expensive—and people eat fruit," Gedda said. "It's a cooking of vegetables that are *mijotés*," meaning they are cooked slowly and thoroughly. "Professional cooks don't cook vegetables the way they should. They're too crunchy, too al dente. If you eat aioli, the carrots shouldn't be firm; the carrot and aioli should mix together on your tongue. In *salade niçoise,* it's right that the beans crunch because the other things are raw and they crunch," he explained, "but in ratatouille it's right that the vegetables be cooked slowly and long."

Provençal cooking is the traditional home cooking of the poor. For generations, "rich and poor ate in the same spirit, with maybe more variety for the rich. You know, twenty years ago, a big property owner still lived modestly. Now, the wealthy have much more money than their grandparents did. The grandfather, even in a château, didn't used to have a car, and today the grandson has one."

He began to define the region's food by saying what it isn't. "Provençal cooking is *not* to put basil or garlic in everything," Gedda said emphatically. "*Not* to put olive oil in everything. One never, never used to put pine nuts in the dishes of Provence. In desserts, yes." Gedda's traditional recipes fill one of his cookbooks, *La Table d'un Provençal.* Lard used to be as important as olive oil, which many peasants could hardly afford to use, because they had to sell the olive oil they produced in order to have money. "My grandmother made many preparations with lard. Olive oil was used above all on raw vegetables and not so much in cooking. Olive oil—it's the media that has talked about it so much." And then he made a clear distinction between what is Provençal, which he loves, and the more contemporary way in which he also likes to cook: "Me, I'm crazy about olive oil."

The traditional Provençal flavorings are nearly all native herbs, often gathered in the wild: thyme, sage, rosemary, basil (a tropical exception), bay laurel, fennel (for seasoning, only the wild sort and mainly the stalks), oregano (mixed with other herbs rather than used alone), and above all the herb that is sometimes still called by its Provençal name—*pebre d'ai,* which means "ass's pepper." In English it's winter savory as opposed to annual summer savory (*sarriette des montagnes* in French as opposed to *sarriette commune*). Gedda picked a branch of *pebre d'ai* for me to taste, and it was very peppery, much stronger than the winter savory I've grown in my New England garden. *Pebre d'ai* is used alone and in combination with other herbs to flavor light meats, salads, fava beans. "Always, savory with goat's-milk cheese and"—as if to say, of course—"white wine from Provence." Another essential seasoning, also Mediterranean, is parsley. Garlic is famously important. So are anchovies preserved in salt. Orange peel appears especially around Nice. The lavender that is now mixed into commercial packets of herbes de Provence never used to be added to food, and it isn't very successful. One of the few costly traditional additions—to bouillabaisse and certain other fish dishes, to *rouille* (garlic mayonnaise with red pepper), to eggplant set with custard to make a *papeton*—is saffron.

"The Provençaux don't like sweet and sour," Gedda said. But the customers of his former restaurant came from many countries, and he had great success with sweet-and-sour dishes based on honey. "The honey from the Var"—the department where he lives—"is the best in the world. It's a question of the flowers or—I don't know." He named the kinds of honey: "rosemary, chestnut, heather, strawberry tree, lavender, many other flowers—thyme, savory."

Provence, bounded to the west by the Rhone River and to the east by Italy, contains just five of the ninety-six French administrative departments: the Bouches-du-Rhône, Var, Vaucluse, Alpes-Maritimes, and Alpes-de-Haute-Provence. "But for the Provençaux," Gedda said, "Provence is above all Arles, Aix, Saint-Rémy de Provence—thus, the Bouches-du-Rhône and the Vaucluse. The real language is above all around Arles." Where he lives now in Bormes-les-Mimosas, the Provençal is influenced by Italian. But Provençal, although for a long time now it has been taught in schools, is fast disappearing; probably no one learns it as a first language. Gedda speaks Provençal with friends from childhood and some others in his generation and older. "It's a very gay language," he wanted me to know, a "sweet" language. And he sang a few lines from a little song.

Aioli, the garlic and olive oil mayonnaise that is part of the foundation of Provençal cooking, is eaten sometimes with just cold meat or fish or steamed potatoes. But it can be eaten with many things, including a selection of boiled vegetables (especially potatoes), hard-boiled eggs, snails, mussels, octopus, and above all salt cod. When a lot of these are present, the meal is a *grand aïoli*. Besides, the sauce provides essential creaminess to the fish soup *bourride*.

A few of the most typical Provençal preparations are made in a mortar, including aioli, tapenade, *pistou* (like Ligurian pesto, it's stirred into vegetable soup to make *soupe au pistou;* the word means "pestle"), and *anchoïade* (a purée of anchovies, garlic, olive oil, and sometimes parsley). "I have a mortar from my great-grandfather who was from Aix and was a great gastronome," Gedda said, "though he didn't cook; he worked in a gristmill." Gedda showed me the white marble mortar, which smelled of garlic. The pestle is always made of olive wood, which is very hard because the trees grow so slowly.

Compared with chopping in a machine, a mortar and pestle give more voluptuous texture. "It's a *pommade*," Gedda said—a "cream." Another dish from the mortar is *brandade,* salt cod with olive oil in a luscious emulsion. The many salt cod preparations "were the dishes of the poor." A mortar is fairly fast and easy to use, though you need a large one, and the only place to find a really good one is an antiques shop, and then only if you're lucky. Gedda served me a platter of *toti à l'anchouiado,* which are toasted slices of bread with *anchoïade;* this version contained well-cooked sliced garlic rather than mashed raw cloves. Gedda poured cold rosé from a bottle with the curves of an amphora.

In salad, he said, "I like it very much when the tomatoes have a little crunch; the Provençaux never eat tomatoes too ripe in salad. On the other hand, for sauce, the tomatoes must be very ripe. Fruits and vegetables have changed a lot. The tomatoes from Holland in summer—*merde!* The zucchini are watery." Provençal produce used to have a concentrated taste that reflected the dry climate. For the reduced quality, Gedda blamed greenhouses and the varieties grown in them. He raises a small vegetable garden with his brother. "Even apples don't taste the way they did. Or peaches. France and the EU try to make everything uniform; it's bad for a small region like ours.

"We still have more than a few fish between Toulon and Saint-Raphaël. I may be a chauvinist, but the fish from the Mediterranean are much better than those from elsewhere. My favorite fish is the sardine. *C'est superbe.* You catch it in the morning, and you grill it at noon." He wrote out a Provençal expression, *"La sardine à la brule dé,"* and gave the rough translation: "'The sardine burns your fingers as you eat.' It's an incredible taste. That's the *real* cooking, with a salad—with olive oil, naturally, very little vinegar, and garlic. After that, a goat cheese and some fruit. My second favorite fish is the eel; unfortunately, there are fewer and fewer." He acknowledged that it was probably impossible to find that kind of food in a restaurant. "All those places down by the ports are fakes."

Gedda never mentioned pasta, which long ago crossed from Italy into Provence. But if you know the pleasure of pasta in

Italy, Provence is not a good place to eat it, because it's pale and overcooked. He did want to be sure that I'd eaten a good plate of long-simmered *pieds et paquets,* and I had. Now, he warned, chefs can buy it ready to cook. Inside the packages of tripe, he explained, there should be salt pork; if there's a regular meat stuffing, you know it's the ready-to-cook kind. At home, the delicious stuffed vegetables of Provence are made with leftover meat (from daube, pot-au-feu, roast veal, roast pork); the meat is chopped and mixed with the insides of the vegetables, with cooked onions and garlic, parsley, and basil.

"I adore freshness," Gedda said, speaking now of rosé wine. "I'm against the use of new wood, especially for rosé—it's all right for red." He meant that in rosé the taste from new oak barrels hides the wine's own flavors of fruit. Gedda used to drink only red and white wine, as his parents did. "It was just twelve years ago that I began to like rosés," he said. "Now I like them too much." What caused the change? "I think it's because the quality didn't used to be very good. Today, the rosé is *formidable.*"

Gedda's terrace always has a breeze, which that morning was strong enough that we had moved inside one of the glass shelters where the restaurant customers used to eat. "There were windmills here for grinding wheat," he said. "The olive-oil mills were in the villages; each village had at least two." The power to turn them came from different sources. "There were windmills, water mills, and *moulins à sang.*" The last, the "blood mills," were the kind, including the ones for olive oil, that were turned by hand.

TWENTY-FIVE

—·—

Ruins

Les Baux, Provence

We each have our experiences in time. I once had a landlady who had lived in Rome in the late 1940s, and when I said I was going there, she told me bluntly, "It's too late." Well, I thought to myself, I wasn't born when you were there. Does that mean I'm not allowed to see the Forum or the Trevi Fountain?

Mass tourism changes whatever it touches, and it has long since altered Provence. That first hit me on a June day about fifteen years ago in Aix-en-Provence, a town that is a centerpiece of visits to the South. I had been before, but this time the streets felt grim with tourists. On the same trip, I passed for the first time the Roman-built Pont du Gard, which, although west of the Rhone, is often counted within Provence, and I discovered it was flanked by two big new parking lots, one on either side of the Gard River. The prolific and blunt James Pope-Hennessy, when his 1952 *Aspects of Provence* was reissued in 1967, described the changes at the famous, crumbling town and château of Les Baux, in their spectacular position on the crest of the Alpilles Mountains. He wrote, "Commercialism has now finally proved that even ruins can be ruined." Of the Fountain of Vaucluse, to which the Michelin green guide still perversely awards three stars, he said, with incomplete self-awareness, "I feel in general no speck of sympathy for those professional admirers of the past who constantly lament the age we live in, but I confess to feeling beside Petrarch's fountain as I have felt in Venice, that here was one place to which I had come a hundred and fifty years too late." What most of us want most when we travel are those moments of contact—with landscape, people, art, architecture, food—that feel intensely personal, or authentic for lack of a better word. Those experiences are almost always unforeseen, and they occur less often in the company of countless others with the same purpose.

There's some good news in Provence. Most visitors are drawn to obvious places, mainly cities and larger towns and seacoast. Things are better away from the sea, off in the countryside. During that same June visit, on a fine afternoon, I saw hardly any cars or people on the two-lane road that leaves Aix and runs east for about twenty-five kilometers, passing through the largely wild land beneath the jutting stone of Mont Sainte-Victoire. I walked among the shrubs of the *garrigue* looking up and heard only sounds of nature. If you have the advantage of speaking French, you can find plenty of people to talk with who have little or no contact with visitors. Certain good restaurants are not filled with foreigners. A lot depends on the time of year.

The walled city of Avignon is larger than Aix and has more indigenous life and better food. Its walls were built by the popes in the fourteenth century and suffered badly afterward. The stones are eroded, yet otherwise the walls are surprisingly complete, due largely to the nineteenth-century work of Eugène Viollet-le-Duc. His fearless alterations, notably at Carcassonne and at Notre Dame in Paris, are easy to criticize, but he was no fool: "To restore a building is not to preserve it, to repair, or rebuild it; it is to reinstate it in a condition of completeness which could never have existed at any given time . . . and, in fact, no civilization, no people of bygone ages, has conceived the idea of making restorations in the sense in which we comprehend them." Similar thoughts might apply to the traditional food of a place.

TWENTY-SIX

Wrapped and Aged in Leaves and Completely Different from All Other Cheeses

Valensole, Provence

Charles Chabot sat me down in his living room before an enormous stone fireplace, unlit in late spring but permanently scenting the room with smoke. His seriousness was underlined by a patriarchal full beard. For two and a half hours he held forth on cheese, his family, and Provence. The experience was a challenge not only to my French at the time (this was in the early 1990s) but to my powers of concentration. Chabot, a farmer and cheesemaker, had utter conviction. He was on a mission to tell me all I should know about the Provençal cheese Banon, and I knew almost nothing.

We were at La Petite Colle, which he farmed with his wife, Simone, in the department of Alpes-de-Haute-Provence. To get there that morning I had passed through the hilltop town of

Banon, which gives its name to the cheese. Then I headed east, crossing the Durance River, largest in Provence, and arriving in the high plateau country northwest of the town of Valensole, an area of open rolling fields of grass. The cheese was once made in a broad area of northern Provence, but the real thing had become hard to find. Chabot, who died a few years ago, was its leading exponent.

Banon is a small round made of goat's milk, tied up in chestnut leaves, the only such leaf-wrapped cheese in France and the most famous cheese of Provence, though it was never widely sold. In the classic Provençal cookbook *Manuel Complet de la Cuisinère Provençale* by the Marseille chef Marius Morard, published in 1886, Banon is the sole cheese in the cheese chapter. Morard begins with a summation: "Superior quality." He says that in Marseille "there are only two places to buy it, but it is known by cheese-lovers who have made excursions now and then in that country of the Basses-Alpes." The cheese is made at the end of September from goat's milk—further on he adds that it's sometimes mixed with ewe's milk—and it's wrapped in vine leaves. "At the end of three months, one has an excellent cheese." Even today, Banon remains somewhat scarce. Production is the second-smallest of any French cheese with an official appellation.

When you untie the raffia of a well-ripened Banon and open the leaves, you find a fully creamy cheese with a particular earthy aroma. But when I saw Chabot, I hadn't experienced that yet. In those days, far more widely available than what he called the "true" Banon was another kind, wrapped in leaves but made in a crucially different way, and that was all I had tasted.

Chabot came from the small village of Marcoux, a little more than fifty kilometers by road to the northeast of Valensole. His paternal grandmother, he said, had grown up by the Lure Mountains above Banon. When she was a girl, at the turn of the twentieth century, she was the last person in her village to defend her flock against a wolf. (For a moment, it was as if he were telling a fairy tale. Wolves persisted in France until the 1920s; now they're coming back.) Marcoux is at six hundred meters, and when Charles and one of his brothers moved to the farm at La Petite Colle, they were the first of the family to live below that altitude. They had descended only twenty meters, but Chabot explained that six hundred meters is a frontier. Below it lies the country of olives, vineyards, almonds, savory, and a strong tradition of the Left.

The old peasant agricultural system persisted until after the Second World War, and nearly every rural family in Haute Provence raised animals and made cheese. Pasture was abundant but dry due to the soil and climate. A herd contained anywhere from 30 to 150 sheep plus 5 to 10 goats. The land and the people were poor, and the peasants raised sheep to sell for meat, not to eat themselves. If for some reason a ewe couldn't feed her lamb, it was suckled by the goats. But the main reason for keeping goats was to provide milk and cheese for the family. When there was any ewe's milk, such as when a lamb had died, it was added to the goat's milk. The farmers ate cheese every day at every meal, as Chabot did himself as a child. Only on feast days would cheese disappear from the table. The men were shepherds; the women did the milking and made the cheese in the farm kitchen. When there was more cheese than a family could eat, they dried it—with the help of the mistral if it was blowing—for eating during the winter. In those days goats used to cease giving milk for four or five months as compared with the three of modern goats. A family with surplus cheese would sell it at winter fairs and markets, particularly in Banon. That occurred as early as the thirteenth century.

Before the dried cheeses were eaten or sold, they were soaked in water to soften them. Chabot's mother used to say, *"Tu trempes une petite nuit"* ("You soak them for a little night"). She flavored the water with savory; each family's method was different. More commonly, I've read, the soaking time was four to ten days. Then after another day or two of drying, the cheeses were often dipped in eau-de-vie or vinegar, which was sometimes flavored with pepper, and then frequently they were tied in brown autumn grape or chestnut leaves. After that they were further ripened on straw or in clay jars, where, if the cheeses weren't eaten within a short time, the taste became powerful.

The area's climate and vegetation are largely Mediterranean, though most of the land is so high that it lacks the Mediterranean's characteristic olives and evergreen oaks. From the early Middle Ages, Chabot said, the region of Banon was different too because, to encourage raising animals, the authorities levied no tax on those who did and they were given free use of grazing lands. In the fourteenth and fifteenth centuries, the plague reduced the population of Haute Provence by more than half, and afterward the people relied more than ever on raising animals, because there was too little labor available for planting crops. Chabot's house, in which we sat, was originally Roman. It was rebuilt around 1600, when prosperity began to return.

Among the cultural differences between the north and south of France, Chabot asserted, even the ways of making cheese were once distinct. A northern-style curd for goat cheese is set by letting the milk cool from udder temperature to something akin to room temperature and then adding whey, full of acid-producing bacteria. Over about twenty-four hours, the gradually rising acidity sets the milk into curd. The northern cheeses, once taken from their molds, ripen from the outside in, mostly through the action of the microorganisms that grow on the surface—many people prefer the cheese while the very center is still almost chalky. The curd that's used to make northern-style goat's-milk cheese, which is the kind you commonly see and eat everywhere today in Provence, is called a *caillé acide*— an "acid curd."

In contrast, Chabot's mother and grandmother, and once, he said, all southerners, made their cheese from a *caillé doux* ("sweet curd") set not by acidity but by about three times as much rennet as northern-style cheesemakers use. The southerners added no whey at all but only rennet, immediately after milking, while the milk was still warm. The curd formed in roughly two hours, before much acidity developed. Chabot proposed that the rapidly formed *caillé doux* was favored in the South because otherwise in the warm climate, while the milk waited for twenty-four hours to set, an explosion of bad micro-creatures could spoil it.

The *caillé doux* cheese is drained in its mold, salted, turned, and, initially, ripened much like other small goat's-milk cheeses. But a fresh *caillé doux* cheese, I found in the *fromagerie,* is quite firm to the touch. The leaf wrapping, which follows in a few days, slows drying and keeps out air, while it allows the cheese to breathe. The surface microorganisms that ripen almost all traditional cheeses require oxygen, but the *caillé doux* doesn't need those organisms and shows little sign of them. Instead, partly due to the enzymes from the large amount of rennet, the cheese turns creamy simultaneously throughout, becoming *crémeux à cœur*—creamy all the way to the heart, like the ripest Camembert, which Chabot reminded me is a mere upstart. (It probably dates from the eighteenth century.)

Cheese has been made from sweet curd, he said, for two to three thousand years. How can we possibly know? I asked. In answer, he showed me nineteenth-century glazed ceramic molds from his family's farm in Marcoux, in use as late as 1950. Such molds were once widely made in Provence. Each one, in the shape of a small dish, is pierced with relatively few large holes, large enough that the delicate *caillé acide* would run through them. The firm *caillé doux* would not. The same molds with the same holes have been uncovered, he said, at a number of archaeological sites in the region of Banon. Where there is pottery, there are cheese molds, he said. Still older evidence from more northern parts of Europe suggests that the *caillé acide,* requiring molds with a large number of small holes, is the more recent invention.

Yet the characteristic southern *caillé doux* almost disappeared, finally, with the help of air-conditioned *fromageries,* which allowed the northern cheese to be made more easily in a warm climate. Chabot, however, believed the main reason for the loss was cultural. As a child in school in the 1940s, he was punished for speaking Provençal—he was put in a corner and made to wear a *bonnet d'âne.* He made the gesture of an ass's ears so I would know what the hat was like. I could feel his resentment. Now he could understand but not speak Provençal.

And most Provençaux, he said, understood only two hundred to three hundred words of their language. They were taught for so long that their language and culture, including cuisine and cheese, were old-fashioned—inferior and superseded by all things French. Chabot said the major cultural break, and the end of the old cheesemaking, came in the 1950s, when the strengthening postwar economy brought the old peasant way of life to a close.

Because, at the time we spoke, there was no restriction on the use of the Banon name, leaf-wrapped "Banons" were being produced widely in France, often from cow's milk. These cheeses were made with an acid curd and ripened inside the leaves to a creamy, slightly sour, powerful, challenging, and by no means entirely pleasant state, with something crude and even manure-y about them. They formed a sharp contrast with goat's-milk cheeses of other kinds, which generally have clean flavors and can be delicate, even lovely. I had tasted the false Banons without understanding that they were in a state of decay that had nothing to do with the true cheese.

The old cheesemaking had retreated, but at the time Chabot first began to make his mother's cheese at La Petite Colle, in 1968, a taste for the old *caillé doux* Banon remained, and he was a success. Yet when he began to speak up for the traditional cheese, dairy experts in France denied to him that it had ever existed. The evidence was unarguable, however, and they came to accept it. One obstacle to reviving the cheese was economic. The acid curd yields 50 percent more cheese, so Chabot had to sell his cheese for a third more and convince his customers the cheese was worth it. In the early 1980s other cheesemakers thought his support for the original cheese was "ridiculous." Yet he insisted that the *caillé doux* was exactly what set Banon apart and could make it thrive amid the mass of other cheeses.

Eventually the other Banon makers came to agree with him, and some used the *caillé doux* for some of their cheeses. They decided to ask that the *caillé doux* be required under the appellation they requested. In 2003 the appellation was approved, and since 2014 it has also required that the goats belong to the old regional breeds, Rove and Commune Provençale, though Alpine and crosses among the three are also permitted. Commune Provençale, the historical goat of Banon, was once down to just three herds and in danger of disappearing. It's true that Banon has been fixed as a slightly narrower type of cheese than the original—no additions of ewe's milk, no drying and soaking, only chestnut leaves and not grape. (The use of grape leaves is older, Chabot told me, because chestnuts were planted around Banon only after 1850.) The cheeses must be aged for five to ten days before they're dipped in eau-de-vie, optionally, and wrapped in leaves, and then they must mature for at least ten more days before they can be sold. Chabot thought six weeks of ripening was ideal.

As at other farms in other French cheesemaking regions, the tasks and equipment at La Petite Colle were simple and offered remarkably little to look at. But what takes place in the milk and cheese is not simple at all. Chabot said, "One learns every day."

Before I left, I bought a Banon to take with me, and when I sat down with it and a loaf of bread, that was the first time I tasted the real thing. It had no precedent in my memory. The flavors were part of the otherness one seeks in traveling. They challenged a little. They were pleasing without being immediately, fully likable. The taste was earthy, rich, sensual. I've had Banon often enough since then to have grown to have a complete liking and even an affection for it. Banon is a part of the enormous variety, complexity, and interest of cheese—explored far more deeply in France than in any other country.

TWENTY-SEVEN

Richard Olney, an Uncompromising French Cook

Solliès-Toucas, Provence

For most of his life, Richard Olney lived on a hillside above the village of Solliès-Toucas, about twenty minutes from the Mediterranean port of Toulon. After he died there, in 1999 at the age of seventy-two, he still loomed so large for me that for years I would catch myself thinking of him as still there, still available to answer a question, to provide some crucial piece of information. Richard's expertise was in French food, but he may have written better about food of any kind than anyone else before or since. Each of us is spoken to by particular voices, and for me there was no one better to learn from than Richard in *Simple French Food,* his second cookbook, published in 1974 and still in print. He wrote four more books, including one based on conversations with Lulu Peyraud of Domaine Tempier in Provence, and he was the chief consultant—really the author—

of the twenty-eight volumes of Time-Life's Good Cook series, published mainly in the 1980s. Back then it went without saying that the content was above all French. He also wrote *Yquem* and *Romanée-Conti,* about wine. He had started out writing a column of menus with recipes for Odette Kahn of *Cuisine et Vins de France.* It took me years to find any aspect of food and drink where he might have been mistaken. (Only one was striking: he was wedded to the old habit of drinking red wine, including great red wine, with cheese, although neither does any favor to the other.) Considering the quantity and level of his work, Richard wasn't particularly well known. The seriousness about pleasure that appealed to some of us must have put off many others. Television for sure was not his medium, and he had no interest in it, which was crippling. Yet he influenced important American professionals, crucially reinforcing and encouraging Alice Waters and forming the importer Kermit Lynch's early understanding of wine (like Richard, both became close to the Peyraud family). Richard was the cook and writer who influenced me most, the reader I most wanted to please. We were friends, although we exchanged only sporadic letters and faxes and we met just twice, albeit at length, at Solliès-Toucas.

He was born in small-town Iowa, one of eight children of a banker. He left to study at the Brooklyn Museum Art School, and then in 1951 at the age of twenty-four he moved to Paris. A decade later, he moved again, to Solliès-Toucas, where he had bought a tumble-down stone house among terraced olive trees. He fixed it up and moved in. The long uphill drive had been "a goat path," he said, and even when it was finally paved, its last abrupt turn remained distressingly steep. He lived in an almost impoverished style with little more than the essential furnishings. His refrigerator was half-size. He washed his vegetables and his dishes in a stone sink.

Those vegetables, often with herbs, played large roles in his recipes. They contrast with the old stereotype of French food as fatty, stuffy, complicated, and centered on meat. The stereotype contained a lot of truth, but it applied especially to restaurant food of a certain two- or three-decade period after the Second World War. And the best places were never rigid or tired, never pointlessly complicated, although certainly they focused on meat. Richard's books supply the missing vegetables, so prominent in markets and home kitchens. He also had an appreciation for starch—in a bread omelette, onion *panade,* bread and squash soup; in potatoes in beer, scalloped, stuffed, as a tart, as fritters, in a daube, with salt cod. (All those appear in *Simple French Food.*)

As I reread this chapter, I see that what's wanted right here is a long quote that shows how Richard described a dish, but the food is so often conveyed through the process, and the steps, if that's the right word, are interconnected and go on at length. Here and there in an introduction, however, a portrait emerges. About a vegetable stew, he says: "The subtle structure of harmonies drawn from a combination of tender young vegetables cooked (or to be more accurate, sweated) together with butter (or olive oil or a combination) in a heavy, tightly covered vessel, each added, raw or precooked, at a specific moment corresponding to its own needs, the complexity of savory autonomies butter-bound in an amalgam of their own fragrances, accented by the caress of an herb or two . . ." Note that at this point you have yet to come to the main verb of the sentence—you're only two-thirds of the way through.

When I bought *Simple French Food* a few years after it came out, I was intimidated by the density of its information. I could read only short sections at a time, hardly taking in the meaning. For a long time I cooked just one recipe, every few months or so (loving it—pork chops and apples in mustard and cream, a combination that no longer much appeals to me). All those things that at first held me at a distance later drew me in.

Richard had moved to France when the wonderful dishes of old-fashioned French cooking could still be found readily in restaurants. He also knew home cooking. He never cooked professionally, but his skills and intellectual engagement were far beyond those of usual cookbook writers, including chefs. Richard wrote well, but what pushed his books to the highest level was his focus on taste, including the role of wine with food, together with his logic and unyielding honesty. When, for a terrine, he called not for grinding the meat but for hand chopping it, because the fibers were less broken and the result was more succulent, he acknowledged that some of his guests couldn't tell the difference. Immediately he reasserted that the difference was "very marked." He said, "It is a question of whether you, the reader, will be satisfied with a decent product or whether you prefer something sublime."

He adored simplicity in food, though he defined it more broadly than most people would—as clarity, purity, focus. He shared the French appreciation for balance and harmony. He was self-taught, a sensualist, driven by the strong pleasure he found in eating and drinking and by his experiences in France. The standards he set were hard ones, for others and for himself. On my first visit to Solliès-Toucas, when I was awed to be in his presence, the main dish was calves' brains with fava beans. He put the brains on the stove to poach. A few minutes later he turned and saw the pan was seething. *"Boiled brains,"* he spat, as if that were the most despicable food in the world. "You can go home and tell everyone that he served you boiled brains." There was a hint of perverse pleasure in the words. But he had caught the error in time, and the brains retained their ideal tender creaminess.

Richard was proudest of The Good Cook series, but his best book was *Simple French Food,* with its tilt toward Provence and the food he cared about most. At the time he wrote, Richard could still say that the streets of his village were

> regularly blocked by the insouciant passage of the shepherd and his troop; the women still beat their laundry along the streams; stuffed eggplant and zucchini are carried through the streets at eleven o'clock in the morning to be installed in the ovens of the local bakery and picked up an hour or so later; the men devote half the year to playing *pétanque* and drinking pastis and the other half to playing cards and drinking pastis, and if, on entering the general store, a couple of housewives happened to be discussing with the shopkeeper the various merits of their respective *ratatouilles* or *soupes au pistou,* one may as well expect to wait a half an hour before being served.

Among all those who have written about food, Richard is perhaps the most sensual. Scrambled eggs are "the softest of barely perceptible curds held in a thickly liquid, smooth, creamy suspension." Small eggplants "swell, retaining the hot air in their skins and each guest should have the pleasure of puncturing his eggplant at table." He expresses the inherent warmth of his sub-

THE FOOD & WINE OF FRANCE

ject. He is completely involved in it, shunning compromise—a cook at the top of his game—and yet kind to the reader. He aims to make a cook out of you if you'll let him. Especially in *Simple French Food,* he explains the why of your actions, teaching almost every kitchen essential and presenting cooking and eating as two parts of a whole.

That book is an unusual combination of relatively informal, sometimes humble dishes with the highest standards and expectations. It's the most complex and personal of his books, not only in its breadth of information but in the way one thought leads to another, with a steady flow of practical asides. Sometimes there's enough detail that you feel you're standing in his kitchen watching him. He urges you to *taste,* knowing that if you don't have confidence in your own palate then the rest is almost worthless.

The style of the food is casual in *Simple French Food,* but one recipe calls for boning an oxtail, using the tip of a small, extremely sharp knife to trace the excruciating complexity of the vertebrae. And under "Eel," Richard wrote: "Rap the back of the head sharply against the edge of a table to knock the eel unconscious, cut a circular incision all around the base of the head, cutting slightly into the flesh, grasp the head firmly in one hand, holding it in a towel to prevent its slipping, and peel the skin, glove-like. . . ."

In person, Richard was often intolerant, and his criticisms could be absurdly strong, sometimes obscene. Big names in food were his targets. That he drank a lot wasn't the reason for this talk. He seemed to be testing his listeners. Yet he was generous to many people, including young cooks who approached him. He opened great wines, including, for me, Romanée-Conti. That meant something, because the most celebrated wines were already becoming inaccessible, as ever greater wealth around the world chased the limited supply.

When I first visited Solliès-Toucas, in 1993, many of the terraced fruit orchards in the valley had already been taken over by housing. Richard never learned to drive. He would walk down to the village, and he used to take the bus to markets farther off. He lived partly out of his garden, his chicken coop, his cellar, and, especially later on when walking became more difficult, his freezer.

On my second and last visit, the main lunch course was squid from the freezer, sautéed for a minute and seasoned with parsley and garlic. It was simple and very good. The principal wine, drunk with the cheeses I had bought that morning at the market in Hyères, was an old Bordeaux, whose name failed to stick in my memory, and it was exceedingly good.

Richard liked improvision in cooking, but within the rules as he understood them. When Nouvelle Cuisine appeared, he was skeptical, seeing it as just another "new cooking" among others that had appeared in the history of French food. "Bizarre marriages and simplistic methods are always part of the baggage," he wrote. "That which is valuable is rarely new and is eventually reintegrated into the mainstream of tradition, while the rest is blessedly forgotten." He would surely have found some of the most uninhibited current creations beyond comment.

His tastes in food and wine were altogether Francophile. I once asked him whether he even *liked* Italian wine. "When I'm in Italy," he answered. Even the nature of Richard's writing was French—romantic, analytical, sensuous, precise. And he was concerned about the gradual internationalization of French and other cuisines. Women, the source and upholders of regional cuisine, were working more outside the home and cooking less, and he saw the regional dishes retreating into restaurants (where they're not often at their best—and depending on the region, unless you have the wonderful good fortune of being invited into the home of some exceptional cook, you may not encounter them at all). Yet he seemed to believe that French cooking would endure. Rather than define it, Richard sidestepped, saying, "Good and honest cooking and good and honest French cooking are the same thing." Beyond that he only pointed to characteristic dishes.

Yet in one particular passage he did say more, about menus— and no one has written with more understanding of the logic of a menu. Assembling multiple courses with their wines can be a greater challenge than doing the cooking. Everything should relate (the courses to each other, the wines to the courses, the wines to each other) and everything should build. There should be no repetition, and each succeeding plate should be a happy, stimulating contrast to what has gone before; the visual is important too. More than the dishes themselves, Richard said, the most French thing about French food is a well-composed menu: "It is the degree to which a menu is based on a sensuous and aesthetic concept that differentiates a French meal from all others."

TWENTY-EIGHT

A Sauce from a Mortar

Avignon, Provence

I counted the seats in the restaurant in Avignon—just eighteen. At lunch, only one other couple was present in addition to our table of three. After we ordered, I saw through a window into the kitchen that a young woman was making the sauce for my fish in a mortar. It was a Provençal *sauce au pistou* ("pesto") for a filet of tuna, which came with a little eggplant-and-anchovy tart (all were perfect). If you have a big Provençal marble mortar and an olive wood pestle, it doesn't take long to reduce garlic and basil to a paste. Still, it was amazing to me to see anyone in a restaurant in France make a sauce to order for just one customer using a mortar and pestle—amazing that anyone would take the trouble, decide the expense in labor was worth it, care enough about freshness, care about the difference in texture, think the customer would notice or deserve that kind of attention. Then I realized that the tapenade placed on the table had also come from a mortar. Its particular smoothness, slipping over the tongue, could have been achieved only in that way. Tapenade can be made ahead because it contains already cured olives and capers. But a sauce of fresh basil leaves is ideally made as close as possible to the last minute. The waitress didn't point out that the sauce was made just for me in a mortar. I knew only because I stood up at the right moment.

Jérôme Gradassi was the chef and owner. After his grandfather died, he closed the restaurant to take over the family wine property, one of the smallest in Châteauneuf-du-Pape. As I was writing the paragraph above, I called him up to learn a little more about him. He speaks with the accent of the South and his voice has a quality almost of happiness in it. He began to apprentice at sixteen, at first in a restaurant as tiny as the one where I ate lunch. He went on to work in other small and large places, including Hiély in Avignon and Baumanière in Les Baux. I asked Gradassi why he had used a mortar, and he said, "Because in a restaurant you welcome people in the same way you welcome them at home." Is it normal in a restaurant to use a mortar? "Less and less. It used to be in every good bistro. Now to find this tradition you have to go to a *grand* restaurant."

TWENTY-NINE

A Slippery White Cheese and a Surprise

Arles and Vauvert, Provence

At the big, exciting Saturday market in Arles, you could buy anything from cheap clothes and hardware to live chickens to take home and cook in your city kitchen. (The customers for those were mostly older.) I bought a goat bell from its maker; the clapper was a goat bone hanging from a strip of goat rawhide, and the warm, deep sound called up everything I love about Provence. At one stand, a young man named Stéphane Lemercier, of Le Mas du Trident, was selling ewe's-milk cheeses from the Camargue. Some were protected in an old glass-and-wood case. Others, half covered in milky brine, sat in neat rows. They were small, white, and round, except where they touched, which squared them off a little; they had been scattered with herbs and ground pepper and a bay leaf had been placed on each. The Camargue is the watery plain of the Rhone delta, a flat landscape that offers nothing to slow the mistral. Once, it was mostly wild, with only a few farmhouses on dry ground. Natural areas have been set aside, but much land was drained for growing rice, grapes, and other crops. Near the sea, enormous quantities of water continue to be evaporated, as they have been for centuries, to produce salt. The Camargue is also known for its ancient race of white horses and for the long-horned black cattle that appear in *daubes de bœuf* and in Provençal bullfights. The cheese sitting in whey was named Le Gardian, after the Camargue cowboys. The cheeses of Le Mas du Trident were all made on the farm from the farm's own milk. "It is very important," Lemercier said, "if you want to make something good." The special reward of Le Gardian was its slippery-smooth tenderness. The texture was wonderfully luscious and light, because ewe's milk is about twice as rich in fat and also has more protein and other solid matter than cow's or goat's milk. It's a paradox that fat, if it isn't greasy and you don't eat too much, makes food taste light. The flavor of Le Gardian, which had only a hint of salt, was rich and clean and somewhat simple (there was a reason for the herbs and pepper). It was as mild and delicate as a glass of ewe's milk.

Stéphane Lemercier was married to Nancy Bouet, whose parents farm Le Mas du Trident outside the town of Vauvert. At the end of a working day I went to the farm to meet Nancy and her father, René. He said the Bouets had herded sheep and made cheese for 150 years. Formerly, sheep in the Camargue were raised for meat, and cheese was made only when milk was available, in spring. The men worked outdoors with the animals and they milked the ewes; women made the cheese. But it was René Bouet who taught his wife, Josiane, to make cheese.

The 250 ewes grazed outdoors the year round. Until a few years before, the flock had been made up only of Mérinos d'Arles, the old breed of the Camarguais shepherds, but each ewe produced less than a liter of milk a day. The Bouets added Lacaunes, the dairy sheep of Roquefort; a ewe supplied more than twice as much milk. Yet they retained some Mérinos d'Arles because the Mérinos' rich milk was needed to supplement the thinner milk of the Lacaunes. Lemercier said the cheese is at its very best from the beginning of March to the end of June, a time when grass is green, plentiful, and "full of healthiness."

I liked Le Gardian a lot, but I was concerned when I saw on the label that the milk was pasteurized. I pressed Bouet about that. He responded that the milk is faultlessly clean, so it doesn't need pasteurization for reasons of safety. I had to think a little before I understood: it's only a coincidence that the heat innate to the process of making the cheese has the same effect as pasteurization. It's the heat that creates the texture, and the texture is at the heart of the appeal. Le Gardian is in effect a cross between the fresh form of the old springtime cheese and *brousse du Rove,* specifically the high heat used to make *brousse,* which is the traditional Provençal ricotta. René Bouet's parents learned to make Le Gardian when they worked for the man who originated the cheese in 1923, in a small, long-since-disappeared dairy in Arles.

I understood Bouet to say that the curd was set with a small amount of rennet over a period of five to six hours. The curd must, I think, be broken up a little before molding, but when I tried to verify the procedure over the phone with Lemercier, he preferred to keep the method secret. Bouet likes the cheese best after about twenty-four hours, while Lemercier prefers it only two to three hours old. "Usually," he said, "the case is everybody eats it immediately"—the day they buy it. When Bouet gave me some of the day's production of Le Gardian to take with me, he repeated several times, emphatically, that it must not be refrigerated.

Besides Le Gardian, the Bouets make *brousse* and aged, pressed raw-milk cheeses, which lie outside the Provençal tradition, plus one additional wholly Provençal cheese, also from raw milk. It had caught my attention at the market and was delicious with ripe cherries at breakfast. This cheese was Le Camarguais. In sheep version, it had the qualities of the old southern *caillé doux,* though the Bouets don't use the term. The flat, round Le Camarguais is slightly smaller than Provence's omnipresent goat's-milk cheeses. And inside its skin, it develops the same fully creamy interior as the leaf wrapped goat's-milk Banon. As the Camarguais slowly dries, it becomes smaller and harder, just as the usual Provençal goat's-milk cheeses do. Like them, it eventually turns into a hard, yellow disk and lasts forever. A little of its excellent, strong caramel taste goes a long way.

Lemercier, having emphasized the care required to make Le Gardian, dismissed the Camarguais as easy: "It's a common way of making the cheese, everywhere in France." Yet, he said, the curd is set immediately after milking, while the milk is at the temperature of the animal, and, as with the *caillé doux,* there's no addition of acidifying whey, which would make it more like other French cheeses. Thirty liters of milk are set by "a common French spoon" of rennet, he said. "It's not very high-tech," he added with a laugh. Within one and a half hours, the curd is set and then ladled—without being first broken to release whey— into molds, where it drains for two days. The cheeses are unmolded, very lightly salted, and turned two or three times a day as they continue to dry. Within eight days, depending on the weather, the cheeses have become soft and entirely creamy, taking on the careless, irregular look of a cheese that almost makes itself. As cheeses go, it could hardly be simpler, or more Provençal in taste, and it's a perfect counterpoint to Le Gardian.

THIRTY

The Importance
of Goose Fat

Samatan, Gimont, and Saint-Martin-Gimois, Gascony

The "fat markets" of southwest France, held once a week in various towns, sell fattened ducks, fattened geese, and foie gras—the products of force-feeding, or *gavage,* to use the softer French word, which can mean simply "stuffing" or "gorging." The biggest *marché au gras* open to the public takes place on Mondays in Samatan, southwest of Toulouse. By eight o'clock, small white vans and a few cars were pulling up in lines in front of the market building. Farmers unloaded plucked carcasses like luggage. Gradually a crowd gathered outside until at 9:30 a whistle blew and the doors opened. Inside a brightly lit white room, the ducks were laid in double rows on long tables, their heads hanging over the sides, with the smaller number of geese in a separate area to one side. Geese, the defining bird of traditional southwest cooking, were the original source of foie gras.

But they're much more expensive to fatten, and in the 1970s they gave way to ducks. Now less than 5 percent of fattened birds are geese. In Samatan, the birds on display—ducks and geese—were whole and uneviscerated, except that the fattened liver had been taken from some. You can and perhaps should wholly disapprove of all force-feeding—it has been a long time since I've eaten foie gras. But the gorging with grain also created the traditional source of the key element of the southwest's richly flavored cooking: delicious goose and duck fat.

At the market the customers' critical assessment was mainly visual. Negotiation was fast—a few questions about breed, price, how many—and then either the sale was abandoned or wallets came out. Some customers bought one bird, some bought many. The price of a whole duck was about four times as much if it contained the liver. The honey-beige fat livers by themselves, in rectangular Tupperware-like containers, were sold in a separate room starting at 10:30. Most foie gras is eaten at the year-end holidays, and the fat market is busiest in November and December, when the price of foie gras also goes up. Some sellers waited longer than others for customers. Those who sold last had to drop their prices. One or two customers carried their purchases in the old style in a basket lined with a white linen cloth. The fat market was over by 11, when the live poultry market opened next door. A *gaveuse,* meaning someone who does the force-feeding, had heard I was a writer and, seeing my notebook, she came up and asked me to be sure to include this: "The quality is in the markets. *Ici, c'est l'authentique.*"

The department of Gers, which includes Samatan, has some of France's prettiest and least spoiled farmland, still a patchwork of fields devoted to varied kinds of farming. The area is part of what was long ago the duchy of Gascony, whose capital, Auch, was already established when the Romans arrived. Gascony, its territory expanding and contracting, eventually joined the duchy of Guyenne, a combination also called Aquitaine. Gascony, however, is a current notion, though not precisely defined, running from Bordeaux south and somewhat east to the Pyrenees, where it meets Basque country and the French province of Roussillon. Some older people in the region still speak Gascon, a Romance language related to Provençal, and almost everyone speaks French with some Gascon accent. The s in Gers is pronounced, sibilant.

The fattening for foie gras is based on the behavior of various wild migratory birds, large and small, that gorge themselves with food before they start on their journeys. Those fat birds are meatier and better tasting and have always been sought for cooking. In Spain, the farmer Eduardo Sousa pursues an extreme, highly ecologically aware form of farming in which he relies on the natural instinct of geese to create foie gras without force-feeding (an approach described in depth and with insight by the American chef Dan Barber in his book, *The Third Plate*). The total amount of foie gras Sousa produces, however, is small and very costly, and there's little potential for scaling up.

All the grain of force-feeding greatly increases the size and the fat of the liver. After roughly three weeks with geese, and in as little as twelve to fourteen days with ducks, the size of the liver has tripled or quadrupled. Corn—maize—is the most effective and economical food. But you don't need foie gras to have a supply of fat or a liver that's more than ordinarily delicious, though not on the level of foie gras. Livers that are merely somewhat fat are more blond in color, less bloody in flavor, and very good. In France, blond chicken livers are commonly sold for a higher price than dark ones.

In the southwest, foie gras used to form part of a thoroughgoing polyculture. Ducks and geese were fattened only in the cold months, after the harvest was over and there was more time. Besides, hot weather is stressful for the birds. A veterinarian on duty at the Gimont market told me, "The foie gras of winter is still the best." The Samatan market began to be held year-round only after air-conditioning was installed to keep the foie gras cool.

The farmers used to fatten only enough birds to provide meat and fat for the family and have a little foie gras to sell; they might also keep a few of the livers to put up in jars for the family. Foie gras, then or now, is seldom prepared at home except in that way. One of the few traditional home recipes for it is *foie gras aux raisins,* braised with grapes, originally tart, half-ripe ones. Farms are no longer so self-sufficient; they're more specialized. Many people have left the countryside. Scarcely anyone fattens just a few geese or ducks. Still, I saw more dooryard chickens in the southwest than I've seen in any other part of France. In the Gers, tradition is especially strong.

France is responsible for three-quarters of the world's production of foie gras and consumes even more than that, because, while it exports a little, it imports more, especially from Bulgaria and Hungary. France used to produce foie gras in Alsace in the far northeast, but now Alsace produces little, and foie gras production has spread to other French regions, with the southwest remaining the leader. Until the mid-1980s most of the foie gras was canned, and this *foie gras de conserve* continues to have a few strong admirers. But it turns out that most people prefer their foie gras much less cooked than that. Chefs make showy dishes of sautéed foie gras, but if you're willing to eat it at all, the best way to understand the appeal is to eat a slice from a plain, minimally cooked (the center should reach only the temperature of rare meat), chilled terrine of whole livers. Classic, perfect accompaniments are clear, diced meat jelly and a glass of lightly sweet wine, often Sauternes. The more you cook foie gras, the less flavor it has, and the more dry and eventually granular it becomes. If you really overcook it, the fat runs out and it's ruined.

Foie gras became troubling to anyone who was paying attention to it starting in the 1970s, when it began to be produced on a much larger scale in much greater quantity in much bigger, more automated operations, using ducks and not geese. Big producers confine their ducks in long, low buildings and sell to large-scale processors. They use more automated feeders that allow one person to feed many more ducks. This foie gras is sold at much lower prices in supermarkets, mostly in emulsified *"bloc"* or mousse form, which has a heavier, greasier texture.

The typical small-scale *gaveur* of the southwest, in contrast, still fattens only twenty to forty birds at a time, from October to March, knows each bird, and more likely sells at a market or directly from the farm. Apart from the feeding, this mostly outdoor production is a model that the world's mass producers of chicken or pork, which use truly inhumane methods, should emulate.

I went to see one farmer, near the "fat market" town of Gi-mont, whose ducks spend most of their lives outdoors. He produces a hundred fattened ducks every fifteen days. Despite the care and organization of the markets, less than a tenth of Gers production is sold there. Most is sold either directly to processors or to retail customers as *conserves à la ferme*. And this farmer sells his foie gras at the farm in the form of conserves, put up in glass jars as his grandmother did.

Some farmers prefer pure Muscovy ducks, but this farmer's birds, like most, were *mulards* ("mules"), which are splotched with white and dark feathers. They're a sterile cross between a dark male Muscovy and a white Pekin or other female. Only male ducks are fattened because they are considerably bigger and have bigger livers. He starts to fatten them, as his mother did, at fourteen to sixteen weeks, one to two weeks later than some farmers. That way the meat, another important product, has more flavor and firmer texture. He feeds them corn for twelve to fourteen days.

The ducks were at that moment in a high-ceilinged barn in six raised wooden-floored pens, beside a big open door. The *gaveurs* raise their own corn, and the Gers maintains the tradition of using white corn; yellow makes yellower foie gras. The birds used to be almost always geese, the farmer explained, and women did the work, selling the foie gras for pocket money. "I never saw my father or grandfather feed a goose." His family ate a lot of confit and cooked with a lot of goose fat. Now the family uses duck fat. People eat less fat in general, he commented, and cook with more oil. (Apart from those who raise birds, cooking with duck and goose fat is no longer typical in the southwest.) Nearby families also used to raise their own grapes for wine; everyone worked together at the harvest, and afterward they ate a big harvest dinner.

The feeding takes about an hour, the farmer explained as he prepared the second feeding at the end of the day. The corn is first softened in water. The feeding may be cruel no matter what, and yet like other small-scale farmers I met in the Gers he seemed thoughtful and kind. The *gaveur* uses a funnel, now usually plastic, which has a small motor attached to stir the grain and keep it flowing. (The *gaveuses* of the past—in France they gained a romantic peasant image—twirled a small stick in a metal funnel.) Instinctively, ducks and geese shy away from people (though in some circumstances geese are aggressive), but during the fattening the feeder is always the same, and after a few days the birds grow accustomed to that person and don't much shy away. The goose or duck is held between the feeder's legs. It doesn't resist, and the tube of the funnel is slid into the neck where it stays for perhaps ten seconds as the bird's crop fills with corn. The crop is the pouch at the bottom of the throat where grain is held before it passes to the gizzard to be broken up. By nature, ducks and geese live on whole grain and naturally swallow even grit and small stones to grind the grain in the gizzard. Their esophagi aren't especially sensitive, though the feeder must be careful.

Sitting on a stool, the farmer quickly touched the base of the duck's neck to feel that the last meal was digested. (I could feel the whole kernels distinctly beneath the feathers.) After this quick feeding, the farmer immediately felt again to be sure the corn was in the crop. Each day the bird was given a little more corn, to make a total of twelve kilos altogether. What I saw didn't look worse than uncomfortable.

In tiny Saint-Martin-Gimois, high on a rounded hilltop, I visited a young couple who lived in a wide old house between the church and the town hall, with their farm buildings behind. Even over the phone, both were outgoing and relaxed. Geese are more delicate, harder to raise than ducks, and they take one and a half to two times as long to fatten, which costs much more in grain. But the wife chose to keep geese because they're more traditional than ducks. Her father had dairy cows, but not as many as farmers do today. She fattened sixty geese at a time, each week selling twenty foie gras and starting twenty more geese. Of the *gavage,* she said, "I've always known it," as if to say that to her it seemed natural. Her geese belonged to the old local breed Masseube, named for a nearby town.

When the geese were four months old, she would fatten them in pens in a stone barn that looked out on an extraordinary rolling panorama of farms with small varicolored fields. She sold her foie gras and birds at three different *marchés au gras,* "because I like to keep the principle of the market, because one likes to defend the quality of one's product"—in person.

As to the difference between goose and duck foie gras, "You can't say one is better." Some duck foie gras, she said, is stronger, more animal-tasting than the other. She acknowledged her own preference. "For me, it's goose. It's finer, milder, creamier— it's more a question of texture. And goose foie gras melts less." She puts up a little foie gras for her family. You don't eat goose foie gras until it's one year old, she reminded me, and she waits two to three years.

The great attraction of foie gras is the combination of smooth, soft texture with rich, mild flavor, mostly from the fat. The French gastronomic writer Curnonsky wrote in the 1950s that foie gras is "a quintessence of aromas and savors that sums up the superior quality of good French things at the table."

Foie gras, dominated by fat, is an adaptable, neutral medium for which chefs have invented countless recipes. To balance the fat, chefs usually call upon acidity in some form—sweet-and-sour sauces and garnishes (sometimes far too sweet, which only adds to the richness and ruins the wine), involving fruit, fruit juices, port, sherry, or Madeira, or sometimes, a tannic element such as spinach or olives. Or they simply balance the richness with a large quantity of something: cabbage, onions, leeks, radishes, endives, scallops, bolete mushrooms.

When we think of French cooking, butter comes quickly to mind, or olive oil in Provence, but until about the middle of the twentieth century, the main cooking fat of most French and other European peasants was lard or, in a few places, both lard and goose fat. In the southwest, the goose or duck fat that distinguishes the traditional cooking gives deliciousness to all sorts of things, not least potatoes or anything else fried in it. And the fat goes into soups or stews—anything. It even goes into pastry.

Beyond fat and confit, traditional Gascon cooking has rich flavors from lamb, wine, Armagnac, sausage, wild mushrooms, garlic, and sweet spices such as cloves. Other typical raw materials are corn, dry-cured ham, hot peppers, vegetables in general (but especially sweet bell peppers, tomatoes, winter squash), wild cèpes, wild birds (especially small ones, like the ortolan, or figpecker, now illegal to eat), confit of pork as well as goose and duck, and freshwater fish—salmon, *alose* ("shad"), trout.

Goose and duck fat play an essential role in preserving meats: duck and goose, also pork (usually in its own fat), sometimes other meats. Apart from the liver, goose and duck used to be prepared almost exclusively as confit. First the birds are cut up and dry-salted for a day or two, along with spices and herbs, not least garlic; then the meat is cooked slowly, immersed in its rendered fat, and finally it is stored in ceramic jars with the hot fat poured over as protection from the air. The meat keeps for months without refrigeration, at least in the cool part of year. After about two months the taste has become much richer. Confit is one of the great flavorful forms of meat. Few old Gascon recipes call for preparing goose or duck in any other way. And confit fat, with its flavor especially of garlic, is extremely delicious for all sorts of purposes.

Both of the southwest's pair of most famous dishes rely on confit. The simpler of the two is *garbure,* a substantial cabbage soup, made of salt pork, leeks, carrots, onions, garlic, beans, herbs, potatoes, and of course cabbage and a piece of confit. The second and more famous dish is cassoulet, whose name is attached to various towns, especially Castelnaudary. It's an elaborate construction based on dried white beans and a selection of meats. And it famously lends itself to loving description, partly because it's one of the dishes for which the elements are first cooked separately, to retain their identities. The beans are cooked with herbs and aromatic vegetables and spices. There's mutton or lamb, a piece of confit, a sausage. All are combined in the *cassole,* a special ceramic dish in the shape of an inverted cone, which gives a wide surface. The contents are then cooked further to make a whole. A crust forms on top, is broken, re-forms. Nothing could be richer in taste than cassoulet, and even in the heat of summer nothing could be more delicious.

THIRTY-ONE

The Last Wine in France: Strong, Dark, and Sweet

Banyuls-sur-Mer, Roussillon

Where the Pyrenees meet the Mediterranean Sea in the French province of Roussillon, the climate is hot and dry. The sun shines an average of 325 days out of 365. Through most of the year the wind is frequent and strong, especially the *tramontana*, which comes from the northwest. In summer, normally it never rains and the wide, flat riverbeds of the valleys are empty. Little will grow on the hillsides but grapes. The grapes become very ripe and sweet and yield a small amount of unusual, strong, superb wine, sometimes dry but mostly sweet.

The greatest of these Roussillon *vins doux naturels* are made from red grapes, and their taste recalls port and sometimes sherry, wines to which they're related. Bottles will age and improve for decades. The color of the *traditionnel* wine is mahogany. The best appellation is seaside Banyuls; a smaller quantity of excellent wine comes from inland Maury; and a little comes from the high-volume, sprawling appellation of Rivesaltes, where quality is more variable. As good as the *vins doux naturels* can be, they're little known. Even some people who are very familiar with the famous regions hardly suspect the existence of such flavors in French wine. Yet within France the wines have had an audience. Into the 1980s more than ten million bottles a year were sold just from Banyuls, and they were consumed mostly within France as everyday apéritifs. Then the wines began to be seen as old-fashioned, even low class, replaced by whiskey and cocktails. In the last thirty years the area planted has been cut in half; much good land is abandoned. But lately more attention is being paid to quality, and in Banyuls there's even a small, organic Collectif Anonyme, which cares about the quality of the wine and not about profit. But few of the area's wines rise to their full potential. For lack of popularity, some excellent bottles remain a good value, if you can find them.

Vin doux naturel means "sweet natural wine," but "natural" is a relative word—the sugar is natural and the method isn't. To keep the sugar in the sweet juice from all being turned into alcohol, the winemaker steps in partway through the fermentation and adds enough pure alcohol to stop the yeasts. Depending on how soon the maker acts, the wine ends up with from 15 to 19 percent alcohol. The sugar and alcohol help to protect the flavors as the wine evolves. (Other sweet wines are made using a filter to remove yeasts or, especially in the past, adding large amounts of sulfur. A tiny number of the world's sweet wines, such as the great Sauternes of Château d'Yquem, are made from grapes that are themselves so sugary—very ripe and often partly dried, frequently because noble rot has made the skins porous— that when the alcohol reaches about 16 percent, more than most yeasts will tolerate, they stop working.) A sweet red *vin doux naturel* is often delicious but simple when young. Then years later a bottle of the same wine may excel in its complexity.

Roussillon belongs to France, but its traditional culture is Catalan, as in Catalonia across the border with Spain, and a number of people speak Catalan. As I drove through the region, I listened to Catalan-language French stations on the radio. Credit for long ago inventing *vin doux naturel* is often given to a Catalan, Arnaud de Villeneuve, who worked at the University of Montpellier and received a patent for the process in 1299, but the wines may be older than that. They might have been developed by the Arabized Christians of Spain (*alcohol* is an Arabic word) or the method might have been brought back to Roussillon by the Knights Templar returning from the Crusades. Over the centuries the *vins doux naturels* have often been celebrated.

Banyuls-sur-Mer is the second-to-last town before the border with Spain (little Cerbère is the last). Although the land meets the sea abruptly, leaving only small beaches or none, the coast attracts summer vacationers who overwhelm the indigenous life of Banyuls-sur-Mer. Its port fills with recreational boats. Fishermen use Port-Vendres a few kilometers north, and just beyond that the small port of Collioure is famous for anchovies. The local cuisine is built on fish and wine. The cooking fat remains olive oil, although olive production in Banyuls was abandoned after a severe freeze in 1956 killed all the trees (and those in an arc running through Provence into Liguria). In recent years, with global warming, there has been little frost at all. The resort ugliness of Banyuls-sur-Mer contrasts with the beauty of the vineyards above; you see them only when you take one of the vacant, narrow roads leading upward.

Three co-ops and twenty-six independent producers make wine in the forty-kilometer-long Banyuls appellation, which takes in the communes of Cerbère, Banyuls-sur-Mer, Port-Vendres, and Collioure. To survive the combined wind, sun, and dryness, the grapes must be tough. The main variety is Grenache Noir, whose strong wood withstands the wind and whose fruit ripens slowly over a long period and is high in sugar. The wine oxidizes easily, a quality necessary for the range of flavors in most *vins doux naturels*. Under favorable conditions, Grenache is lush and high yielding, but in the dryness and poor soil of Banyuls, the growers rarely achieve thirty hectoliters of wine per hectare, an unusually low yield, which is also the maximum allowed under the appellation.

A short way from the beachfront, up a tree-lined main street, a low white building displays a sign in big red letters: Domaine du Mas Blanc. That's the appellation's most respected producer. *Mas* means "farm" or "farmhouse," but of the original Mas Blanc, only the foundations survive in one of the vineyards. The domaine's proprietor is Jean-Michel Parcé. His father, Dr. André Parcé, starting in the 1950s, and his grandfather, Dr. Gaston Parcé, in the 1920s and 30s, were the chief forces behind the wines. The appellation was among the first in France, granted in 1936.

Jean-Michel Parcé was both assured and serious, as if he felt the weight of his family's achievement. The *cave* was small and full of barrels and everything connected with wine. Parcé was busy, energetic; I wasn't his highest priority. While we were speaking, he was repeatedly called to answer the phone, to assist his three workers, and once to run a forklift during the lengthy loading of pallets of bottles from a tractor trailer. But he spoke with authority, and eventually he gave me his full attention.

Before phylloxera destroyed the vineyards at the end of the nineteenth century, he said, up to 40 percent of the grapes had been Mourvèdre and varieties other than Grenache. The growers replanted on resistant American rootstocks, but the first they chose weren't adapted to the acidic soil. Mourvèdre and Syrah didn't produce; only Grenache did. This accident led to the dominance of Grenache, with its high sugar and alcohol. And so *vin doux naturel* became much more important than the area's "regular" dry wine.

That too used to be sold as Banyuls, he explained, and it was called *nature* ("plain"). But when the appellation was established, it recognized only *vin doux naturel*. The producers resisted the decision, and finally in 1971, after the perseverance especially of Parcé's father, the dry red and rosé wine was granted its own appellation of Collioure, with a territory identical to that of Banyuls.

The schist soil is poor and thin; some old vines send their roots directly into broken rock. The vineyards are steep, and the work is necessarily by hand. Most plots are small, tended by owners who work part-time and sell their grapes directly to the co-ops. The vines are trained in the ancient goblet shape common to warm Mediterranean locations. The vines are kept low, so they aren't broken by the wind. From a short, thick trunk, a few arms rise around an open center.

Countless walls and terraces cut across the vineyards, creating strangely irregular shapes. To the unknowing eye, the walls appear random. They're a thousand-year-old response to storms, which are rare but violent, the wettest ones blowing in from the sea. "When our ancestors put a vineyard in place," Parcé said, "they first left it bare all winter, waiting for rain. Then they saw where the water ran. And they built the little walls across to break the speed of the water." The walls feed into stone-lined ditches called *agulles* ("needles") in Catalan. The effect is to slow erosion and allow badly needed water to soak in. The diagonals often meet at a single point, which gives the pattern its name: *peu de gall* ("rooster foot") in Catalan. Parcé said, "The system is very, very effective." Visually, the appellation is one of the most deeply interesting in all of wine, unusually architectural and affecting. The abandonment of so many vineyards has left the landscape threatened, but growers who continue to produce under the appellation are required to preserve it.

The grapes for Mas Blanc's Banyuls and Collioure are transported in ninety-liter plastic *comportes* to the winery, where they're stemmed and crushed. Removing the stems eliminates their tannin, in order "to respect the tannin in the grapes." The skins macerate in the juice for three weeks as the wine ferments. Then the Collioure is pressed and put into three-year-old oak barrels, purchased from good Bordeaux estates. A year later the Collioure is clarified by decanting and adding egg whites; some bottlings are dominated by Grenache, others by Mourvèdre or Syrah. Because Parcé makes no dry white wine, I asked, What do you drink with fish? "We drink young Collioure," he said. The fish, typically rockfish, are cooked in the regional style "with rosemary, olive oil, basil, tomato—not with cream." A good Collioure, though the warming climate has increased the alcohol, gives a lot of pleasure with food, especially Mediterranean food. Rich and strong but somehow delicate, it tastes of fruits such as cherry and raspberry. The tannin is not bitter but ripe and soft from the heat.

The Mas Blanc Banyuls is 85 percent Grenache Noir with the rest a mix of Carignan, Syrah, and Mourvèdre. The vines yield merely eighteen to twenty hectoliters per hectare; the grapes, picked later than those for Collioure, are riper. Under the appellation rules, they must contain at least 252 grams of sugar per liter, which is to say the juice is at least one-quarter sugar. After three to seven days, Jean-Michel Parcé stops the fermentation by adding a carefully calculated amount of nearly pure alcohol, made from wine and bought from a distillery. The sweetness or dryness of the Banyuls depends on how far the fermentation has gone when the alcohol is added.

As the wine ages, it's taken in one of several different directions. The wine called Rimage (from the Catalan word for "grape") has a more modern taste of fresh fruit, though it too has a long history. Like most wines, it's matured without air contact. The kind of container, Parcé said, doesn't matter— stainless steel, wood—as long as oxygen is kept out. The dearth of oxygen both preserves the fruit flavors and allows them to develop. The wine's color remains more or less red. Aging lasts up to six or seven years, according to how tannic or refined a wine the producer wants to sell, and then the wine is bottled. It's best to drink Rimage "very young or very old," Parcé said. "There are no half measures." By "very young," he meant within three years of bottling; "very old" was after twenty-five years. Young Rimage shares the pleasing, accessible red-fruit flavors of Collioure. With age, those give way to prune, fig, raisin, cooked fruit, and nuts.

In contrast with Rimage, Banyuls *traditionnel* is matured

through intentional oxidation—air contact—in barrels or casks that have empty space at the top. Often, traditional Banyuls is "shocked" by placing it in glass demijohns for a year or two outdoors, where the day-to-night and seasonal temperature swings are extreme. Parcé, however, keeps his traditional wine indoors, where the differences are milder. Oxidation, through exposure to the air at the top, turns Banyuls *traditionnel* brown and replaces fresh flavors with those of walnut, almond, prune, coffee, orange, pepper, sometimes chocolate. Bottles can last for decades. The 1921 made by his grandfather, Parcé said, remained excellent.

In certain years the wine gains a *rancio* taste. That Spanish word (*ranci* in Catalan) broadly means "rancid." In wine, in Parcé's definition, it's specifically an odor "between hazelnut and rancid walnut." *Rancio* "destroys other aromas and one senses only that. It is extreme oxidation—pushed; it has eaten everything else." Producers make specific *rancio* bottlings. Most of those who know Banyuls consider the *rancio* positive. But it's an acquired, esoteric taste—very different from the accessible fresh fruit of young Rimage. At the table, *rancio* Banyuls "needs a dish that is fairly sweet," Parcé said. "Something I consider marvelous is bitter-orange marmalade put in a *pain d'épices* with a perimeter of very bitter chocolate. That takes *rancio* to a sublime level."

A third kind of Banyuls, of which very little is made, is traditionally raised in a solera system, like that used to age sherry. Over a period of years, younger wines are gradually added to older ones to make a homogeneous aged wine. The barrels used to be stored in the heat and cold under an attic roof (like Tuscan *vin santo*, which in its once-dominant, drier version resembles traditional Banyuls). "It wasn't a commercial system," Parcé said. "It was a system to give pleasure." At one time Mas Blanc was the sole house to continue the tradition, but now others have revived it. At the Domaine du Mas Blanc, the solera barrels are stacked in three *sostres* ("layers"). As the wine evaporates, the barrels are topped up only every two months, allowing a "half oxidation." The bottom layer is refilled from the middle, the middle from the top, and the top is filled with more wine from a good vintage. Being at least five years old, the solera Banyuls qualifies to be labeled Hors d'Âge, meaning wine is "beyond age" and has no vintage.

To Parcé, drier Banyuls remains an apéritif, as it always was, and sweet Banyuls is for dessert. Both dry and sweet are ideally served at 16 degrees C (60 degrees F), except that in summer the sweet should be 2 degrees cooler. An open bottle of the traditional Banyuls aged through oxidation keeps for a month or more in the refrigerator, he said. Open Rimage lasts only a short time.

The most confusing aspect of Banyuls is that the wine's dryness or sweetness has nothing to do with whether it's Rimage or traditional and isn't indicated on the label, except implicitly. If the alcohol is 16 percent, then the wine is very sweet; if the alcohol is 17.5 percent, the wine is half-dry; if the alcohol is 18 or 19 percent, then the wine is dry. The appellation allows fifteen permutations of Banyuls. Parcé offers eleven. Even the large, presumably consumer-friendly (though not so quality-oriented) co-op Terre des Templiers, which represents three-quarters of production, offers as many as nine choices. As historic as the varied forms may be, they seem a crazy way to make and sell wine, baffling to new consumers.

Tasting the different kinds makes clear the different paths that Banyuls can take, or rather down which it is led. Besides Banyuls from red grapes, there is a little white and rosé Banyuls. The white has the full dose of sugar; the juice is wholly unfermented. Parcé's white Banyuls, from a blend of Grenache Blanc, Muscat d'Alexandrie, and the indigenous Tourbat, was full-bodied but tasted to me too much like cooked sugar, like jam without the fruit.

A three-year-old, distinctly sweet Rimage from La Coume vineyard had a prune aroma. About an eighteen-year-old Banyuls *traditionnel,* Parcé commented, "It's natural, it's older. *Ça c'est bon.*" I tasted cooked fruits; the wine was lighter than the previous ones, leaving the mouth clean and filled with alcohol. After that, the Hors d'Âge from the solera system seemed at first much more restrained, yet the flavors remained in the mouth much longer. I thought silently to myself that the Hors d'Âge was the most delicate and refined Banyuls, but Parcé volunteered that it was less delicate and more rustic, because it contained a blend of vintages. A nearly quarter-century-old *rancio,* tasted last, was very long and balanced, with a *rancio* flavor that to me was pleasing and not aggressive (and due to the alcohol and full oxidation, quite different from the oxidized wines of the Jura).

Besides apéritifs and dessert, very occasionally Banyuls is proposed with a main-course dish such as duck with bitter orange or sour cherries, and I've read a recipe for pheasant with cocoa beans as a complement to Banyuls. Before dessert, sweet Banyuls is sometimes drunk with blue cheese, especially cow's-milk blue cheese. And sweet Banyuls goes with cantaloupe, prunes, and walnuts.

(Who drinks dessert wines? you may ask. So many people love dessert and so few people love sweet wines. For lack of demand, prices aren't nearly as high as the low yields and extra labor would seem to require. I love them, and so do most food and wine professionals as well as amateurs who really know wine. But when I serve them to friends who don't fall into those categories, almost no one finishes a glass. The only bottle I remember ever being truly appreciated by them was the sweet Barsac of Château Climens in Bordeaux, which contains a lot of balancing acidity—and it's among the candidates for greatest sweet wine in France.)

But what's special with sweet Banyuls is chocolate. While chocolate is the enemy of most wines, making them taste acidic and thin—without a trace of fruit or much else that would give pleasure—a well-chosen red Banyuls, especially *traditionnel,* is outstanding with chocolate. There's a sympathy of concentrated flavors, and the body and high alcohol to carry them, as long as the wine is sweeter than the chocolate. Banyuls isn't the only drink that goes with chocolate, but nothing is better.

THIRTY-TWO

What Is French Food?

France is the greatest country for bread, cheese, and wine, and its culinary techniques are the foundation of the training of nearly every serious Western cook and some beyond. When I write that, the statement seems so strong that for a moment I feel nothing I can add will stand up to it. I pause, and then I think of underlining the point by saying that bread, cheese, and wine form a trinity of fermented foods that have sustained France for centuries and more—wine was introduced to Provence by the Greeks, bread was already being made by the Gauls when the Romans arrived, and the Romans introduced hard cheeses. And maybe it's key, even in this age of vegetables, that of all countries France has the most appreciation for meat. As to the vegetables, especially around Paris, France developed advanced market gardens, as well as a gastronomic culture built partly around the *halles,* where all sorts of raw materials were sold. No other Western country has taken haute cuisine to such an advanced level, which is not at all to diminish France's less elaborate and rustic cuisines. Then there are the country's practitioners of other highly evolved gastronomic crafts—charcuterie, pastry, chocolate, *confiserie*. When I talk with accomplished winemakers, cheesemakers, charcutiers, pâtissiers, they're so committed, sincere, careful, and intelligent.

And yet if you sat down to a meal in France, could you, could I, answer the question: What makes this food French? You might have obvious clues: bread on the table throughout the meal; a cheese course; wine with lightness, complexity, and a long aftertaste; food with harmony, freshness, and complementary flavors. Yet you can find those things in other Western countries. More indications might be butter in the cooking, sauces containing stock, a famous French dish or two. If you're attuned, you might possibly recognize a high-level professional meal as French by its analytical precision paired with a strong sensuality, a combination pursued nowhere else to the same degree. But with any French food, apart from well-known old-fashioned dishes, it's very hard to say whether it is truly French or, if so, what makes it that way.

In its diversity, French food was always messy to define. And it's confusing that there are two Frances, Paris and the rest. Paris leads, with its concentration of wealth and power, sophistication, and steady influx of energizing outsiders from other parts of the country and abroad. As consumers, Parisians, especially, have become more demanding of raw materials—their freshness, flavor, sustainability; the use of organic and biodynamic methods. And the food changes because the French look outward. They like new things; they're modern.

The old French way of eating was stiffer and involved more ritual. The biggest break with the past may be that people don't want to be so serious when they eat. Like the rest of us, the French want to be relaxed and have fun. In restaurants they aren't focused on cultural knowledge and intellectual engagement. They're looking for food that's simpler and yet contains diverse influences, more variety and stimulation. They're much more open than they were to mashups of flavors, dishes, cultures, sensibilities. It's not necessarily a problem to combine raw with cooked, for instance, going far beyond a garnish of chervil or lemon. Maybe few people any longer expect the food on a plate to automatically make sense or even to know what that might mean.

The critic and historian Bénédict Beaugé writes more insightfully about modern French cooking than anyone else. He's anchored in facts, and he certainly takes an intellectual approach. He has collaborated on books with the celebrated chefs Pierre Gagnaire and Michel Troisgros. One of his recent books, purely his own, is *Plats du Jour: Sur l'Idée de Nouveauté en Cuisine,* devoted to three hundred years of the pursuit of newness in fashionable cooking. A few years ago Bénédict said, "People don't want a complex cuisine, and even critics may not understand more complex cuisines." He wasn't criticizing, he was just commenting.

Richard Olney in the 1980s asserted that what more than anything else made a meal French was the logical structure of a menu: the sequence, the build, the relationships, the steady stimulus from beginning to end. Now I begin to think even the idea of a menu will disappear. But at the moment I write this, Bénédict says that at top restaurants in Paris there's a slight decline in the lengthy, chaotic tasting menu in favor of a more classical structure, even as fashions continue to come in from abroad, especially Japan.

Paris restaurants and their customers have a two-century-long history together. When service was, and is, very good in France (it could always be awful), both you and your server understand your roles. You bring an interest, a respect, even a sense of purpose, and at least a minimum of knowledge of what's likely to be on offer. In a small place, the proprietor might be the server. (Once, in a now-gone Paris bistro, the chef-owner realized we weren't French, and she called from the kitchen window, "You ordered a salad. Does that mean you want the kidneys grilled?" No, I'd meant it when I asked for the kidneys sautéed and with Madeira; the salad was for afterward. She wanted to be sure we were playing our parts, so she could play hers.) The server knows you are there to accomplish something serious, even if that serious thing is pleasure, and knows it's the server's job to assist. The server shares the view that not only is the sensual an important part of life but even that it's unbecoming for anyone not to know how to enjoy good food and drink. I've certainly never heard it spoken, and it sounds a little grand to say it, but the server seems to believe that knowing how to enjoy yourself at the table is a part of French civilization. But is that relationship disappearing, too much a part of the old seriousness?

When a surge of energy occurs in French food, it seems to start in Paris bistros. The first economy-luxury restaurant, though no one put it that way back then, was La Régalade, launched in 1992 out in the 14th arrondissement. To run it, the chef Yves Camdeborde left the luxury of working with Christian Constant at the Hôtel de Crillon; instead he pursued a bistro where placed on your table to start was a terrine with a knife stuck in it, accompanied by the requisite bread, mustard, and cornichons, all for you to help yourself at will. The price of a meal was a bargain. When I spoke with Camdeborde at the time, he invoked with admiration the names of the great chefs of Nouvelle Cuisine. But at La Régalade he made humbler dishes— authentic, "classic," and yet "one improves them always. . . . You add more seasoning, more spices; you always remove butter, cream, grease. You use more olive oil." And why cook traditional food? "Because I like to eat traditionally and drink traditionally." Camdeborde came from Pau in the Béarn in the southwest. The menu reflected that, and you could hear it in his accent. In his region, he said, "the cooking remains strong. One stays very long at the table *chez nous*. Everything takes place at the table. You talk, you discuss. . . . *On est très, très traditionnel chez nous.*" In 2005 he opened Le Comptoir du Relais off Boulevard Saint-Germain, a more luxurious place still based on tradition.

The genre of highly skilled, sometimes very free cooking at moderate prices became *bistronomie: bistro* plus *gastronomie*. The phenomenon of "natural wine" started in France, and added to the bistro mix were natural-wine bars, such as Raquel Carina and Philippe Pinoteau's still-admired Le Baratin. Pierre Jancou opened Racines in the Passage des Panoramas and moved on to other places, strongly underlining the organic and sometimes biodynamic origins of his food and drink, and coming up with the English phrase "more than organic." The chef Iñaki Aizpitarte's Le Chateaubriand became the most famous of the innovative genre, filled with customers from around the world. But is any of the latest French food, at whatever level, evolving in a way that's distinctly French? In a word, *no*.

A vital cuisine requires a mass of people eating, talking, cooking—converging on a point, however large—and that mass grows smaller as fewer people cook. The best-known, really distinctive dishes could survive indefinitely, and the regional cuisines are still alive, although they've long since ceased to evolve, apart from becoming more modern, which is to say less regional. The French who cook at home, especially in cities, don't necessarily cook specifically French food. Immigrants have brought their own cuisines, influencing the rest.

France is big—the biggest country in Western Europe, with both Atlantic and Mediterranean coasts as well as the heights of Mont Blanc. The land, although it changes a little as the climate grows warmer, provides much of the diversity of French food and drink. It's the most enduring component.

Some foodstuffs have disappeared or nearly so. The market gardens closest to Paris have given way to housing. Small wild birds have become endangered and are no longer caught. Meats overall, as Bénédict Beaugé, who does cook, has told me more than once, are not what they were. Restaurants tend to serve a cheapened version of their regional cuisine, except the luxe places, which can prepare a dish exceedingly well, although they often revise it until it's almost something else. (You might find the dishes unadorned at one of the *fermes-auberges,* "farm-inns," which at their best offer local dishes made from the farm's own and other local products.) Haute cuisine kitchens and those inspired by them are more and more international, enriched by takings from around the world. Chefs talk more and more across borders.

French food at times, as I've seen when I've questioned a producer, still reflects the analytical approach that the French take to almost anything. This approach explains, I think, the technique in the kitchen, including the *fonds* ("stocks") of classical French cuisine (as set in stone by Escoffier), as well as the detailed rules of each appellation (given in its *cahier des charges*). It supports the balance and harmony that are still typical of much French food and drink, and it's surely allied to a respect for the past, which for better or worse can inhibit a chef from taking chances.

No tendency toward rational thought explains the extraordinary diversity in traditional French food and drink. Mere variety comes from a red-wine eel stew, Basque dishes hot with Espelette pepper, the surprisingly conservative taste of chicken braised with forty cloves of garlic, and the thick, even funky old-school version of Provençal oil, whose earthy flavor runs through the traditional cooking. Canned sardines with bread and butter are very French, as are radishes with butter and salt and dark bread. The range of cheeses is so famous it's almost beyond mentioning, from wide flat tender wheels of Brie to hard, aged Savoie cheeses with their clean, primordial mountain flavors. On the other side of the country are hot buttered Breton buckwheat *galettes* with a glass of lightly bubbly Breton cider. Dessert can consist of a glass of densely sweet wine tasting of noble rot, one of the greatest joys of all.

The wackiness of some things, not just Banon cheese, *vin jaune,* and *tourteau fromagé,* is totally in tune with some contemporary cooking. *Aligot,* the long stringy cheese-potato purée from Auvergne, is theatrically prepared for you, the spoon raised overhead with long strings still attached to the mass in the pot. There's intensely perfumed Muscat de Beaumes-de-Venise, like drinking a rose. The small Burgundian cheese Époisses, with its stinky orange rind, may nearly collapse from its own creaminess. Nice has squares of *socca,* the vast flat chickpea pancake (borrowed from Liguria) with a grinding of black pepper. And it has *pan bagnat* made of the much-discussed ingredients of a *salade niçoise* put inside a fresh long roll and set aside for the bread to begin to imbibe the juices. The curiously sweet-and-sour peasant *pounti* from the Rouergue is a loaf made of eggs, flour, chard, salt pork, and prunes. *Civet de lièvre* is braised hare served in its blood-thickened sauce. *Tête de veau* is calf's head taken from the bone and cooked slowly in water for two hours, often served cold in long, narrow slices and its fatty gelatinousness cut with a vinaigrette. Familiar and yet very special are all the textures based on flour and butter, including brioche, croissants, éclairs, and millefeuilles. And the different, triple textures of the elusive perfect *macaron,* with its outer crunch, inner soft filling, and tender resistance between.

If the standard for a great meal is that it affects you emotionally, that's much more likely to happen with something that you've never before encountered and is unique to where you are. And it's more likely to happen with traditional food, as your reactions bounce back and forth along the line connecting past and present. When you don't bring cultural references, you don't know all that's going on, but still the excitement is there.

France continues to offer a powerful experience of food and drink, dazzling and fascinating, if you know where to look. There's haute cuisine, no longer uniquely French, but defined by its luxury, fashionableness, and utter refinement. And the rest of French food ranges so wide as to be beyond definition. You may think to yourself that you'll know it when you see it, but very often you won't. It's a huge source of fun and enjoyment.

The last French cooking to change the way the rest of the West thinks about food was Nouvelle Cuisine, forty years ago. It too began in Paris bistros. After that, despite the work of some exciting chefs, such as Joël Robuchon, there was no cohesive style, no broad source of energy. Then in the 1990s, Spanish chefs drew the world's attention, followed in the 2000s by the New Nordic chefs, with their deep exploration of place by way of ingredients.

I can imagine a fresh wave of energy coming from France and rippling outward. It would come from looking back to the Frenchness of food that's so nearly forgotten it seems new. France has such an extraordinary gastronomic wealth that it seems it almost must for a time return to the center. There are the dishes, the foods themselves, the *volupté* and sense of appetite, the calculated flow and surprise of a menu. If a new wave did come, it would surely freely appropriate and combine anything it liked from classical, bourgeois, and regional cuisines down to the most rustic, and probably add whatever was new at the moment. I can see French cooking becoming again part of the zeitgeist. Swept into the currents that animate our time.

INDEX